INDIA'S POLITY IN THE AGE OF AKBAR

HEDGEHOG AND FOX

ASHOKA UNIVERSITY
HISTORY SERIES

the fox knows many things,
but the hedgehog knows one big thing

SERIES EDITOR

RUDRANGSHU MUKHERJEE

IQTIDAR ALAM KHAN

India's Polity in the Age of Akbar

permanent black

in association with

ASHOKA UNIVERSITY

Published by

PERMANENT BLACK
'Himalayana', Mall Road, Ranikhet Cantt,
Ranikhet 263645
perblack@gmail.com

in association with

ASHOKA UNIVERSITY

Distributed by

ORIENT BLACKSWAN PRIVATE LTD
Bangalore Bhopal Bhubaneshwar Chandigarh Chennai
Ernakulam Guwahati Hyderabad Jaipur Kolkata
Lucknow Mumbai New Delhi Patna
www.orientblackswan.com

ISBN 978-81-7824-466-2

Typeset in Adobe Garamond Pro
by Guru Typograph Technology, Crossings Republic,
Ghaziabad 201009
Printed and bound by Sapra Brothers, New Delhi 110092

in memoriam

Professor S. Nurul Hasan

Contents

Preface

THE ESSAYS PRESENTED in this volume comprise my researches over the years I was teaching a postgraduate course on the rise of the Mughal Empire (1526–1605). Some of these, published in scholarly journals, were widely commented upon. In the Introduction which follows I have tried to summarize my overall assessment of the rise of the Mughal Empire and the orientation it was given by Akbar.

While working on the themes in this volume I had the privilege of working at a number of leading libraries, including the National Library (Calcutta), the British Library (London), and the Bibliotheque Nationale (Paris). The Research Library of the Centre of Advanced Studies in History, Aligarh Muslim University (AMU) at Aligarh, was where the major part of my research material was collected. I thank the staff of these libraries for their help.

As always, I am beholden to Professor Irfan Habib for many suggestions towards improving the reach of research and presentation; and to the Aligarh Historians Society and its Secretary, Professor Shireen Moosvi, I am grateful for sponsoring this book. Mr Barkatullah made the text of this book ready for publication.

For transliterating Persian terms I have generally followed the system adopted in Steingass' *Persian–English Dictionary*, retaining only two diacritical marks, the 'raised comma' and the 'inverted comma', for *alif-hamza* and '*ain*, respectively.

When in footnoted citations the names of publishers and other details of publication are not in evidence, it is for one of three reasons: (1) they have been cited earlier in the book; (2) they can be found in the Bibliography at the end of the book; (3) the original source does not carry them.

Despite her painful illnesses, Kamo bravely tried to ensure the early completion of this book.

The material in this book was first published as shown below. In the course of being edited it has sustained changes in phrasing and syntax wherever these seemed required, but the substance and arguments remain those in the original versions.

Chapter 1 in *Researches in the History of India: 1200–1750*, New Delhi, 1992

Chapter 2 in *Medieval India: A Miscellany*, vol. I, Delhi, 1969

Chapter 3 in *Journal of the Royal Asiatic Society*, 1980

Chapter 4 in *Studies in History*, vol. II, no. 1, January 1980

Chapter 5 in *Akbar and His India*, ed. Irfan Habib, Delhi, 1997

Chapter 6 in *A Shared Heritage: The Growth of Civilizations in India & Iran*, ed. Irfan Habib, New Delhi, 2002

Introduction

India's Polity in the Age of Akbar

THE BEGINNING OF THE sixteenth century has been taken to represent an important turning point in Indian history because it marks the appearance of certain significant political and economic processes.[1] We witness in particular a tendency towards the sharing of political authority and social surplus among culturally diverse ruling groups within states controlling large stretches of territory. This phenomenon matured in the second half of the sixteenth century, with the emergence of a rejuvenated Mughal Empire under Akbar, but its origins can be traced to the rise of the class of hereditary chiefs, later designated *zamindars*, who at the end of the sixteenth century claimed from 10 per cent to 25 per cent of the assessed revenue within the Empire. As is evident from 'The Account of the Twelve Subas' in Abul Fazl's *Ain-i-Akbari,* the *zamindars* in each *pargana* generally belonged to the dominant Hindu castes and employed a number of horsemen and foot retainers. They formed 'a semi-military class, who could not

[1] For a characterization of the 'Mughal era' as the 'early modern' period of Indian history, see Osamu Konda, *The Early Modern Monarchies in Mughal India,* Kyoto, 2012, pp. v–vi. Cf. Catherine B. Asher and Cynthia Talbot, *India before Europe*, New Delhi, 2006, p. 115. It is maintained that the (Mughal) imperial ideology and institutions served 'as a catalyst for the growth of a new kind of Indian culture and society.'

be ignored politically by any regime.'[2] This situation was a crucial element in the emergence of the Mughal Empire, characterized by John F. Richards as the 'end product of a millennium of Muslim conquest, colonization and state building in the Indian subcontinent.'[3]

There is distinct evidence of the sporadic presence of Hindu officers in high positions under the Khalji and Tughlaq Sultans of Delhi,[4] as also under the Lodi and Sur rulers (witness the phenomenon of Hemu, for example);[5] or for that matter the rise of Purbia chiefs in the Khalji kingdom of Malwa in the early decades of the sixteenth century;[6] or the coming to power in Bengal of Raja Ganesh.[7] Without the support of Hindu agrarian magnates and officials it was now obviously becoming difficult to run a state system. This social reality also seems to underline the startlingly novel theory of the state evolved in the Mughal Empire, from roughly 1580, as a highly centralized political structure capable of accommodating ruling groups with diverse cultural and religious affiliations.

The process of integration of these different social groups was accompanied by an independent factor, viz. the flow of American silver into India via Europe well before the time Sher Shah came to power (1540). This eased the scarcity of precious metals felt

[2] For a discussion of the rise of *zamindars* as a distinct social category, see Irfan Habib, in *The State and Society in Medieval India*, ed. J.S. Grewal, New Delhi, 2005, pp. 149–51.

[3] John F. Richards, *The New Cambridge History of India*: *The Mughal Empire*, Cambridge, 1993, p. 2.

[4] See Iqtidar Alam Khan, 'Hindu Chiefs in Sultanate Polity (Thirteenth and Fourteenth Centuries)', *Studies in People's History*, vol. I, issue 1, June 2014, pp. 24–8.

[5] Cf. Iqtidar Husain Siddiqui, *Some Aspects of Afghan Despotism in India*, Aligarh, 1969, pp. 19, 21, 23, 24, 56–9, 60, 105.

[6] For the prominent role of the Purbia Rajputs in the service of the Khalji sultans of Malwa during the first half of the sixteenth century, see D.H. Kolff, *Naukar, Rajput and Sepoy*: *The Ethnohistory of the Military Labour Market of Hindustan, 1450–1850*, Cambridge, 1991, pp. 87–9, 160–3.

[7] See K.R. Qanungo, in *History of Bengal*, vol. II, ed. J.N. Sarkar, Dacca, 1948, pp. 122–9.

acutely in many parts of North India since the end of the fourteenth century.[8] The expansion in the money economy that the inflow of precious metals brought about doubtless made it possible to restore, if not entirely establish, the cash nexus in revenue extraction, and so substantially strengthened the financial stability of the state. Another long-term tendency was the growth of urban manufactures and the expansion of a free-born artisan class—as against the extensive existence of slave labour in the fourteenth century and earlier. This change is reflected in the fact that Babur noticed multitudes of artisan labourers in India without alluding to slavery. At the same time, his observation regarding the availability of 'unnumbered and endless workmen of every kind' testifies in a more generalized context to the ongoing expansion of handicraft production.[9] Slavery too was on the way out as a universal institution in light of Rafiuddin Ibrahim Shirazi's testimony (supported by 'Arif Qandhari and Abul Fazl) that, in his seventh regnal year (1562–3), Akbar not only prohibited the enslavement of prisoners of war but also made trading in slaves a punishable offence.[10] This is supported by evidence of the absence of open slave markets in Mughal towns.[11]

I

If the economic and social situation was now different in important ways from what had prevailed before the sixteenth century, can we

[8] For a detailed discussion, see Najaf Haider, 'Coins and Silver Crises', in *Economic History of Medieval India, 1200–1500*, ed. Irfan Habib, New Delhi, 2011, pp. 149–61.

[9] *Babur-nama*, tr. A.S. Beveridge, London, 1921, 2 vols (continuous pagination), p. 520.

[10] Cf. Irfan Habib, in *The State and Society in Medieval India,* ed. J.S. Grewal, New Delhi, 2005, p. 435.

[11] There is no mention of regular slave markets in the descriptions of towns in the Mughal Empire by European travellers. Manrique's notice (*Travels 1629–43*, tr. C.E. Luard and H. Hoston, London, 1927, vol. II, p. 272) of 'markets and fairs' where villagers seized for non-payment of tax were sold is obviously not a reference to a regular slave trade. Cf. Irfan Habib, in *The State and Society in Medieval India*, p. 436, fn. 52.

say that the forms of empire-building under the Surs (particularly Sher Shah) and the first three Mughal emperors also were qualitatively different from those obtaining in the earlier phase of Islamic presence in the subcontinent? It is important to remember in this regard that state policies and forms of governance identified with Akbar's drive to systematize the organs of state control and, at times, even measures reflecting his spirit of universal reconciliation (*sulh-i kul*), can be traced back to trends that had appeared earlier under Afghan rulers.

One may here recall Athar Ali's perceptive observation pertaining to 'the survival of the administrative framework of the Delhi Sultanate, especially that relating to land revenue administration under Khaljis and Tughlaqs, in Sher Shah's measures carried forward by Akbar.' But, according to him, in certain vital respects Akbar's administrative systematization originated only with Sher Shah:

> For example *zabt*, the cornerstone of Akbar's land revenue administration as well as the system of *dagh* (branding of horses) originated only with Sher Shah. Islam Shah strengthened the same trend by attempting to bring the whole of his empire under direct control of the central authority. Anticipating a similar move by Akbar in 1574, Islam Shah had converted his entire empire into *Khalisa*, i.e. land under control of central authority, which would imply [the] placing of nobles on cash salaries.[12]

We may now consider the development of certain trends in the early-sixteenth-century polities that laid the basis for these new developments.

The growing influence of Hindu officials serving in the assessment and collection of land revenue became particularly visible under the last two Lodi Sultans (1489–1527). A letter of 'Abdul Quddus Gangohi during Babur's time suggests that to the presence of Hindu officials in the revenue department (*diwani*) was being attributed the

[12] See Athar Ali, 'Towards an Interpretation of the Mughal Empire', in idem, *Mughal India: Studies in Polity, Ideas, Society and Culture,* New Delhi, 2006, pp. 60–1.

demand for *'ushr* (tithe) levied on behalf of the state on theologians' revenue grants.[13] Badauni, incidentally, mentions Dankar, a Hindu scholar of Persian and Arabic who 'used to give instruction on scholarly subjects' during Sikandar Lodi's reign (1489–1517).[14] Firishta says that Sikandar Lodi encouraged Hindus (the reference obviously is to officials) to learn to write in the Persian script.[15]

There has survived evidence testifying that, from the very beginning, Islamic states in India were not always averse to extending financial support to non-Muslim religious establishments in the form of some kinds of grants. Such grants may be traced back to the time of Arab rule over parts of Sind and Punjab in the eighth century; the Arab commander Muhammad Ibn Qasim is reported to have asked Brahmans to present their leading divines so that they might be given 'generous grants' (*in'am-i wafir*).[16] If one goes by local traditions and the occasional epigraphic evidence, the state's support to Hindu religious establishments was not entirely ruled out during the fourteenth and fifteenth centuries.[17] But 'Abbas Khan's testimony, that Sher Shah provided separate facilities in state-owned *sarais* for Hindu travellers to have their meals prepared by Brahmin cooks, speaks of a degree of state accommodation for upper-caste Hindus

[13] Cf. *Maktubat-i Quddusia*, Matb'-i Ahmadi, letter 169, pp. 335–7. Here, Shaikh 'Abdul Quddus Gangohi protests against Babur's decision, sometime around 1528, to demand *'ushr* from the grant holders. Shaikh 'Abdul Quddus demands in his letter the exclusion of Hindus from offices in the department of *Diwani* and insists that the office of *amin* be given only to pious Muslims.

[14] 'Abdul Qadir Badauni, *Muntakhab ut-Tawarikh,* vol. I, p. 323.

[15] *Tarikh-i Firishta,* vol. 1, Nawal Kishore, p. 187.

[16] Anonymous, *Chachnama,* Persian translation by 'Ali Kufi, ed. Umar Daudpota, Delhi, 1939, p. 210; see Irfan Habib, *Medieval India: The Study of a Civilization*, New Delhi, 2007, p. 31.

[17] For Muhammad Tughlaq's financial support to a Hindu temple (*Go-math*) see inscription dated 3rd *Vaisakha*, 1387 *Vikram* Year/AD 1328, located at Batihagarh, District Damoh, Madhya Pradesh; cited by Mehdi Hasan, *Tughlaq Dynasty*, reprint, Delhi, 1976, pp. 34–5.

not discernible in the earlier period.[18] That at a popular plane a spirit of religious tolerance was growing is shown by the wide appreciation among contemporaries, including many Muslim theologians, for Kabir's preachings attacking the rigidities of existing orthodoxies. This is, for example, the testimony of the prominent Islamic divine of the sixteenth century, Shaikh 'Abdul Haq Muhaddis. Sometime around 1522 his grandfather, a spiritual preceptor, described Kabir to him as a 'monotheist' (*muwahid*), which, it goes without saying, amounted to a deliberate refusal to condemn the Bhakti saint as a non-believer (*kafir*).[19] This situation, one may speculate, promoted a favourable ideological climate for the rise of a political culture identified with Akbar's *sulh-i kul*.

II

Rushbrook Williams' reading of the situation in India at the time of Babur's invasion (1526), however, tends to project a picture of heightened tensions between Islamic powers and resurgent Hindu chiefs.[20] He characterizes Babur's success in Hindustan as a victory of the forces of Islam over a Rajput (i.e. Hindu) confederacy, led by Rana Sangram Singh, which was all set to establish its dominance after overthrowing the 'greatly weakened Muhammadan powers'. A subsequent assessment, from an essentially Muslim standpoint, of the cultural scene in North India on the eve of Babur's invasion, even tends to suggest, again without any firm evidence, the existence of proselytizing movements of Hindus seeking to create 'apostates' (*murtid*) among Muslims.[21] Both these views naturally portray Babur

[18] 'Abass Khan, *Tarikh-i Sher Shahi*, MS. India Office, Ethe 219, f.108b. See also Iqtidar Alam Khan, 'The Karwan Sarays of Mughal India: A Study of Surviving Stuctures', *The Indian Historical Review*, vol. XIV, nos 1–2 (July 1987 and January 1988), pp. 111–12.

[19] Cf. Irfan Habib, 'Kabir', in *Religion in Indian History*, ed. Irfan Habib, New Delhi, 2007, p. 148.

[20] L.E. Rushbrook Williams, *An Empire Builder of Sixteenth Century*, reprint, Delhi, n.d., pp. 18–19.

[21] Cf. K.A. Nizami, *Salatin-i Dehli ke Mazhabi Rujhanat* (Urdu), Delhi, 1958, p. 450.

as a defender of Islam, and of Muslims in India, against the supposedly rising tide of Hindu militancy and cultural aggression.

It may, however, be pointed out that Rushbrook Williams' thesis overestimates the political consequences of the Battle of Khanua (1527), which was only an episode, though an important one, in the long-drawn struggle for supremacy in North India between the Mughals on the one hand and the remnants of the Lodi Empire and their supporters among the Rajputs and other chiefs on the other. This struggle continued down to the Mughal victory in the Second Battle of Panipat (November 1556).

Rushbrook Williams does not take into account the fact that the so-called Rajput confederacy was formed at the initiative of Hasan Khan Mewati and was joined by Mahmud Lodi (son of Sikandar Lodi), and that Mahmud Lodi was set up as the king and is reported to have issued a gold coin from Rana Sangram's camp which carried his name as the reigning sultan.[22] Moreover, from the list of chiefs forming this 'confederacy' given in Shaikh Zain's *Fathnama*, one knows that out of 101,000 troops commanded by Rana Sangram at Khanua, 22,000 were retainers of his Muslim allies.[23]

If the testimony of two renowned contemporaries of Babur, namely Guru Nanak and Shaikh 'Abdul Quddus Gangohi, is any indicator of the popular response to Babur, initially a vast majority of not only Hindus but of Muslims as well would appear to have been intensely hostile to the invading Mughals. They were seen by both communities as the enemies of religion. In Guru Nanak's words, Babur's coming led to Muslims losing their 'five-time prayer' and Hindus 'their hours of worship'.[24] Shaikh 'Abdul Quddus, in one of his sayings recorded in *Lataif-i Quddusi*, characterizes Babur's advance into the Punjab as an impending calamity (*chiz-i bala*) to *dar al-Islam* in India. Shaikh

[22] Rizqallah Mushtaqi (d. 1581) (*Waqi'at-i Mushtaqi*. MS. Br. Library, Or. 1929, f. 44a) wtites: 'Hasan Khan Mewati raised Sultan Mahmud, son of Sultan Sikandar, to kingship and brought around the Rana.'

[23] *Babur-nama*, tr. A.S. Beveridge, London, reprint 1969, p. 562.

[24] M.A. Macauliffe, *The Sikh Religion: Sacred Writings and Authors*, vol. I, reprint, Delhi, 1963, pp. 112–13.

Rukn al-Din, the compiler of *Lataif-i Quddusi*, records the burning down of 'Abdul Quddus Gangohi's hospice (*hujrah*) at Shahabad by the invading Mughals and the loss of his own books, including a rare Islamic treatise on '*ilm-ul-Kalam*'. Shaikh 'Abdul Quddus himself was taken prisoner and treated most brutally. Rukn al-Din also alludes to the massacre of non-combatants, including people connected with mystic establishments at Rudauli.[25]

III

The state system that arose in North India with Babur's victories at Panipat (1526) and Khanua (1527) had features that demarcated it profoundly from other post-Abbasid sultanates, including the Delhi Sultanate and its fifteenth-century successors. This difference was particularly marked in two respects: (a) Unlike them, in the Timurid system the status of Islamic *shari'at* as the guiding principle of the state was not fully established; and (b) there also existed a great deal of uncertainty about the Timurid rulers' entitlement to sovereignty, their high aspirations and claims of noble lineage notwithstanding. This situation may be ascribed to the strong influence on the Timurid polity of the pagan code of the Mongols, according to which the choice of sovereign was limited to the circle of direct descendants of Chingiz. Babur himself considered the *Tura-i Chingizi* an important element in his heritage and, as far as possible, was anxious to conform to its tenets. He also clearly admits that before him the Timurid rulers did not use for themselves any royal title higher than that of Mirza.[26]

The impact of the Mongol code on the Timurid polity, however, appears to have been weakened by the end of Humayun's reign

[25] *Lataif-i Quddusi*, Delhi, 1311 H, pp. 8, 31, 35, 63–4. Cf. Simon Digby, 'Abd al-Quddus Gangohi (1456–1537): The Personality and Attitudes of a Medieval Sufi', *Medieval India: A Miscellany*, vol. III, Bombay, 1975, pp. 10–11.

[26] *Babur-nama*, p. 344.

(1530–56), which may be ascribed partly to the influx of a large number of nobles and a still larger number of troops of diverse, mostly non-Turani, origins.[27] This weakening of the Mongol impact did not, however, automatically lead to a strengthening of the role of Islamic *shari'at* in the Timurid state—or the Mughal Empire, as it came to be called in India after 1526. On the contrary, this development appears to have created a theoretical vacuum which was seemingly sought to be filled by borrowing convenient ideas that became familiar to the Timurids through the non-Turani elements that joined their service in different capacities during this time.

According to one estimate, out of 145 nobles who served under Babur in Hindustan, 33 were identified as Afghans or Indian Shaikhzadas.[28] That there was an influx of Iranis in the lower grades of the nobility under Humayun during 1545–5 is borne out by Abul Fazl's list of nobles who accompanied him to Hindustan in 1555. Out of 51 nobles in this list, only 16 may be identified as Turanis, some of them occupying high positions.[29] The accretion of troops of Indian origin is attested to by Babur's random mention of Shaikh Ghuran, an Indian Shaikhzada stationed at Jalali (near Aligarh), commanding 3000 '*tarkashbandan*' (*dhanuks?*).[30] The influx of Indian troops is also shown by Babur's statement, recorded on 30 November 1526, that the contingent of one of his Afghan officers consisted of 250 or 300 Turanis and 2000 Hindustanis, suggesting that already by this date the ratio between the two categories of troops in the contingents of several of his officers was in the range of 1:8 or 1:10.[31]

[27] In a list of 145 nobles of Babur, prepared sometime in the eighteenth century from several texts, 33 can be identified as Afghans or Indian Shaikhzadas, while 52 of them may be regarded as 'Mughals' hailing from Central Asia. See *Tazkirat ul-Umara* (bound in a volume entitled *Haft Risala-i Taqwim al-Buldan*), MS. 45, Buhar Collection, National Library, Calcutta.

[28] See *Haft Risala-i-Taqwin al-Buldan*, cited above.

[29] *Akbar-nama*, vol. I, ed. Agha Ahmad Ali, Calcutta, 1873, p. 342.

[30] *Babur-nama*, p. 526.

[31] Ibid., p. 538.

Babur and Humayun as well as many of their leading nobles also had the opportunity of interacting closely with the hereditary chiefs (the *zamindars*) of territories conquered in India. Mention may be made in this regard of the Ghakkars and Janjuhas of the Salt Range, the Khanazads of Mewat, the Bachgotis of Awadh, the Baghelas of Bhatta, and some of the Purbia chiefs of Malwa. Such interactions with mostly Hindu hereditary chiefs perhaps represented an additional channel through which new ideas and information relating to the working of power structures at the local level in India could have come to the Mughals during these early years (1527–56).

Babur's favourable notice of the fiscal and military arrangements within the territory of the Janjuha chiefs of the Salt Range, his remarks on the 'permanent' nature of royal offices in Bengal, and Shaikh Zain's reference to the 'established Indian practice [*qa'da-i mustamarra-i-Hind*] of calculating the strength of contingent of a chief at the rate of a hundred horsemen per revenue unit (*vilayat*) of one lakh [copper *tankas*?]',[32] illustrate the kinds of new ideas, practices, and customs relating to the art of governance that were becoming familiar to the Timurids in India. Some of these, like the Bengali custom of not touching the predecessor's treasure, which appeared to Babur 'strange', were rejected. But others, like the custom of maintaining a ratio between the strength of contingents and revenue of the assigned territories, became in due course established practice within the Timurid military organization. The basic principle underlining the *mansab* organization introduced by Akbar was evidently derived from this Indian practice.[33]

[32] Ibid., pp. 379, 482, 562.

[33] Cf. Shireen Moosvi, 'The Evolution of Mansab System under Akbar until 1596–7', *Journal of the Royal Asiatic Society*, no. 2, 1981, p. 175. Re-examining Abul Fazl's passage interpreted by Moreland as suggesting the introduction of a second (*sawar*) rank, she holds that the passage only lays down a system of fixing the number of horsemen to be maintained keeping in view three different categories of *jagirs*. This system appears to have been conceived after the Indian practice noticed by Shaikh Zain.

The process of admitting into the nobility persons belonging to diverse social, ethnic, and religious backgrounds that gained momentum during Akbar's reign appears to have begun in the time of Babur. During the months separating the First Battle of Panipat (20 April 1526) from the Battle of Khanua (17 March 1527), Babur appears to have made a concerted attempt to take into his service as large a number of ex-officers of the Lodi Empire as was possible in the circumstances. To gain this objective he offered to many of them not only a restoration of the assignments held by them, but sometimes also promised to enhance these appreciably.[34] A count of the names of nobles mentioned in connection with military campaigns and court ceremonies shows that out of 145 nobles serving Babur in India, 33 were Afghans and Shaikhzadas recruited after Ibrahim Lodi's defeat. It is true that many of them stayed with Babur only for a short while. But some, like Araish Khan, still counted in the highest echelon of the Mughal nobility during the early years of Humayun's reign.[35] Several other nobles of the same category joined Humayun's service during 1533–6.[36]

The inclusion of Shi'a Iranis in Humayun's service after his return from the Safavid court to the Kabul–Qandahar region in 1545 was a significant development from this point of view. For the first time so many Irani Shi'as came to be included in the service of a Timurid ruler on a regular basis.[37] Before this, in no state ruled by a

[34] *Babur-nama*, pp. 477–8, 526–7.

[35] Cf. Gulbadan Begam, *Humayun-nama*, ed. A.S. Beveridge, London, 1902, p. 25.

[36] Khwandamir (*Qanun-i Humayuni*, ed. Hidayat Husain, Calcutta, 1940, pp. 12, 97) refers to a seating arrangement introduced by Humayun in 1535 which was planned after the signs of the zodiac. In this arrangement nobles of Indian origin were allotted the house (*daira*) of Saturn. This points to the presence, around this time (1535), of a number of Indian Shaikhzadas in Humayun's service. They were obviously in addition to Afghan chiefs who joined Humayun's court in 1533.

[37] The influx of Iranis (most of them Shi'as) in lower grades of the nobility under Humayun during 1545–5 is borne out by Abul Fazl's list of nobles

Muslim dynasty did Shi'as and Sunnis coexist in the nobility in such remarkable amity.

Many of the state personnel of Irani origin who joined Humayun's service during 1548–55 as minor functionaries rose to high positions during the first twenty years of Akbar's reign. Already by 1575 Iranis, many of them known to be Shi'as, constituted about 27 per cent of the total strength of the nobility, and formed over 38 per cent of those with the *mansab* of 500 and above.[38]

The next decisive step in the transformation of the Mughal nobility into a truly composite body was the influx of Rajput chiefs, which also commenced during the years 1556–75. Along with the Rajputs, many more Indian Muslims, most of them Shaikhzadas, were included in Akbar's nobility during the same period. This created a situation where Indian Muslims and Rajputs came to form respectively 14 per cent and 10 per cent of the total strength of the nobility and over 9 per cent and 8 per cent of the *mansabdars* of 500 *zats* and above.[39] Towards the end of Akbar's reign (1595), the strength of the Rajputs and other Hindus among nobles of 500 *zat* and above stood at over 22 per cent.[40]

IV

From its very inception the Mughal Empire manifested a tendency towards an intensified centralization of political and administrative authority as well as of the resources it controlled. The assignment system and organization of military hierarchy brought by Babur

---

accompanying Humayun to Hindustan in 1555. Out of 51 nobles listed, 16 may be identified as Iranis. *Akbar-nama,* vol. I, Calcutta, 1873, p. 342.

[38] See Iqtidar Alam Khan, 'The Nobility under Akbar and the Development of his Religious Policy, 1560–80', *Journal of the Royal Asiatic Society,* nos 1 and 2, 1968, pp. 30–2, 35

[39] Ibid., pp. 31–2, 35.

[40] Athar Ali, *The Mughal Nobility under Aurangzeb*, Bombay 1966, p. 31.

appear to have carried the seeds of this tendency. For example, the terms that Babur uses for the assignments conferred by him on his nobles in India indicate that there was an attempt to separate their stipulated personal income (*wajh*) from what was meant for salaries (*'alufa*) or support (*istiqamat*) to their retainers.[41] There is also some basis for imagining that at times a clear demarcation was sought to be made between the *wajh* jurisdiction and the routine military-cum-civil administration within a *pargana* or *sarkar*. This would have facilitated the apportioning of a fixed amount of revenue, of particular territories as *khalisa* revenues managed by officials of the *diwani*.[42]

Similarly, a scrutiny of the terms which Babur occasionally uses to denote the status of individual military personnel is revealing. It points to the existence of a military hierarchy, from petty officers like *jawanan-i jirga, jawanan-i yakka*, and *yegits*, to the highest rank of *beg*. Some of Babur's statements also suggest a system of promotions from lower to higher ranks.[43] This organization evidently was later incorporated in the system of twelve grades (*maratib*) introduced by Humayun in 1535, where the salary (*'alufa*) was linked to the rank (*martaba*) of a noble in the military hierarchy.[44] Similarly, the tendency

[41] See Iqtidar Alam Khan, 'The Mughal Assignment System during Akbar's Early Years, 1556–1575', in *Medieval India I: Researches in the History of India*, ed. Irfan Habib, Delhi, 1992, pp. 67–8. The expressions *wajah-i istiqamat* and *Wajh-w 'ulufa* have been misread by A.R. Khan as *Wajah-wa-istiqamat* and *wajh-w 'ulufa* in his 'Babur's Settlement of his Conquests in Hindustan', *Proceedings of the Indian History Congress,* 29th session (Patiala 1967), Patna, 1968, p. 218.

[42] For example, under Babur the territory of Delhi was not assigned to any noble. It was apparently administered by a team of *shiqdars* and *diwans*. Again, in May 1529, while in the territory of Bihar 50 lakhs (*bahlulis*?) were assigned to Muhammad Khan Nuhani, an Afghan noble; the remaining revenues of one crore, reserved for *khalisa*, were possibly collected by Murshid Iraqi appointed as the *diwan* of the territory on 13th April the same year. Cf. *Babur-nama*, pp. 476, 662, 776.

[43] Ahsan Raza Khan, 'Gradation of Nobility under Babur', *Islamic Culture* (Hyderabad), vol. IX, no. I, January 1986.

[44] Khwandamir, *Qanun-i Humayuni*, pp. 41, 43–50. See also Shireen

towards an enhanced share of *khalisa* revenues so clearly documented for Akbar's reign may be seen taking shape under Babur.[45]

The tendency towards centralization in the Mughal imperial system was reinforced by the increasing use of firearms when putting down local resistance. Babur's use of firearms at Panipat (1526) and Khanua (1527) showed that the primitive cannon pieces (*zarbozans*) cast in bronze or brass (already known in India by then), if deployed in a formation not hindering the free movement of cavalry, could in fact enhance the effectiveness of mounted archers. One firearm of great effectiveness, not known till then in India but used by Babur, was the Turkish matchlock (*tufang*), in which fire was led by a rope into a frying pan that then set off an explosion of the gunpowder that had been rammed down the barrel. In the battles of Panipat (1526) and Khanua (1527), Babur's matchlockmen, taking shelter behind some kind of barricade (at Panipat), or moving with carts carrying field pieces (*zarbozans*), seem to have played a decisive role in breaking the enemy's offensives. Under Akbar these matchlocks came to be regularly used in localized military operations.[46] As Abul Fazl seems to imply in the *Ain-i Akbari*, firearms were perceived as contributing to (a) the strengthening of central authority within the realm; and (b) rapid military conquests leading to the annexation of vast territories.[47] While one may have some reservations about the last statement, there is no doubt that the wide use of *tufang* under

---

Moosvi, 'The Evolution of *Mansab* System under Akbar until 1596–7', *Journal of the Royal Asiatic Society*, no. 2, 1981, p. 174, where she interprets this passage as an attempt to introduce 'some sort of classification of nobles' and the fixing of their salaries 'according to that gradation'.

[45] See *Babur-nama*, p. 617: Babur's reference, on 22 October 1528, to his imposing a cut of 30 per cent of *wajahs* 'to be used for war material and appliances' was simultaneously a rather drastic increase in *khalisa* revenues.

[46] Iqtidar Alam Khan, *Gunpowder and Firearms: Warfare in Medieval India*, New Delhi, 2004, pp. 72–3, 132–5.

[47] *Ain-i Akbari*, ed. H. Blochmann, vol. I, Calcutta, 1872–7, pp. 82, 149–51.

Akbar in localized operations did contribute to reinforcing the central authority's control over localities.[48]

The imperial system inherited by Akbar received its fulfilment in the wholesale systematization and centralization that the empire underwent from 1574. Athar Ali correctly assigns to Akbar himself a pivotal role in bringing about this transformation. The introduction of *mansab*, or number-rank, the division of the empire into *subas*, *sarkars*, and *mahals* where the administration of one province was a replica of the other, and the practice of linking the *mansab* obligation to expected income from assignments, were some of the aspects of this process which did not have precedents either in Timurid history or in that of the Delhi Sultanate. These cannot but be ascribed to the genius of Akbar.[49] But no one has suggested that this system was perfected by the end of Akbar's reign: criticism on this count directed against historians identified with Aligarh is surely misplaced.[50] Such criticism does not, for example, take into account Athar Ali pointedly acknowledging Moreland and Irfan Habib's contributions on the changes taking place in the *mansab* system under Jahangir and Shah Jahan. Athar Ali also mentions in this context the extension of the Mughal *zabt* system to the Deccan by Murshid Quli Khan.[51]

The cultural ethos of an entirely new type of state system, sought to be run by Akbar with the help of a composite nobility, translated itself, after an initial experiment with a royal version of the *shari'at*, into a supra-religious theory of sovereignty. Its articulation in Abul Fazl's writings carried the stamp of his magisterial learning and

[48] See the chapter titled 'The Matchlock Musket as an Instrument of Centralization', in Iqtidar Alam Khan, *Gunpowder and Firearms: Warfare in Medieval India,* New Delhi, 2004, pp. 143–63.

[49] Cf. Athar Ali, 'Towards an Interpretation of the Mughal Empire', *Mughal India: Studies in Polity, Ideas, Society and Culture,* New Delhi, 2006.

[50] For the criticism that Aligarh historians tend to suggest the perfection of the Mughal imperial apparatus by Akbar, see Muzaffar Alam and Sanjay Subrahmanyam (ed.), *The Mughal State, 1626–1750,* Delhi, 1998, p. 30.

[51] Athar Ali, *The Mughal Nobility under Aurangzeb*, p. 41.

originality of thought. As Irfan Habib points out, Abul Fazl has two variants of this theory, which can be traced to heterodox tendencies in medieval Islam, marked amongst them being the doctrines of the Unity of Existence (*wahdat ul-wajud*) of Ibn 'Arabi (1181–35) and of the Divine Light (*farr-i izidi*) of Shihab al- Din Suhrawardi Maqtul (d. 1191).[52] This theory, projected by Abul Fazl as *sulh-i kul*, became the guiding principle of the Mughal state. Boiled down, this provides a new definition of royalty which precludes entirely the identification of state authority with a particular religion and enjoins upon a just ruler to extend his benevolence and protection equally to all his subjects without exception. Within the framework of this theory there was no scope for the operation of those provisions of the *shari'at* which imposed certain disabilities on the *zimmis*. This theory, in other words, makes it obligatory for kings to establish universal reconciliation (*sulh-i kul*) and ensure that religious differences among people do not lead to mutual antipathy. It was a new concept of sovereignty directly linked to Akbar's religious policy which, according to the author of *Dabistan-i Mazahib*, was aimed at holding together various elements without allowing any one faction to gain dominance.[53]

V

In the writings of I.H. Qureshi there is the assertion that after Akbar's death the idea of Islamic monarchy was revived by his successor,[54] as against the contrary view presented, for example, by Irfan Habib in 'The Political Role of Shaikh Ahmad Sirhindi and Shah Waliul-lah'.[55] In taking the position that Jahangir was influenced

[52] Irfan Habib, 'A Political Theory for the Mughal Empire: A Study of the Ideas of Abul Fazl', *Proceedings of the Indian History Congress*, 59th (Patiala) Session, pp. 332–4.

[53] Cf. *Dabistan-i Mazahib,* ed. Nazar Ashraf, Calcutta, 1809, pp. 431–2.

[54] I.H. Qureshi, *The Administration of the Mughal Empire,* Karachi, 1966, p. 39.

[55] This was presented at the Aligarh session of the Indian History Congress, 1960.

by Nur al-Din-Khaqani's *Akhlaq-i Jahangiri*, Muzaffar Alam and Sanjay Subrahmanyam seem implicitly to suggest that, after all, I.H. Qureshi's thesis suggesting the revival of Islamic monarchy after Akbar has some basis.[56] Unfortunately, they do not cite any passage from this unpublished text. If the contents of another text with the same title by 'Abd ul-Wahab Ilhami is any guide, the term *akhlaq* in such texts only means 'ethics', wherein sometimes there is found advice to a king with reference to the Prophet's and pious caliphs' traditions. Jahangir's name is inserted in the title as a token of respect for the reigning sovereign. It implies no pretension to set forth the fundamental doctrines of the Mughal state.[57]

Of the documents issued by Akbar's successors reiterating the basic principles of the theory of sovereignty evolved by him, the most significant, perhaps, is Aurangzeb's *nishan* to Rana Raj Singh of Marwar, written in 1658 to win the latter's support in the war of succession. While reiterating the basic principles of the theory of sovereignty evolved under Akbar, he says rulers are bound to ensure that men belonging to various communities and different religions should live in the vale of peace and pass their days in prosperity, and no one should interfere in the affairs of one another. Kings who resorted to 'intolerance', according to a memorable statement in this letter, 'become the cause of dispute and conflict and of harm to the people at large.' This is a 'habit deserving to be rejected and cast off.' The letter concludes with the solemn promise that were Aurangzeb to succeed in seizing the throne, 'the revered practices and established regulations of my great ancestors' would continue to be observed.[58] In view of Aurangzeb's attempt in the last twenty years of his reign

[56] Cf. *The Mughal State*: *1526–1750*, ed. M. Alam and Sanjay Subrahmanyam, Delhi, 1998, p. 23.

[57] MS., Maulana Azad Library, AMU, Subhanuallah Collection, 891. 0026

[58] See Athar Ali, *Mughal Empire in History*, Presidential Address, section II (Medieval India), Indian History Congress, 33rd Session, Muzaffarpur, 1972. The text of the letter can be seen in Shyamaldas, *Vir Vinod*, II, p. 20.

to partially enforce a version of the orthodox *shari'at*, this statement appears rather ironic. But the fact that for winning support within the nobility in 1658, he had to make an announcement to this effect indicates the wide acceptability that the supra-religious theory of sovereignty established by Akbar had come to gain among the Mughal governing class. The strong commitment of Rajput and other Hindu chiefs to the Mughal Empire, which evolved in the sixteenth century under Akbar, appears to have remained largely unshaken down to 1739. This is illustrated, for example, by a story narrated by Muhammad Bakhsh Ashob of the unequal fight an unnamed Rajput *zamindar* and his retainers put up against Nadir Shah's troops near Ghiraunda. It was, perhaps, the only occasion during Nadir Shah's invasion when a body of Indian troops made a stand and died fighting. The royal officers, Ashob informs us, came to know of this 'incident' only when they, after having surrendered before Nadir Shah, passed through Ghiraunda en route to Delhi.[59] It would, indeed, appear that Aurangzeb's attempt to deflect the Mughal Empire from the supra-religious character acquired by it under Akbar was not wholly successful. The Rajput chiefs serving the empire as nobles or bound to it in some other way seemed to be confident down to the first half of the eighteenth century that the basic character of the empire was the same as handed down by Akbar to his successor. Jai Singh Sawai's and Girdhar Bahadur's objection to a proposal to reimpose *jiziah* at a consultative assembly in 1739, on the grounds that the Mughal emperor was the ruler of both Hindus and Muslims,[60] is very suggestive of the prevailing sentiment. It speaks of the deep imprint of Akbar's *sulh-i kul* carried by the Mughal Empire down to the time of its decline in the eighteenth century.

[59] *Tarikh-i Shahadat-i Farrukh Siyar wa Muhammad Shah Badshah,* Br. Library, Rieu, iii, 944–5, ff. 204b–206a.

[60] *Iqbal-nama* (anonymous author, eyewitness to developments down to 1734), Rampur. MS, cited by Satish Chandra, *Parties and Politics at the Mughal Court*, Bombay, 1979, p. 169, fn. 4.

1

The Mughal Assignment System during Akbar's Early Years, 1556–1575

IN THE DELHI SULTANATE, as also in the regional states which succeeded it during the fifteenth century, but most prominently during the Mughal period, the appropriation of the agricultural surplus and its orderly distribution amongst different segments of the ruling class was conducted mainly by an elaborate system of revenue assignments introduced in India originally by the Ghorians. The central feature of this system consisted of an arrangement whereby the management and appropriation of revenues of different territorial units vested in members of the ruling group under the supervision of the central authority. Individual holders of an assignment were not allowed to acquire hereditary rights over the regions that fell under their jurisdiction. Such an assignment was designated *iqta'* in the Delhi Sultanate and *jagir* or *tuyul* in the Mughal Empire. With the passage of time, the system tended to change in a variety of ways, often affecting or defining the degree of political centralization.

As Irfan Habib has pointed out, Firuz Tughlaq's 'policy of letting son succeed father to official posts' amounted 'to a complete capitulation to the sentiment in favour of permanent and semi-hereditary rights in the assignments.' Under the Lodis, this process went a step further when 'the nobility consisted of Afghan tribal leaders, whose control over the revenues of their territorial charges tended to be hereditary and derived only partly from the king's favour.'[1] But with the establishment of the Mughal Empire this trend was reversed. In the Mughal system of assignments, identified with *jagirs* or *tuyuls*, a noble's income from his assignment approximated to his salary fixed according to his rank in the hierarchy and the expected or actual strength of his armed contingent. It was closer to a pure revenue assignment than to an administrative-cum-fiscal charge like the *iqta'* of the Sultanate period. 'It was never a fixed territorial unit, and had no connection except for convenience in assignment, with the administrative units, *sarkars* and *parganas*.' The practice of frequently transferring assignments also reasserted itself under the Mughal rulers. Ordinarily, the *jagir* of a Mughal noble was transferred from one place to another after every three or four years.[2]

It is important to understand how and when this reversal of the earlier trend occurred under the Mughals. Was the emergence of the assignment system of the Mughals, with its pronounced centralizing features, dictated, as Rushbrook Williams suggests, by the theory of kingship that Babur brought with him?[3] Or was it an entirely novel arrangement conceived and enforced by Akbar along with his other far-reaching measures of 1574–5 (19 R.Y.) devised consciously for tightening control over the nobles? Or, again, would it be more

[1] 'The Social Distribution of Landed Property in Pre-British India', in *Indian Society: Historical Probing*, ed. R.S. Sharma and V. Jha, New Delhi, 1977, p. 294.

[2] Ibid., p. 303.

[3] *An Empire Builder of the Sixteenth Century*, reprint, S. Chand, n.d., Delhi, p. 161. Rushbrook Williams' view may be summarized thus: Babur, being the 'very embodiment of absolute kingship' and 'divine right', was determined to be 'no Sultan hampered by all the limitations which had beset the Lodi dynasty.' But lacking an aptitude for administration, Babur 'found it necessary to carry on the administrative plan of the Lodis.' An entirely new arrangement 'bridging the gulf between the central and local authorities' could materialize only under Akbar.

correct to assume that it was an arrangement meeting the special requirements of the Mughal polity in India which evolved under the strains and stresses of the period 1526–75, when the Mughals were struggling desperately for survival in the face of persisting local hostility? Before we attempt to answer these questions on the basis of fresh research, let us briefly notice the treatment that the subject has received from Moreland and Irfan Habib, both of whom have paid little more than passing attention to the evolution of the Mughal assignment system during the first twenty years of Akbar's reign.

The distinctive features of the Mughal assignment system towards the close of the sixteenth century are mainly discernible in the abundant source material that becomes available for the period 1595 onwards. Unfortunately, this material does not throw much light on the working of the system prior to 1574–5. It tends, moreover, to create the impression that the Mughal assignment system, with the features that we associate with its working during the seventeenth century, came into existence only with the introduction of *mansabs* in 1575. Such an impression is implicit in Moreland's as well as Irfan Habib's treatment of the subject. Both seem to proceed on the assumption that prior to 1575 the assignments in the Mughal Empire were not substantially different from the permanent administrative-cum-revenue charges of the Lodi period. According to Moreland, for instance, there is no important reference in the sources of Akbar's reign indicating that the assignee was permitted to realize only his sanctioned income and was 'required to account to the central treasury for any sums which he might collect in excess.' He goes on to suggest that this practice may have been 'developed gradually as an alternative to frequent revision of valuation' during the last twenty years of Akbar's reign.[4] Irfan Habib, on the other hand, implicitly suggests that in as late as the 13th regnal year of Akbar, i.e. 1568–9, the practice of frequent transfers was not decisively established.[5]

[4] *The Agrarian System of Muslim India*, reprint, Delhi, 1968, p. 98.
[5] *The Agrarian System of Mughal India*, Bombay, 1963, p. 260.

These suggestions are very useful in so far as they enable one to locate the problems that need to be examined in order to appreciate the working of the Mughal assignment system prior to Akbar's measures of 1575. At the same time, it is obvious that these two authorities have drawn purely tentative inferences from a limited survey of the extant evidence. Moreland himself has alluded in passing to references in the chronicles to assignments (with various designations) given to or held by nobles at different points of time—references that represent a store of information which, if arranged and sifted properly, could illuminate many aspects of the working of the Mughal assignment system during the early years of Akbar's reign.[6]

The insights provided by this evidence go to highlight the following problems as deserving of particular attention from researchers: (1) What were the different terms used in the sources to describe assignments as well as assignees, and to what extent do these reveal changing nuances in the system? (2) Were the assignments of individual nobles, as also of nobles belonging to the same clans, composed of compact territorial units, or were they parcelled out in small fragments scattered over different territories? (3) Were the assignments in the nature of revenue-cum-administrative charges or did they imply the separation of administrative and fiscal jurisdiction that was so patently established in the subsequent period? (4) What was the frequency of transfer of assignments and in what way was this related to other developments such as the separation of administrative and revenue charges, or the fragmentation of *jagirs*?

To find answers to these questions, as well as to address the wider issue of the reversal of the trend from the semi-hereditary or permanent control by nobles of their assignments, it is necessary to examine contemporary references pertaining to the receiving and holding of assignments by nobles. About 400 cases of such assignments made under Akbar down to 1581 have been gathered from *Tarikh-i Akbari*

[6] Cf. *The Agrarian System of Muslim India*, p. 94, where Moreland refers to chronicles showing 'the frequency of appointments and promotions'.

by 'Arif Qandahari, *Tazkira-i Humayun wa Akbar* by Bayazid Bayat, *Akbar-nama* by Abul Fazl, *Tabaqat-i Akbari* by Nizamuddin Ahmad, and *Muntakhab-ut-Tawarikh* by 'Abdul Qadir Badauni, and a list of assignments made which covers the first twenty-four years of Akbar's reign.[7] Individual cases of assignments are arranged in chronological order and information classified under the following five heads: 'Date', 'Nomenclature', 'Locale', 'Name of Assignee', and 'References'.[8]

Let us first examine the nomenclature. Such an exercise is aimed at gaining insights into the dynamics and orientation of the changes that the Mughal assignment system underwent during the first five decades of Mughal rule in Hindustan. It is largely based on a table showing the frequency with which different terms denoting assignments or assignees are used in my list of assignments.[9]

Next, I shall focus on the actual working of the Mughal assignment system down to 1567, drawing upon other more general evidence gleaned from the sources. To illustrate the frequency of *jagir* transfers during this period, information furnished by the list of assignments is presented in a separate appendix, where it is arranged under two heads: 'List of Assignments held by Thirteen Leading Nobles'; and 'List of Nobles holding *sarkars* Multan, Etawa, Narnaul, Kalpi and Sambhal as Assignments'.[10]

II

The term *jagir*, commonly used in seventeenth-century official papers to describe the revenue assignment, does not occur in any work compiled before Akbar. Its occurrence seems to have synchronized with the transition from the semi-permanent territorial assignments of the Lodi period to the revenue assignments of the Mughal Empire.

[7] See Appendix I.

[8] For the nature of information furnished under these heads, see introductory note to Appendix I.

[9] Appendix II.

[10] Appendix III.

The term *jagir*, which by the end of the sixteenth century came to be accepted as the standard word for a revenue assignment, is actually a shortened form of the Persian *jaygir*, meaning 'possessing, occupying a place, fixing a habitation, making a settlement'.[11] It possibly originated in the popular administrative jargon of petty officials during the early years of Akbar's reign and came to be used in official papers only gradually. A tendency on the part of both Abul Fazl and Badauni to spell the term as *jaygir*, and Abul Fazl's deliberate attempt in the third volume of *Akbar-nama* to substitute for it the archaic expression *iqta'*, indicates the reluctance of these writers to use this term of vulgar origin.

Accounts of the period 1556–60 contain the term *jagir* much less frequently than those of the period 1561–75.[12] From the table in Appendix II below it can be seen that of the total of 68 references for the period 1556–60, only 22, i.e. 32.3 per cent, mention the term *jagir*, while in the remaining 67.7 per cent cases the terms used for the assignments or the position of assignees are *hukumat/hakim* or some other vague expression like *hirāsat, sardārī, dawārī,* or *iyālat*. On the other hand, the corresponding respective percentages for 1561–75 come to 60.57 per cent and 39.43 per cent. As a matter of fact the frequency of use of the term *jagir* by chroniclers seems to increase dramatically from 1561 onwards, and persists down to 1575. But then, significantly enough, it declines in narratives of the period 1575–80. We know this as the period when in a major part of the empire revenue assignments were kept in abeyance. In the narratives of these years the term *jagir/jaygir* occurs only in 9.9 per cent of cases.

It may be assumed that the varying frequency of the term *jagir* was caused by the changing nomenclature for different kinds of assignments in the original documents consulted by the chroniclers. This is forcefully suggested by the sudden drop in the frequency of

[11] Muhammad Ghiyasuddin, *Ghiyas ul-Lughat* (compiled AH 1242/AD 1825–6), Kanpur: Nawal Kishore, 1878, p. 115. Cf. Steingass, *Persian–English Dictionary*, Indian edition, 1973, s.v. *jaygir.*

[12] Appendix II.

the term *jagir* during the period 1575–80. The sudden and startling shift from the extensive use made of the term during the preceding period was presumably caused by its absence from the royal orders conferring charges on the nobles during this period. Proceeding on the assumption that the varying technical terms used by chroniclers reflect the changing administrative jargon of official papers, one might interpret the table given in Appendix II as suggesting that the original documents available to chroniclers for the first four years of Akbar did not always use the term *jagir* as the standard technical term for assignment. This in turn goes to confirm the inference drawn by Irfan Habib from his reading of two of Akbar's *farmans* (dated AH *Jumada* I 971/December 1563–January 1564 and AH 24 *Sha'ban* 979/9 January 1572) that during the early years of Akbar's reign 'the term [*jagidar*] was meant to designate the lesser assignees of revenue, and not the great nobles or commanders holding large charges.'[13]

There is another significant aspect of the nomenclature used in the chronicles of Akbar's reign for assignments. It almost entirely excludes the expressions *wajah-wa-'alufa, istiqāmat-wa-wajah, wajah-wa-istiqāmat,*[14] terms used by Babur to describe different kinds of assignments made by him. Interestingly enough, in his Persian translation of the Turkish text of the *Babur-nama* prepared during the

[13] Irfan Habib, 'Aspects of Agrarian Relations and Economy in a Region of Uttar Pradesh during the Sixteenth Century', *The Indian Economic and Social History Review*, vol. IV, no. 3. September 1967, p. 209.

[14] Cf. A.R. Khan, 'Babur's Settlement of His Conquests in Hindustan', *Proceedings of the Indian History Congress*, 1967, p. 218. The expression *wajah-wa-istiqamat* being misread as *wajah-i istiqamat* can lead to a serious error in the study of Mughal nomenclature. For a correct reading of the formula, see A.S. Beveridge, *The Babur-nama, The Haiderabad Codex*, London: Luzac and Co., 1905, reprint 1971, ff. 304b, 326b, etc., as well as *Tuzak-i Baburi*, MS. BM Or. 3714, ff. 501, 531, etc. For Tatar Khan's assignment in Bayawa (that is Payanwan, cf. A.S. Beveridge, trans. *Babur-nama*), p. 540n.; and Irfan Habib, *An Atlas of the Mughal Empire,* Delhi, 1982, p. 28) and Khusrau Kokaltash's assignment in Alwar, as in most other cases, the formula used read *wajah-wa-istiqamat* not *wajah-i istiqamat.*

1580s, 'Abdur Rahim scrupulously avoids use of the newly coined term *jagir*, taking care to retain the original expressions.[15] One might well suppose that in doing so he was guided by awareness that the *wajahs* of Babur represented in many respects a very different kind of assignment system from the one identified, in the 1580s, with *jagirs*. And perhaps it was again for the same reason that in the official papers of the first four years of Akbar's reign (when the term was yet to be fully accepted in the standard administrative parlance), instead of employing the term *wajah*, vague expressions like *hukumat, sardārī, dāwarī, iyālat, hirāsat*, etc., were preferred.[16] It follows that the basic change in the nature of the assignment system, necessitating the coining of a new term to describe it, perhaps came about some time after Babur but before Akbar's accession. One might also consider whether this change did not occur under the Surs. It could have been the outcome of Sher Shah's policy of appointing *sarkar*-level military commanders, which was apparently a decisive step in the direction of separating the revenue assignments from the administrative charges of nobles.[17] This process is known to have been carried further by Islam Shah, who attempted to put all the 'soldiery' serving under him on cash salaries.[18]

III

At the time of Humayun's death (January 1556), the Mughal Empire appeared to be divided into seven or eight military zones, commanded by leading nobles from their headquarters at Kabul, Qandahar, Lahore, Multan, Delhi, Agra, Etawa, Kalpi, Kol, and Sambhal. These

[15] See *Tuzak-i Baburi*, MS., British Library, Or. 3714.

[16] See Appendices I and II.

[17] A rather obscure passage in the *Tarikh-i Sher Shahi* (India Office, Ethe, 219, f.114a), where Shuja'at Khan's appointment as the *hakim* of Malwa is mentioned, indicates that the salaries of troopers serving under a noble were paid through assignments made by the central authority within the territory under his administrative charge.

[18] 'Abdul Qadir Badauni, *Muntakhab-ut Tawarikh,* vol. I, Calcutta, 1864–9, p. 384.

nobles were entrusted with the responsibility of establishing regular administration after suppressing Afghan and other local resistance in the territories put under their control. Within these military zones, there existed smaller charges held by nobles placed in a subordinate position to the commanders (*hakims*) of larger territories. Side by side with military commands and charges there also existed revenue assignments (sometimes termed *jagir*) of the individual nobles. The *jagir* (revenue assignment as distinct from the military–administrative charge) of a high noble covering a number of contiguous *parganas*, sometimes even *sarkars*, would mostly be located within the territory controlled by him. But it would not always be concomitant with his military–administrative charge. Speaking in terms of the territory covered by the two kinds of assignment, one might say that the military–administrative charge of a high noble would always extend much beyond that of his revenue assignment. On the other hand, in the case of an ordinary noble holding charge of a *sarkar* or *pargana* in a subordinate position to a high noble, the meagre evidence we have suggests that the confines of his *jagir* often conformed to the territory of his charge.

The system of commands and *jagirs* obtaining at the time of Humayun's death may be inferred from the incidental evidence shedding light on arrangements obtaining in the military zones administered from Delhi, Kabul, and Qandahar. For instance, it suggests that the territory controlled from Delhi extended over a number of surrounding *sarkars*. To the south-east of Delhi the territory is known to have covered the *sarkars* of Mewat and Narnaul. Tardi Beg administered this entire territory from Delhi, but his own *jagir* was located in Mewat.[19] The *sarkar* of Narnaul apparently comprised the military charge as well as revenue assignment of one of Tardi Beg's subordinates, Majnun Khan Qaqshal.[20] A similar arrangement seems

[19] See *Akbar-nama*, vol. II, p. 14, for Abul Fazl's cryptic remark: 'servants of Tardi Beg maintained order in Mewat.'

[20] Ibid., p. 20. After Majnun Khan Qaqshal, who is described as the *jagirdar* of Narnaul, was expelled from there by the Sur noble Haji Khan,

to have existed in Kabul. While the overall military–administrative charge of *sarkar* Kabul rested with Mun'im Khan, and he also exercised the powers to appoint or dismiss commanders of different places within that *sarkar*,[21] not all the revenues of Kabul were under his control.[22] His personal *jagir* or revenue assignment comprised only a part of the total estimated revenues of *sarkar* Kabul. Several places located within the Kabul *sarkar* are known to have been held as *jagirs* by nobles serving as Mun'im Khan's subordinates. In this connection mention may be made of Mir Hashim's *jagir* comprising Kahmard, Ghorband, and Zuhak,[23] or of Khwaja Jalaluddin Mahmud holding the *hukumat* of Ghazni.[24]

The evidence on arrangements existing in *sarkar* Qandahar is still more revealing. The *sarkar* of Qandahar is described by Abul Fazl as Bairam Khan's *jagir* administered by his deputy, Shah Muhammad Qalati.[25] But he also seems to suggest that Zamindawar, described in the *Ain-i Akbari* as one of the '*vilayats*,' constituting '*Gharbi-i* Qandahar'[26] was held by Bahadur Khan Uzbek as his military and revenue assignment.[27] From this one might infer that the revenue

---

Tardi Beg came there to re-establish Mughal authority. This suggests that at this time the protection of *sarkar* Narnaul was his responsibility.

[21] For Mun'im Khan's position as the *hakim* of Kabul, see Iqtidar Alam Khan, *The Political Biography of a Mughal Noble*, New Delhi, 1973, pp. 35–51.

[22] From an incidental statement in Bayazid Bayat's memoir (*Tazkira-i Humayun wa Akbar*, ed. Hidayat Hosain, Calcutta, 1941, p. 221) that in 1557 Mun'im had gone to Nangnahar and Mandrawar to collect revenue, one might suppose that his *jagir* was located in the region around Ju-i Shahi (later Jalalabad).

[23] *Akbar-nama*, vol. II, p. 17.

[24] Ibid., p. 53.

[25] Ibid., p. 14.

[26] *Ain-i Akbari*, Bib., Ind., vol. I, p. 589.

[27] *Akbar-nama*, vol. II, p. 52. Abul Fazl uses the term *dawari* to describe Bahadur Khan's position at Zamindawar. Beveridge has by a slip rendered the word *dawari* as *diwani*. See English trans., vol. II, p. 53.

assignment of Bairam Khan was actually confined to only a part of *sarkar* Qandahar. This inference finds support in Nizamuddin's more cautious statement that Bairam Khan's *jagir* consisted of 'the town (*balda)* of Qandahar and its environs (*muzafat*).'[28]

The available evidence on the working of this arrangement during the first four or five years of Akbar's reign indicates also a growing tension between the commandants (*hakims*) of the different regions and the central authority over the question as to what kind of jurisdiction was to be allowed to them within the territories under them. One specific point of dispute appeared to be whether the commandant of a larger territory should control the entire revenues of the area or whether his fiscal authority should remain confined to his personal *jagir*, so that all the *mahals* and *sarkars* of his charge not within his own *jagir* and also not reserved for the *khalisa* might be given as *jagirs* to other nobles by the central *diwan*. Conflicting orientations of the central authority and regional commandants on this issue can be seen at work in the court's relations with 'Ali Quli Khan, the commandant of Lucknow and the adjoining *sarkars*, during 1558–60. Sometime in 1558, *pargana* Sandila was assigned by 'Ali Quli Khan to one of his relatives, Ismai'l Khan. But this assignment was superseded by the central *diwan*, which assigned it in *jagir* to Husain Khan Jalair. Although Ismai'l Khan tried to resist Husain Khan Jalair's taking over charge of the *pargana*, he was not successful. 'Ali Quli Khan, who initially encouraged Ismai'l Khan in his resistance, subsequently, appears to have accepted the *fait accompli.*[29]

There is yet another incident which throws light on this tension from a slightly different angle. In 1557, Mun'im Khan, the commandant of Kabul, arbitrarily removed Khwaja Jalaluddin Mahmud from his charge of Ghazni and, then, anxious to prevent

[28] Nizamuddin Ahmad, *Tabaqat-i Akbari,* ed. B. De, Calcutta, 1931, vol. II, p. 128.

[29] *Akbar-nama*, vol. II, pp. 68–9.

the aggrieved noble from reporting the matter to the court, had him imprisoned. From Mun'im Khan's behaviour on this occasion it becomes apparent that he was not very sure if he really had the authority to remove an assignee and for this reason feared that he might be accused of acting beyond his competence.[30]

Contrary pulls operating within the Mughal assignment system during the early years of Akbar's reign seem to have given rise to a number of the features assumed by the system as it operated down to 1575. One of these features appears to be the growing demarcation between the revenue assignments and the jurisdiction of the commandants over the territories controlled by them. The revenue assignment or *jagir* of a noble was increasingly conceived in terms of a fixed income assigned against specific *mahals* rather than a portion of the revenue collected from the territory administered by a noble. Also the locale and the nominal value of the *jagirs* of all the nobles, including the *jagirs* of those serving in different regions in subordinate positions to the superior *hakims*, would be decided by the central *diwan*. This is illustrated by an interesting passage in Bayazid Bayat, who tells us that in 1560, 'Ali Quli Khan, then *hakim* of Jaunpur and adjoining *sarkars*, assigned *sarkar* Banaras to his younger brother, Bahadur Khan, in a manner that bordered on defiance of the royal wishes. But he took care to make this assignment formally on behalf of the king (*az qibl-i padshahi*), which was apparently the reason why the court was eventually persuaded not to make an issue of this episode.[31] This was an exceptional case, however, insofar as the actual decision on assignment was taken by the commandant of a region without prior authorization. The standard procedure of the distribution of *jagirs* within a region appears to be that at the time of the appointment of a high noble as the *hakim* of a certain region, an official of the central *diwan* would be deputed to supervise the distribution of *jagirs* among the nobles stationed there. Abul Fazl

[30] Ibid., p. 71. See *Political Biography of a Mughal Noble*, p. 52.

[31] Bayazid, *Tazkira-i Humayun-wa-Akbar*, p. 244.

reports this procedure in connection with the assignment of *jagirs* in Malwa in the year 1562.[32] One might also suppose that the locale and value of the *jagirs* of even the highest nobles were expected to be properly defined through *sanads* issued by the central *diwan*, and refusal by the commandants of the regions to fully abide by this procedure was not condoned. It seems that one of the causes of the breach between the Uzbek nobles and the court in 1565 was the refusal of 'Ali Quli Klan and other Uzbek nobles to accept such control.[33] But, at the same time, one does come across occasional instances of the king virtually delegating his authority of assigning *jagirs* in different regions to local commanders.[34]

Down to 1560 or 1561, apparently, the revenue assignments covered a compact territory of contiguous *parganas* or *sarkars*. This is suggested by references in the sources to the assignment of *jagirs* and appointments of *hakims*. Before October 1560 one does not come across any case where one part of the salary of a noble was assigned against a fraction of the revenues of one *pargana* and the other

[32] At the time of 'Abdullah Khan Uzbek's appointment to Malwa in the 7th R.Y/1562–3, Muinuddin Khan Farankhudi, then a *wazir* in the *diwan-i buyutat*, was deputed to supervise the distribution of *jagirs* there. He was under instructions to return to Agra after performing this task (*Akbar-nama*, vol. II, pp. 168–9).

[33] It is noteworthy that while agreeing to stop military operations against 'Ali Quli Khan in 1565 without insisting on his surrender, Akbar still insisted that he would only be allowed to reoccupy his *jagir* after obtaining a formal *sanad* from the central *Diwan*. Again, during the brief peace of 1566, 'Ali Quli Khan was persuaded to send his agent to Agra to obtain formal papers of his *jagir* from the court. Cf. *Akbar-nama*, vol. II, pp. 260, 285: *Tabaqat-i Akbari*, vol. II, p. 181; *Muntakhab-ut Tawarikh*, vol. II, p. 82. See also *Tazkira-i Humayun-wa-Akbar*, pp. 339–40.

[34] One such case pertains to 1574, when Mun'im Khan was authorized by Akbar to recommend the assignment of *jagirs* in the eastern *sarkars*. Akbar is reported to have told Mun'im Khan: 'I recognize your handwriting. [A noble] will be assigned a *jagir* (only) after receiving a recommendation in your handwriting.' Bayazid, p. 339. It may be assumed that this practice had existed earlier as well.

part against a fraction of the revenues of some other *parganas*. It would appear that till 1560 the salaries of the nobles were arbitrarily settled in terms of the *jama'* of the *parganas* against which they were assigned.[35] Under this practice, a noble could hold as his *jagir* part of a *pargana*, one whole *pargana*, or several contiguous *parganas*, and a fraction of another adjacent *pargana*, but it was never assigned in parts against the partial *jama'* of two or more *parganas*. When around December 1560 an attempt was made by the officials of the central *diwan* to fragment the *jagir* of a senior noble by assigning it against the partial *jama'* of two different *parganas*, it provoked the noble to accuse the officials of vindictiveness.[36] There is also other evidence which suggests that earlier the *parganas* assigned to a noble were always contiguous ones. Bayazid Bayat tells us that in December 1560 'Ali Quli Khan was assigned (*jagir kardand*) *sarkars* Jaunpur, Banaras, Ghazipur, and some of the *parganas* of *sarkars* Manikpur and Awadh.[37] Apparently, part of 'Ali Quli Khan's salary that exceeded the total *jama'* of *sarkars* Jaunpur, Banaras, and Ghazipur was assigned against some of the *parganas* of the two neighbouring *sarkars*. It is significant that both the *sarkars* bordered upon

[35] This was apparently a practice dating from Babur's time. Babur's use of the term *pargana* for *wajah* is an indication that he perceived assignments basically in terms of fiscal units. For a reference of this kind, see, for instance, *Tuzuk-i Baburi*, f. 411b, where resumption of the nobles' assignments is described as resumption of their *parganas*.

[36] *Akbar-nama*, vol. II, p. 120. In Shamsuddin Muhammad Atka's letter to Akbar, written around December 1560, he complains bitterly that of one crore copper *tankas* sanctioned as his *juldu*, the authorities had assigned 40 *lakhs* (80 lakh *dams*) against Firuzpur. We know that at the time of the compilation of the *Ain-i Akbari* (Bib. Ind., L p. 554) the *jama'* of Firuzpur amounted to 1,14,79,404 *dams*. This indicates that the rest of the revenues of the *pargana* were either assigned to some other noble or were reserved for the *khalisa*. The remaining 60 *lakh* copper *tankas* (120 lakh *dams*) of Shamsuddin Muhammad Atka's assignment were to be given to him elsewhere. This was, apparently, viewed by him as a deviation from established practice.

[37] *Tazkira-i Humayun-wa-Akbar*, p. 239.

sarkar Jaunpur. This would strongly suggest that these *parganas* were contiguous to the rest of the territory of 'Ali Quli Khan's *jagir*, of which *sarkar* Jaunpur was a part. Thus one would be quite justified in interpreting this evidence as indicating the current emphasis on compact *jagirs*.

During Akbar's early years the *mahals* of the *khalisa* were not clearly demarcated. The Centre's share in the revenues of the different regions was no doubt fixed, but its collection and transmission to the central treasury were made the responsibility of the *hakims*. This situation is suggested by two statements furnished by Bayazid Bayat. First, he vaguely alludes to the existence of an arrangement, down to the beginning of 1561, where the responsibility for collecting central revenues rested with the senior nobles acting as *hakims*.[38] Secondly, he makes a cryptic reference to '*sarkar* Banaras' being 'in excess of his ['Ali Quli Khan's] *jagir*' in 1560. This *sarkar* was assigned by 'Ali Quli Khan to his brother Bahadur Khan 'on behalf of the king'.[39] From this statement it may be construed that before *sarkar* Banaras came to be assigned to Bahadur Khan at the beginning of 1561, its revenues were at par with those of the *khalisa*, but these were actually managed by the *hakim* of the Jaunpur region, of which Banaras was a part. Thus there emerges a general picture of high nobles managing the *khalisa* revenues of the regions administered by them, which they could always be tempted to misappropriate. Such a tendency was bound to be aggravated by the inflated *jama'* on the basis of which the value of the assignment was calculated. It was, perhaps, because of the general tendency of the regional *hakims* to withhold central revenue that towards the beginning of 1561 the central treasury was completely exhausted.

[38] Ibid., p. 244. While commenting on the depletion of the central treasury around December 1560, Bayazid observes: 'After His Majesty started paying attention to the affairs of his *sarkar (sarkar-i khwud)*, the people have seen how much treasure has accumulated in each one of the towns, *parganas* and villages of Hindustan.'

[39] *Tarikh-i Humayun-wa-Akbar*, p. 244.

One noteworthy consequence of the working of the *jagir* system during the first four years of Akbar's reign was the concentration in particular regions of *jagirs* of nobles belonging to the same clans. This emerges from evidence relating to the Turani nobles during 1563–7. Already by 1565 the following concentrations seem to have existed: Uzbeks in the Jaunpur region; Qaqshals in Kara-Manikpur, Jalairs in Lucknow and Awadh; Mirzas in Sambhal; and the Atka clan in the Punjab. A number of factors seem to have contributed to this situation. Firstly, it could have been created by the Court's policy, down to 1560, generally to assign *jagirs* to members of a clan in a region administered by their leader. One comes across several such instances. In 1559, for instance, the entire Jalair clan was assigned *jagirs* in and around *sarkar* Lucknow. In August–September 1560, Akbar decided to confer the 'whole of Punjab on him [Shamsuddin Muhammad Atka] and his brothers.'[40] Again, the concentration of clans in particular regions was also facilitated by an overt tendency on the part of high nobles to procure *jagirs* for their own clansmen within the territory of their charges. Sometimes this was sought to be achieved even by violating or twisting the rules.[41]

From the central authority's point of view, one negative result of this development was the marked slowing down of the process of transfer of *jagirs*. The list of assignments I have prepared shows that transfers were more frequent during the first four years of Akbar's reign than during 1560–7. This result is derived from Appendix III. It comes out clearly from the list of assignments held by Muhammad Qasim Barlas, Bahadur Khan, 'Ali Quli Khan, Qaya Khan Gung, and Iskandar Khan. The same trend is also suggested by the list of nobles holding assignments in *sarkars* Multan, Etawa, Narnaul, Kalpi, and Sambhal. The concentration of different clans in particular regions by 1560 was responsible, at least partly, for this slower rotation of *jagirs* during the ensuing six years.

[40] *Akbar-nama*, vol. II, pp. 82, 116.

[41] As in the case already mentioned, 'Ali Quli Khan's assigning Banaras as *jagir* to his brother on the presumption that he was doing it on behalf of the king (*az qibl-i padshahi*). Cf. *Tazkira-i Humayun-wa-Akbar*, p. 244.

IV

In the evolution of the *jagir* system under Akbar, 1561 appears as a crucial turning point. It is around this time that certain far-reaching changes in the working of the *jagir* system become discernible. These changes may be regarded as the precursors of Akbar's measures of 1574–5. In this section, I propose briefly to notice some of these changes, and, to the extent that the available evidence permits, I propose to investigate the question of how the changes of 1561 were related to the better-known developments of 1566–7 and 1574–5.

A significant change introduced around 1561 pertains to the manner in which *jagirs* were assigned. From the second half of 1560 onwards, the *jagirs* of great nobles came to be assigned in fragments scattered over a number of *parganas* located at considerable distances from each other. It seems this was done as a matter of conscious policy. The change seems to have synchronized with the rise of a new concept of assignment, which, in the post-1561 period, was increasingly perceived as pre-sanctioned income determined in accordance with the status and obligations of the assignee.

The basic evidence suggesting this change is vague, even problematic in nature. The earliest indication of it is furnished by Shamsuddin Muhammad Atka's letter of December 1560 to Akbar, referred to in the preceding section, in which he accuses the officials of the central *diwan* of being slow in assigning to him and his son certain *jagirs* already sanctioned by the king. He also complains of these officials being vindictive towards him and makes two specific points: that the full assignment of *jagirs* sanctioned by the king in October 1560 was being delayed indefinitely; and that an attempt was being made to fragment his *jagir* by assigning it in pieces in various *parganas*. The second point is not directly made but clearly implied in the statement: 'out of the entire amount [of one crore copper *tankas*] the authorities have assigned [only] forty lakhs (i.e. 80 lakh *dams*) on Firuzpur.'[42] The implication of this statement becomes clear in the

[42] *Akbar-nama*, vol. II, p. 120.

light of the *A'in-i Akbari's* figure for the *jama'* of *pargana* Firuzpur, which in 1595 stood at 1,14,79,404 *dams*,[43] which means it outstripped the *jama'* of Shamsuddin Muhammad Atka's assignment against the same *pargana* by 34,79,404 *dams*. The corresponding *jama'* figure for 1560 would have been still higher owing to the fact stated by Abul Fazl himself that the earlier *jama' raqami* figures were inflated. It can thus be seen that in assigning only 40 lakh copper *tankas* (i.e. 80 lakh *dams*) out of Shamsuddin Muhammad Atka's sanctioned income of one crore or two crore *dams*, against a *pargana* whose *jama'* exceeded one crore fourteen lakh *tankas*, the officials of the central *diwan* were seen to be deviating from the norm followed till then.

It may, however, be pointed out that Shamsuddin Muhammad Atka's grouse was not fully justified. Official deviations from the norm hitherto adhered to were not confined to his case. Sometime between 1561 and 1563 Mun'im Khan's compact *jagir* at Hisar Firuza was also reduced by almost half, and for this he was compensated by being assigned *jagirs* in the widely scattered *sarkars* of Etawa and Khairabad, and the *parganas* of Shahpur (in *sarkar* Bari Doab), Jalandhar (in *sarkar* Bet Jalandhar Doab), and Indri (in *sarkar* Saharanpur).[44]

[43] *Ain-i Akbari*, Bib. Ind., Calcutta, 1867–77, vol. I, p. 554

[44] *Tazkira-i Humayun-wa-Akbar*, pp. 240, 248, 299: In October 1560, *sarkar* Hisar Firuza was given to Mun'im Khan as his *jagir*. Presumably, the entire revenues of Hisar Firuza were assigned to him. He appears to have held this *jagir* without change till 1561, when an order was issued for the transfer of *sarkar* Hisar Firuza to the *khalisa*, but on Mun'im Khan's agreeing to its being governed by a *hakim* appointed by the central *diwan* he was allowed to hold a *jagir* there. (See also *Akbar-nama*, vol. II, p. 189.) The extent to which Mun'im Khan's *jagir* in *sarkar* Hisar Firuza was reduced can be gauged by comparing the figure for its income in 1567 furnished by Bayazid Bayat, i.e. 3 crore (*dams*?), with the *jama'* of the *sarkar* given in the *Babur-nama* (1,30,75,174 copper *tankas*, equal to 2,61,50,346 *dams*) and *Ain-i Akbari* (5,23,54,905 *dams*). Bayazid has not specified the currency in which he has stated the *hal-i hasil* of Mun'im Khan's *jagir* at Hisar Firuza.

Till April 1561 *sarkar* Hisar Firuza was administered by a certain Khwaja Kalan, described by Bayazid as a servant of Mun'im Khan. In April 1561 the same *sarkar* was placed under a *hakim* appointed from the central *diwan*. The person entrusted with this charge was Bayazid Bayat who had, till this time, been a personal servant of Mun'im Khan; his appointment as *hakim* of Hisar Firuza was considered a promotion to the position of an officer of the king. His new status was underlined by the conferment of the title *sultani*.[45] It is very likely that the curtailment of Mun'im Khan's administrative jurisdiction in *sarkar* Hisar Firuza suggested by the above change not only accompanied but actually resulted from the decision of the authorities to reduce his assignment in that *sarkar*.

Here it would not be out of place to note that the identical cash rates given in the schedule of *Ain-i dahsala* for the widely dispersed *dastur* circles comprising Kishni and Ibrahimabad in Awadh are quite different from the rates sanctioned for Awadh, but similar to those of Manikpur and Rae Bareli. Regarding these *dastur* circles, Shireen Moosvi's guess that these were 'included in the *jagirs* of some big nobles who held the other circles within their *jagirs* and wished to have identical *dasturs* in various parts of their *jagirs*', seems very plausible. Thus the pattern of cash rates shown for different *dastur* circles in *Ain-i dahsala* may also be interpreted as testifying to the fragmentation of the *jagirs* of some of the high nobles during 1575–80, when these rates were actually worked out.[46]

Shamsuddin Muhammad Atka's letter is perhaps the earliest document where the value of the *jagir* of a noble is stated in terms of sanctioned income rather than the yield of the *parganas/sarkars* against which it was assigned. This evidence seems to point to a quite

---

But it could not be a figure in copper *tankas*. If Bayazid's figure for the actual collection in 1567 is treated as being stated in copper *tankas* then it would exceed the *jama'* of the *sarkar* both for 1526 as well as 1595.

[45] *Tazkira-i Humayun-wa-Akbar*, pp. 249–50.

[46] Shireen Moosvi, 'Formulation of Land Revenue Rates under Akbar', *Indian Historical Review*, January 1978, vol. IV, no. 2, pp. 324-5.

different conception of the system from the one where a revenue assignment was conceived basically as the allocation of the revenues of a territory to a person entrusted with its administration. It is in this sense that Atka Khan's reference to the pre-sanctioned value of his *jagir* represents an entirely different situation from what is suggested by the statements in *Babur-nama* specifying the amounts assigned to individual nobles against different *parganas/sarkars*. Moreover, it is integral to the conception of a *jagir* representing the pre-sanctioned income of a noble that its value would be fixed keeping in view the status of the noble and the actual strength of his contingent. In this context, Shireen Moosvi's interpretation of the passage in *Akbar-nama* on the fixing of the strength of the nobles' contingents in 1566 seems to be especially relevant.[47] It is very likely that the money rates per horseman mentioned there were used for specifying the strength of the contingent against the expected income of *jagirs* under the newly established *jama*'. But it is also possible that these criteria were formulated on the basis of previous practice, having been worked out by taking into account the ratio to be maintained between the strength of a noble's contingent and his actual income.

This is partly borne out by the figures furnished by Bayazid Bayat for the *hal-i hasil* of Mun'im Khan's *jagirs* in *sarkar* Hisar Firuza, and the strength of the contingent that he maintained on that income. In 1565, 700 to 800 horsemen were maintained on the income of Mun'im Khan's *jagirs* in *sarkar* Hisar Firuza,[48] and the actual collection (*hal-i hasil*) of the same *jagir* in 1567 came to three crore *dams*.[49] From these figures the rate of payment per horseman works out to 42,857 *dams* if the strength of the contingent is taken as 700, and 37,500 *dams* if it is accepted as 800. The rates

[47] Shireen Moosvi, 'The Evolution of the *Mansabdari* System under Akbar until 1596–7', *Journal of the Royal Asiatic Society*, no. 2, 1980, p. 175.

[48] *Tazkira-i Humayun-wa-Akbar*, p. 285.

[49] As already argued, this figure could not have been in copper *tankas*. It is obvious that Bayazid has converted the original figure of copper *tankas* into *dams*.

per horseman fall within the range of the second category (32,000) and third category (48,000) of horsemen given by Abul Fazl. One might even conjecture that the new conception of the *jagir* suggested by Shamsuddin Muhammad Atka's reference to the pre-sanctioned value of his assignment tended to make the income of a noble's *jagir* and the number of troops commanded by him contingent on each other.

The process of the fragmentation of *jagirs* and the consequent separation of *jagir* from administrative jurisdiction inevitably impeded the regional concentration of the *jagirs* of the nobles. But there also arose a definite policy of not allowing the clans to remain concentrated in particular regions. During 1564–7 even the groups siding firmly with the king in his conflict with the recalcitrant Turani nobles were not exempted from the operation of this policy. Soon after the suppression of the Uzbek nobles in 1567, members of the Atka Khail were transferred from the Punjab. Subsequently, their *jagirs* were scattered all over the empire. Akbar regarded Atka Khail's dispersal a greater achievement than the suppression of defiant sections of the nobility.[50]

In conclusion, it would be useful to specifically enumerate some of the important points that emerge from this discussion.

An analysis of the nomenclature used for the Mughal assignments strengthens the impression that the system identified with the *jagirs* of Akbar's reign was a different kind of arrangement from the one represented by the military-cum-revenue assignments of Babur. Insofar as this suggests that the origin of the Mughal assignment system lay in the administrative policies of the Sur rulers, it points to a line of inquiry which has yet to be pursued with vigour. It also goes to underline Athar Ali's emphasis on the contribution made by the Sur regime to the structure of the Mughal polity.[51]

[50] *Tazkira-i Humayun-wa-Akbar*, p. 253.

[51] 'Toward an Interpretation of the Mughal Empire', *Journal of the Royal Asiatic Society*, no. 1, 1978, p. 39.

The division of the Mughal Empire at the time of Humayun's death into a number of military zones administered by senior nobles seems to resemble the administrative plan that, according to Abul Fazl, was contemplated by Humayun in 1555, a scheme characterized by S. Nurul Hasan as aimed at the decentralization of authority.[52] But from references to assignments during the first four years of Akbar's reign it appears that the organization of military command inherited by him from Humayun was actually superimposed on a system of revenue assignments closely regulated by the central authority. This in turn points to a similarity with the structure of commands and assignments established by Sher Shah. From its very inception, then, this arrangement appeared to carry an inbuilt tendency towards the separation of the revenue assignments from the assignees' military and administrative jurisdictions.

The working of this system during the last two years of Bairam Khan's regency, when he was forced to act in important matters in consultation with leading nobles,[53] seems to have given rise to certain features which thwarted its intrinsic centralizing propensity. But this imperfection of the Mughal assignment system in the early years of Akbar's reign was speedily remedied after he had succeeded in establishing his personal authority in the central government around 1561. One might even suggest that the changes discernible in the Mughal assignment system between 1561 and 1567, such as the linking of a noble's income with his status and military obligation, the fragmentation of *jagirs*, and the clear demarcation of the *jagir* jurisdiction from routine administration went much beyond the structural possibilities of the system handed down by Humayun. In many respects it now tended to resemble the *jagir* system of the

[52] S. Nurul Hasan, 'New Light on the Relations of Early Mughal Rulers with Their Nobility', *Proceedings of the Indian History Congress*, 1944, pp. 389–97.

[53] For the curtailment of Bairam Khan's powers around April 1558, see Iqtidar Alam Khan, 'The Mughal Court Politics during Bairam Khan's Residency', *Medieval India—A Miscellany*, vol. I, Delhi, 1969, p. 33.

post-1575 period, which, it goes without saying, was increasingly conditioned by the operation of a new mode of revenue assessment and collection, and also by the gradual introduction of an elaborate system of military hierarchy and obligations.

Appendix I

This Appendix seeks to assemble information pertaining to the assignments conferred upon, or held by, individual nobles at different points of time during the first twenty-four years of Akbar's reign (1556–80). The references listed have been taken from the four major histories of Akbar's reign, namely, *Tarikh-i Akbari* by 'Arif Qandahari, *Tazkira-i Humayun-wa-Akbar* by Bayazid Bayat, *Akbar-nama* by Abul Fazl, *Tabaqat-i Akbari* by Nizamuddin Ahmad, and *Muntakhab-ut Tawarikh* by 'Abdul Qadir Badauni. The available information is presented under five heads:

Date: This is either established with the help of specific dates furnished by the chronicles or is suggested by the sequence of reporting in Abul Fazl's chapters arranged by regnal years.

Nomenclature: If, in a particular reference, the fact of a noble holding an assignment is alluded to only by implication without using any specific expression to denote the nature of his jurisdiction, the entry in this column simply reads: '(assignment)'.

Locale: Where the place assigned is identified with the *pargana* headquarters or a small town (*qasba*) located within a *sarkar*, its name is entered under *Pargana/Qasba*. For the purpose of this list, the *tumans* of *sarkars* Kabul and Qandahar are also identified as *parganas*. The name of the *Sarkar* within which the *pargana/qasba* under reference was included is entered under the column *Sarkar* within parentheses. (In the case of *qasba* Kahmard situated in Balkh this rule could not be adhered to as it was not included in any of the *sarkars* listed in *Ain-i Akbari*.) To indicate whether a particular place name in this column refers to a *pargana* or *qasba*, the letter 'Q' is written within parentheses against the names of the *qasbas*: e.g. 'Mama Khatun (Q)'. The locations of places other than *pargana* or *sarkar* headquarters have been determined with the help of Irfan Habib's *Atlas of the Mughal Empire* (Delhi: Oxford University Press, 1982). In a few cases, where the information is vague and alludes only to the assignment of unspecified *parganas* in a particular *sarkar*, it is entered as '*Parganas*' in the column '*Pargana/Qasba*' with the name of the *sarkar* within parentheses under '*Sarkar*'.

If the place is identified with the name of a *sarkar* headquarters or the territory of a *sarkar* (e.g. *sarkar* Punjab), it is placed under *Sarkar*; this applies to cases where the same place happened to be the *suba* headquarters as well, in view of the fact that during our period, i.e. down to 1580, regular *subas* did not exist.

In all cases where the place assigned is identified by the sources with a territory that later came to comprise a *suba* (e.g. Malwa, Punjab, etc.) or appears to have corresponded to a territorial unit that was larger than a *sarkar* but was not constituted into a *suba* in 1580, it is placed under '*Vilayat/Suba*', and against the latter type of territory 'V' is added in parentheses: e.g. 'Badakshan (V)'.

The spellings of place names given by Irfan Habib in his *Atlas* are generally used.

References: The following abbreviations are used:

'Arif	'Arif Qandahari, *Tarikh-i Akbari*, Rampur, 1962
Bayazid Bayat	*Tazkira-i Humayun-wa-Akbar*, Calcutta, 1941
AN	Abul Fazl, *Akbar-nama*, Calcutta, 1873–87
TA	Nizamuddin Ahmad, *Tabaqat-i Akbari*, Calcutta, 1931
Badauni	'Abdul Qadir Badauni, *Muntakhab-ut Tawarikh*, Calcutta, 1864–9

Where the sources cited for the same reference have varying versions of technical terms or of names, etc., the earlier version is preferred.

Appendix I

List of Assignments: AD 1556–80

Date	Nomenclature	Locale			Name	Reference
		Pargana/Qasba	*Sarkar*	*Suba/Vilayat*		
1556						
March	*ba-aramash w asaish-t mulk*			Badakhshan [V}	Mirza Sulaiman	*AN*, II, p. 14
March	*intizam dasht*		Kabul-wa-Ghazni		Mun'im Khan	,,
March	*jagir*		Qandahar		Bairam Khan	,, *TA*, II, p. 128
March	*nizam-i Sarkar*		Sambhal		'Ali Quli Khan	*AN*, II, p. 14
March	*hukumat*		Agra		Sikandar Khan Uzbek	,,
March	*ba-sardari*		Kalpi		'Abdullah Khan Uzbek	,,
March	*amniyat bakhsh*			Mewat (V)	*mulazman-i* Tardi Beg	,,
March	*lawazim-i khidmat*		Kol-wa Jalali		Qaya Khan Gung	,,
March	*ijra-i ahkam-i padshahi namud*	Bayana	(Agra)		Haidar Muhammad Khan	,,
March	*jagir*	Ghorband	(Kabul)		Mir Hashim	*AN*, II, p. 17
		Kahmard (Q)				
		Zuhak	(Kabul)			
March	*jagir*		Narnaul		Majnun Khan Qaqshal	*AN*, II, p. 20
March	*sawab-i intimā*		Delhi		Tardi Beg Khan	,,

(*contd.*)

Appendix I (*contd.*)

Date	Nomenclature	Locale			Name	Reference
		Pargana/Qasba	*Sarkar*	*Suba/Vilayat*		
September–October	*hakim*		Agra		Sikandar Khan Uzbek	*AN*, II, p.129
,,	(assignment)		Etawa		Qaya Khan Gung	Badauni, II, p. 13
,,	(assignment)		Kalpi		'Abdullah Khan Uzbek	,,
,,	(assignment)	Bayana	(Agra)		Haidar Muhammad Khan	,,
November	(assignment)		Sambhal *ba-sair-i pargana-ha-i mian-i doab*		'Ali QuIi Khan (titled Khan-i Zaman)	'Arif, p. 52 *AN*, II, p. 45
,,	*ikhtisas bakhshidand*		Kalpi		Abdullah Khan Uzbek (titled Shuja'at Khan)	*AN*, II, p. 45
,,	*ba intizam namzad shud*		*dar-ul mulk Agra-wa an hudud*		Qaya Khan	,,
November	*ba hirasat*		*Shahar-i* Lahore		Haji Muhammad Sistani	Ibid., p. 47
,,	*ba hirasat*		Delhi		Mahdi Qasim Khan	Ibid., p. 48
,,	*hukumat*		Ghazni		Khwaja Jalaluddin Bujuk	Ibid., p. 55
December	*jaygir*	Sialkot	(Rachnao Doab)		Sikandar Khan	Ibid., p. 47
1557						
March	(assignment)		Multan		Muhammad Quli Khan	*AN*, II, p. 53

(*contd.*)

Date	Nomenclature	Locale			Name	Reference
		Pargana/Qasba	*Sarkar*	*Suba/Vilayat*		
March	*jagir*		Multan		Bahadur Khan Uzbek	*AN*, II, p. 53
March	*jagirdar*		Nagaur *wa an hudud*		Muhammad Quli Barlas	Ibid., p. 53
23 July	*jagir*		Kharid, Bihar *wa an hudud*		Sikandar Sur	Ibid., p. 59
23 July	*hirasat*		Qila-i Mankot		Abul Qasim	Ibid., p. 59
December	*hukumat*		Lahore		Husain Khan	Ibid., p. 46
1558						
March	*mutakafil-i intizam*		Ajmer		Muhammad Qasim Khan Nishapuri	Ibid., p. 66
March–October	*jaygir*	Surharpur	(Jaunpur)		'Abdul Rahman Beg	Ibid., p. 83; *TA*, II, p. 137; Badauni, II, p. 23
1558	*jaygir*	Sandila	(Lucknow)		Sultan Husain Khan Jalair	*AN*, II, p. 69
1558	*jagir*	Fathpur Haswa, etc.	(Kara-Manikpur)		Kamal Khan Ghakkar	Ibid., pp. 78, 192 *TA*, II, p.161
1558	*jagir*	Hatkant	(Etawa)		Adham Khan	*AN*, II, p. 78

(*contd.*)

Appendix I (*contd.*)

Date	Nomenclature	Locale			Name	Reference
		Pargana/Qasba	*Sarkar*	*Suba/Vilayat*		
1558	*wajah-i jaygir*	Bayana	(Agra)		Habib 'Ali Khan	Badauni, II, p. 31
1558	*muqarrar shud*	Bhasawar Toda Bhim	(Agra)		Chaghtai Khan	Ibid.
1559 March–September	*jaygir*		Dipalpur		Bahadur Khan Uzbek	*AN*, II, p. 102; Badauni, II, p. 11
1559	(assignment)		Lucknow		'Ali Quli Khan	*AN*,II, p. 82 *TA*, II, p. 141
1559	*ba taskhir*		Jaunpur		'Ali Quli Khan	Ibid.
1559	*supurda*		Lucknow		Jalairs	*AN*, II, p. 82
1559	*hakim*		Hisar Firuza		Beg Mirak	Bayazid, p. 279
1560						
March	(assignment)	Indri	(Saharanpur)		Husain Khan	Badauni, II, p. 35
March	*hakim*		Delhi		Shahabuddin Ahmad Khan	*AN*, II, p. 94; *TA*, II, p. 143
March	(assignment)	Sikandra Rao	(Kol)		Muhammad Baqi Baqlani	*AN*, II, p. 94
March	(assignment)	Bhera	(Chinhat Doab)		Shamsuddin Muhammad	Ibid., p. 95

(*contd.*)

Appendix I (*contd.*)

Date	Nomenclature	Locale			Name	Reference
		Pargana/Qasba	*Sarkar*	*Suba/Vilayat*		
March	(assignment)		Lahore		Qasim Mahdi Khan	Ibid., *AN*, p. 95
March	(assignment)		Lahore		Mir Muhammad, Khan-i Kalan	*AN*, II, p. 95
			Alwar		Bairam Khan	Ibid., p. 98
March–April	*hakim*		Dipalpur		Durwesh Uzbek	'Arif, p. 61; Bayazid, p. 226
,,	*jagir*	Bhatnair	Hisar Firuza)		Sher Muhammad Diwana	'Arif, p. 61; Bayazid, p. 225; *AN*, II, p. 109; *TA*, II, p. 147; Badauni, II, p. 40
May	*hukumat*		Kabul		Haidar Muhammad Khan Akhta Begi	*TA*, II, p. 162
April–May	(assignment)		Bahraich		Qaya Khan	*AN*, II, p. 100
April–May	*muqarrar shud*		Nagaur		Mirza Sharfuddin Husain	Ibid., p. 104
April–May	*jagirdar*	Pathaura / Thara	(Bari Doab)		Mirza 'Abdullah Mughal	Bayazid, p. 225; *AN*, II, p. 110

(*contd.*)

Appendix I (*contd.*)

Date	Nomenclature	Locale			Name	Reference
		Pargana/Qasba	*Sarkar*	*Suba/Vilayat*		
August–September	(assignment)		Multan		Muhammad Quli Khan Barlas	*AN*, II, pp. 114–15
,,	*jaygir*		Multan		Muhammad Qasim Nishapuri and others	Ibid.
,,	*jaygir*	Etawa	(Etawa)		Bahadur Khan	*AN*, II, p. 115
July–August	*hukumat*		Delhi		Khwaja 'Abdul Majid	Ibid., p. III .
August–September	*hukumat*			Punjab	Shamsuddin Muhammad Atka and brothers	*AN*, II p. 116
October	*juldu*	Firozpur	(Dipalpur)		Shamsuddin Muhammad Atka	Ibid., p. 121
	jaygir			Nagaur	Mirza Sharfuddin Husain	Ibid., p. 128
October–December	*Jagir*	Patiali			Husain Khan	Badauni, II, p. 43
December	*jagir*	*Parganas*	Jaunpur Baranas Ghazipur (Awadh & Manikpur)		'Ali Quli Khan-i Zaman	Bayazid, p. 239

(*contd.*)

Appendix I (*contd.*)

Date	Nomenclature	Locale			Name	Reference
		Pargana/Qasba	*Sarkar*	*Suba/Vilayat*		
December	*diwan*		Hisar Firuza		Khwaja Muzaffar 'Ali	Bayazid, p. 240
December	*jagir*		Hisar Firuza		Mun'im Khan	"
	hukumat		Kalpi		'Abdullah Khan Uzbek	Badauni, III, p. 6
1561						
January–March	(assignment)		Etawa		Bahadur Khan Uzbek	Bayazid, p. 244
"	*Jagir*		Banaras		Bahadur Khan Uzbek	"
March	*sardari-i suri*			Malwa	Adham Khan	*AN*, II, p. 138
"	*Ikhtisas yaft*		Sarangpur		*Adham Khan*	*AN*, II, p. 138
"	*sardari-i ma'navi*			Malwa	Pir Muhammad Khan	*AN*, II, p. 138
1561						
March	*muqarrar shud*		Mandu		Pir Muhammad Khan	*AN*, II, p. 138
			Ujjain			"
	mufauwaz gasht		Handia		Qaya Khan Gung	"
March	*namzad kardand*		Mandasor *wa an hudud*		Sadiq Khan	"
March	*Jaygir*		Kalpi		'Abdullah Khan	"
April	*Jagir*		Hisar Firuza		Mun'im Khan	Bayazid, p. 249

(*contd.*)

Date	Nomenclature	Locale			Name	Reference
		Pargana/Qasba	*Sarkar*	*Suba/Vilayat*		
24 May	*jagirdars*	*[Parganas]*	*an hudud* (Jaunpur and the eastern *sarkars* in general)		Ibrahim Khan Uzbek Majnun Khan Qaqshal Shaham Khan Jalair Kamal Khan Ghakkar	*TA*, II, p. 154
August	*hakim*		Jaunpur		'Ali Quli Khan	'Arif, p. 68
August	*jagir*		Banaras		Bahadur Khan	*TA*, II, p. 154
August	*hakim*		Kalpi		'Abdullah Khan	Badauni, II, p. 49
August	*hukumat*		*Sarkar* Punjab		Shamsuddin Muhammad Atka (titled Khan-i A'zam)	Bayazid, p. 245; *TA*, II, p. 155
October–November	*hirasat*		Chunar (Q)		Hasan 'Ali Khan Turkman	*AN*, II, p. 150
1562						
January	*jaygir*		Mewat (V)		Mirza Sharfuddin Husain	Ibid., p. 155
January	*hukumat*		Malwa		Pir Muhammad Khan	'Arif, p. 68; *AN*, *AN*, II, p. 152; *TA*, II, p. 156
1562						
January–February	*jaygir*		Ajmer		Mirza Sharfuddin Husain	Badauni, II, p. 50

(*contd.*)

Appendix I (*contd.*)

Date	Nomenclature	Locale			Name	Reference
		Pargana/Qasba	*Sarkar*	*Suba/Vilayat*		
January–February	*jaygir*		Ajmer		Tarsun Muhammad Khan Shah Budagh Khan 'Abdul Muttalib Khurram Khan Muhammad Husain Shaikh	*AN*, II, p. 157
March–April	*jaygir*	Sakit	(Kannauj)		Ibrahim Badakhshi	Ibid., p. 163
March–May	*jaygir*	Birka	(Bet Jalandhar Doab)		Jan Muhammad Bihsudi	Ibid., p. 169
July–August	*jaygir*	Sarut	(Saharanpur)		Mir Muhammad Munshi	Ibid., p. 180
,,	*shiqdar*	Sarut	(Saharanpur)		Qasim 'Ali Sistani	Ibid.; *TA*, II, p. 159; Badauni, II, p. 54
August	*hakim*		Mandu		'Abdullah Khan Uzbek	'Arif, p. 68; Bayazid, p. 243; *AN*, II, p. 168; *TA*, II, p. 157
,,	*jaygir*	(*Parganas*)		Malwa	Qaya Khan Gung Shah Muhammad Qalati Habib Khan	*AN*, II, p.168

(*contd.*)

Date	Nomenclature	Locale			Name	Reference
		Pargana/Qasba	*Sarkar*	*Suba/Vilayat*		
1563						
January	*jaygir*	Mama Khatun (Q)	(Kabul)		Tulak Khan	*AN*, II, p. 184
,,	(assignment)	Ghaznin	(Kabul)		Mirza Khizr Khan Hazara	Ibid., p. 186
March	*jaygir*		Kara		Khwaja 'Abdul Majid (Asaf Khan)	Ibid., p. 182
,,	(assignment)	Peshawar	(Kabul)		Hamza 'Arab	Bayazid, p. 255
,,	*hakim*		Multan		Muhammad Quli Khan Barlas	*AN*, II, p. 187
,,	*jaygirs*	(*Parganas*)	Hisar Firuza		Mun'im Khan	Ibid., p. 189
		(*Parganas*)	Etawa			
		(*Parganas*)	Khairabad			
		Shahpur	(Karli / Bari Doab)			
		Kalanaur	(Karli / Bari Doab)			
		Jalandhar	(Bet Jallandhar Doab)			
		Indri	(Saharanpur)			
,,	(assignment)		Kabul		Ghani Khan	*TA*, II, p. 162
April–May	*hirasat*		Chunar		Hasan Khan Turkman	Badauni, II, p. 63
August	*shiqdar*		Narnaul		Gesu Khan	'Arif, p. 73; *TA*, II, p. 165;

(*contd.*)

Date	Nomenclature	Locale			Name	Reference
		Pargana/Qasba	*Sarkar*	*Suba/Vilayat*		
						Badauni, II, p. 60
1563						
August	*jagir*	*Pargana*	(Narnaul)		Khanzadas	*TA*, II, p. 166
August	*jaygirs*			Punjab	Mir Muhammad Khan Qutbuddin Khan Mahdi Qasim Khan Sharif Khan Jan Muhammad Bahsudi Raja Kapur Deo Raja Ram Chand	*AN*, II, p. 193, Bayazid, p. 270
September	*darai*	*Parganas*	(Punjab)		Kamal Khan Ghakkar	'Arif, p. 72; *TA*, II, p. 161
September	*jagir*		Ajmer, Nagaur		Husain Quli Beg	*AN*, II, pp. 195–6
September	(assignment)	Qil'a Merta	(Nagaur)		Jag Mal	*AN*, II, p. 196
September	*muqarrar shud*		Narnaul		Shuja'at Khan	Ibid., p. 199
September	(assignment)	Hajipur	(Jodhpur)		Husain Quli Khan	Badauni, II, pp. 59–60
September	*jagir*	Ponian	(Hisar Firuza)		Shah Qurban	Bayazid, p. 278

(*contd.*)

Appendix I (*contd.*)

Date	Nomenclature	Locale			Name	Reference
		Pargana/Qasba	*Sarkar*	*Suba/Vilayat*		
1563	*hakim-i vilayat*	Danduana	(Nagaur)		Husain Quit Khan	'Arif, p. 73
1563	*jagirdar*	Sahaswan	(Badaun)		Qulich Chaugan Begi	Badauni, III, p. 121
1564 January	*hakim*		Delhi		Tatar Khan	Bayazid, p. 284
1564 January	*jagirdar*	Safadaon	(Delhi)		Nuruddin Muhammad Tarkhan	Bayazid, p. 284
March–June	*jaygirdar*		Kara Bhatta Garah-Katanga		'Abdul Majid Asaf Khan	*AN*, II, p. 209; *TA*, II, p. 170
June–July	*hukumat*		Sarangpur		Muhammad Qasim Nishapuri	*AN*, II, p. 224; *TA*, II, p. 172
July–August	*hukumat*			*Vilayat-i Malwa wa Mandu*	'Abdullah Khan Uzbek	'Arif, pp. 79–80; *TA*, II, p. 172
July–August	*guzashta bud*		Handia		Khan Quli	*AN*, II, p. 230; *TA*, II, p. 174

(*contd.*)

Appendix I (*contd.*)

Date	Nomenclature	Locale			Name	Reference
		Pargana/Qasba	*Sarkar*	*Suba/Vilayat*		
July–August	*jaygir*		Handia		Muqarrab Khan	*TA*, II, p. 174,
July–August	*hukumat*		Mandu		Qara Bahadur	*AN*, II, p. 232; *TA*, II, p. 174
Sept. 1564–March 1565	*hukumat*			Punjab	Mir Muhammad Khan (title Khan-i Kalan)	*TA*, II, p. 174
,,	*hakim*		Multan		Muhammad Quli Khan	"
,,	(assignment)			Punjab	Qutbuddin Khan	"
					Mahdi Qasim Khan	
					Hasan Sufi Sultan	
					Jan Muhammad Bihsudi	
					Kamal Khan Ghakkar	*AN*, II, p. 239
					Fazil Muhammad Khan	Ibid.
					Muhammad Quli Khan	Ibid.
1565						
March	*jagir*		Jaunpur		'Ali Quli Khan-i Zaman	*TA*, II, p. 180; Badauni, II, p. 75
March	*jaygir*		Awadh		Sikandar Khan Uzbek	'Arif, p. 85; *AN*, II, p. 249; *TA*, II, p. 180; Badauni, II, p. 75

(*contd.*)

Appendix I (*contd.*)

Date	Nomenclature	Locale			Name	Reference
		Pargana/Qasba	*Sarkar*	*Suba/Vilayat*		
March	*jaygir*	Surhurpur	(Jaunpur)		Ibrahim Khan Uzbek	*AN*, II, p. 249; *TA*, II, p. 180; Badauni, II, p. 75
March–June	*hukumat*		Garah-Katanga		'Abdul Majid Asaf Khan	*TA*, II, p. 181
,,	*jagir*		Kara		'Abdul Majid Asaf Khan	,,
June	*jāygirdar*		Manikpur		Majnun Khan Qaqshal	*AN*, II, p. 249
June	*jagirdaran*			Awadh	Shaham Khan Jalair Shah Budagh Khan Amir Khan Muhammad Amin Diwana	*AN*, II p. 250
1565					Sultan Quli Khaldar	
June					Chalma Tawachi Shah Tahir Badakhshi Khalilullah Gada 'Ali Tolkchi Khan Quli Sarban Yusuf Taghai, etc.	
June	*jagirdar*	Nimkhar	(Khairabad)		Amir Khan-i Jamil	Bayazid, p. 286
June	(assignment)	Nimkhar	(Khairabad)		Shah Budagh Khan	'Arif, p. 84

(*contd.*)

Appendix I (*contd.*)

Date	Nomenclature	Locale			Name	Reference
		Pargana/Qasba	*Sarkar*	*Suba/Vilayat*		
September	*jagir*		Kara		Khwaja 'Abdul Majid Asaf Khan	Bayazid, p. 287
1566						
January	(assignment)		Jaunpur Banaras Ghazipur		Mun'im Khan	Bayazid, pp. 294–5
January	(assignment)		Banaras		Bayazid Bayat	„
January	(assignment)	Zamania (Q)	(Ghazipur)		As'adullah Khan Tabrizi	Bayazid, p. 296
January–March	*faujdar*	Samana (Q)	(Sirhind)		Muhammad Tarkhan	*AN*, II, p. 263
„	*mahamm-i vilayat*			Malwa	Shahabuddin Ahmad Khan	Ibid., p. 271
March–July	*nazim-i ashtat*		Garaha		Mahdi Qasim Khan	Ibid., pp. 272, 273
1566						
March–July	*ta'yin namuda*		Garaha		Shah Quli Khan Naranji Kakar 'Ali Khan	*AN*, II, p. 273; Badauni, II, p. 85
March–July	*jaygir*	Azampur	(Sambhal)		Ibrahim Husain Mirza	Ibid.
November–December	*shiqdar*		Balda-i Sirhind		Hafiz Rakhna	*TA*, II, p. 202
	sarkardari		Sirhind		Hafiz Rakhna	Ibid.
„	*muntazim*		Kabul		Mirza Faridun	*AN*, II, p. 275
„	*mahammat*					

(*contd.*)

Appendix I (*contd.*)

Date	Nomenclature	Locale			Name	Reference
		Pargana/Qasba	*Sarkar*	*Suba/Vilayat*		
1567						
January–March	*ba-kharch-i maishsat*	Azampur	(Sambhal)		Muhammad Sultan Mirza	*AN*, II, p. 279
,,	*jaygir*		Sambhal		Ibrahim Husain Mirza	Ibid., pp. 279–80
,,	*jaygir*	Nihtaur	(Sambhal)		Ulugh Mirza Shah Mirza	Badauni, II, p. 91
,,	*jaygir*	Nimkhar	(Khairabad)		Yar Shahi	*AN*, II, p. 280
,,	*muqarrar shuda*			Malwa	Muhammad Quli Khan Barlas	Ibid.
,,	*istahkam dad*		Ujjain		Khwaja Hadi	Ibid.
,,	(assignment)		Handia		Qadam Khan	Ibid.
,,	(assignment)	Satwas(Q)	(Handia)		Muqarrab Khan	Ibid.
January–March	*jaygir*	Patyali Shamsabad	(Kannauj)		Husain Khan	Badauni, II, p. 86
22–23 March	*hukumat w darai*			*Vilayat-i* Punjab	Mir Muhammad Khan	'Arif, p. 94; *AN*, II, p. 286; *TA*, II, p. 207
,,	*taqsim namudand*	(*Parganas*)		Punjab	Mir Muhammad Khan Qutbuddin Khan and their relations	*AN*, II, p. 286

(*contd.*)

Appendix I (*contd.*)

Date	Nomenclature	Locale			Name	Reference
		Pargana/Qasba	*Sarkar*	*Suba/Vilayat*		
,,	*muhafzat*		Kara Manikpur		'Abdul Majid Asaf Khan Majnun Khan Qaqshal	*AN*, II, p. 283; *TA*, II, p. 207
,,	*jaygir*	Hindaun	(Agra)		Junaid Kararani	*AN*, II, p. 284
,,	*hukumat*		Delhi		Tatar Khan	Ibid., p. 288; *TA*, II, p. 208
,,	*jaygirdar*	Bhojpur (Q)	Delhi		Shahabuddin Khan Turkman	Ibid.
March	*jaygir*	Surhurpur	(Jaunpur)		Ibrahim Khan Uzbek	*AN*, II, p. 289
,,	*hakim*		Kannauj		Mirza Yusuf Khan	'Arif, p. 97; *AN*, II p. 289; Badauni, II, p. 94
April–May	*jaygirdar*			Manikpur	Muhibb 'Ali Khan	*AN*, II, p. 291
,,	*dar qala'*			Manikpur	Majnun Khan Qaqshal	'Arif, p. 100
,,	*hakim*			*Qala'-i* Chunar	Hasan Khan	Ibid., p. 106
June	*jaygir*		Jaunpur Banaras Ghazipur Chunar		Mun'im Khan	'Arif, p. 107; Bayazid, p. 299; *AN*, II, 298; *TA*, II, p. 213; Badauni, II, p. 101

(*contd.*)

Appendix I (*contd.*)

Date	Nomenclature	Locale: *Pargana/Qasba*	Locale: *Sarkar*	Locale: *Suba/Vilayat*	Name	Reference
June	*jaygir*		*Qasba* Kora		Farhat Khan	*AN,* II, p. 298
June	*gumashta-i Khan-i Khanan Mun'im Khan*	Zamania	(Ghazipur)		Qasim Mushki	Bayazid, p. 300; *AN*, II, p. 325
June	*supurdand*	Sultanpur & a few other *parganas* of Hasan Khan Bachgoti	(Awadh)		Asadullah	Bayazid, p. 300
July–August	(assignment)		*Qasba-i* Etawa		Shuja'at Khan	*AN*, II, p. 298
September	*jagir*	Bayana	(Agra)		Haji Muhammad Khan Sistani	*TA,* II p. 215
,,	*jagir*	Bayana Bhasawar Wazirpur Mandalgarh	(Agra) (Agra) (Agra) (Mewar)		Asaf Khan	Ibid.; Badauni, II, p. 102
,,	*jaygir*		Awadh		Muhammad Quli Khan Barlas	*AN*, II, p. 300; *TA*, II, p. 214
1567						
September–October	*hukumat wa hirasat*	Qila'-i Siwi Super	(Ranthambhor)		Nazar Bahadur	*AN*, II, p. 303; *TA*, II, p. 215 Badauni, II, p. 102

(*contd.*)

Appendix I (*contd.*)

Date	Nomenclature	Locale			Name	Reference
		Pargana/Qasba	*Sarkar*	*Suba/Vilayat*		
Septembe–October	*hukumat*	Kota	(Hadauti)		Shah Muhammad Khan	*AN*, II, p. 303; *TA*, II, p. 215 Badauni. II, p. 102
September–October	*jaygir*			Vilayat-i Malwa	Shahabuddin Ahmad Khan Shah Budagh Khan Murad Khan Haji Muhammad Khan Sistani	*AN*, II, p. 313 *TA*, II, p. 215 Badauni, II, p. 102
September–October	*jaygir*		Gagraun		Asaf Khan Wazir Khan	*AN*, II, p. 313
1568						
January	(assignment)		Rohtas		Muhibb Ali Khan	Bayazid, p. 302
February	*jagir*	Daryabad	(Awadh)		L'al Khan Badakhshi	Ibid.
February–March	*makarmat* *farmud*		Chittor		Khwaja Abdul Majid Asaf Khan	*AN*, II, p. 324 *TA*, II, p. 219

(*contd.*)

Appendix I (*contd.*)

Date	Nomenclature	Locale			Name	Reference
		Pargana/Qasba	*Sarkar*	*Suba/Vilayat*		
1568						
February–March	*jagirdar*		Ujjain		Murad Khan	*AN*, II, p. 330
,,	(assignment)	(*Parganas*)	Ujjain		Mirza 'Aziz Mashhadi	*TA*, II, p. 222; Badauni, II, p.106
,,	*hakim*	Saronj	(Chanderi)		Shahabuddin Ahmad Khan	Ibid.
,,	*hakim*		Sarangpur		Shah Budagh Khan	Ibid.
August–September	*hukumat*			*Vilayat-i* Punjab	Husain Quli Khan	*TA*, II, p. 223; Badauni, II, p. 106
,,	*jagir*		Sambhal		Mir Muhammad Khan-i Kalan	*AN*, II, pp. 332–3; Badauni, II, p. 106
,,	*mukaramat shud*			*Sarkar* Malwa	Qutbuddin Muhammad Khan	*AN*, II, p. 333
,,	*makhsus gasht*		Kannauj		Sharif Khan	Ibid
June–December	*jaygir*		Lucknow		Husain Khan	Badauni, III, p. 18
,,	*jaygir*		Lucknow		Mahdi Qasim Khan	Ibid., II, p. 125; *AN*, II, p. 336
,,	*wajah-jaygir*	Kant Gola	(Badaun)		Husain Khan	Badauni, II, p. 126

(*contd.*)

Appendix I (*contd.*)

Date	Nomenclature	Locale			Name	Reference
		Pargana/Qasba	*Sarkar*	*Suba/Vilayat*		
1569						
February–March	*jaygir*	Saronj	(Chanderi)		Shahabuddin Ahmad Khan	*AN*, II, p. 331
,,	*hukumat*		Sarangpur		Shah Budagh Khan	Ibid.
21 March	*hukumat w hirasat-i qila*		Ranthambhor		Mahtar Khan	Ibid., p. 338; *TA*, II, p. 224
June –August	*jagir*	(*Parganas*)	Kalinjar		Majnun Khan Qaqshal	*TA*, II, p. 226
,,	*muhazfizat w hidrasat-i qila*		Kalinjar		Majnun Khan Qaqshal	Ibid.
,,	*jaygir*	Arail	(Allahabad)		Raja Ram Chand of Bhatta	Badauni, II, p. 120
1570						
September	*jaygirdar*	Pakpattan	(Bet Jalandhar Doab)		Mirza 'Aziz Koka, titled Khan-i 'Azam	Ibid., p. 133
,,	(assignment)		Lahore		Husain Quli Khan	Ibid., p. 134
October–November	*hukumat*		Nagaur Ajmer Jodhpur & the frontier of Gujarat		Mir Muhammad Khan titled Khan-i Kalan	'Arif. p. 131; *AN*, II, p. 357

(*contd.*)

Appendix I (*contd.*)

Date	Nomenclature	Locale			Name	Reference
		Pargana/Qasba	*Sarkar*	*Suba/Vilayat*		
1571						
March–April	*jaygir*	Dipalpur	(Punjab)		Mirza 'Aziz Koka titled Khan-i Azam	'Arif, p. 132; *AN*, II, p. 363 *TA*, II, p. 232
,,	*hakim*		Punjab		Husain Quli Khan	'Arif, p. 133; *AN*, II, p. 364; *TA*, II, p. 232
,,	*hakim*		Multan		Sa'id Khan Mughal	*TA*, II, p. 233; Badauni, II p. 134
,,	*jaygir*		Multan		Muhibb 'Ali Khan	*TA*, II, p. 233; Badauni, II, p. 134
1572						
June–July	*jagir*		*Khitta-i* Lucknow		Sikandar Khan Uzbek	'Arif, p. 155; *AN*, II, p. 368; Bayazid, p. 307; *TA*, II, p. 235
June	*jagir*	Saraon	(Manikpur)		Qulij Khan	Bayazid, p. 307
,,	*jagir*	Saraon	(Manikpur)		Mun'im Khan	Ibid.

(*contd.*)

Appendix I (*contd.*)

Date	Nomenclature	Locale			Name	Reference
		Pargana/Qasba	*Sarkar*	*Suba/Vilayat*		
July–August	*hukūmat wa dārāi*		Nagaur Ajmer Jodhpur upto Gujarat frontier		Mir Muhammad Khan	'Arif, p. 157
18 September	*Jagir*		Lucknow		Sikandar Khan Uzbek	'Arif, p. 155; Badauni, II, p. 135
7 November	*marahmat farmud*		Patan		'Abdur Rahim, titled Mirza Khan	*AN*, III, p. 6
,,	*shiqdārī*		Patan		Saiyed Ahmad Khan Barah	'Arif, p. 159; *AN*, III, p. 6; *TA*, II, p. 238; Badauni, II, p. 140
December	*hukūmat*		Ahmadabad		Mirza 'Aziz Koka titled Khan-i A'zam	'Arif, p. 162; *AN*, III, pp. 8–9; *TA*, II, p. 241 Badauni, II, p. 164
,,	*hukūmat*	Bandar Khambayat	(Ahmadabad)		Hasan Khan Khazanchi	*AN*, III, p. II
,,	(assignment)			Malwa	Qutbuddin Muhammad Khan	Ibid., p. 18

(*contd.*)

Date	Nomenclature	Locale			Name	Reference
		Pargana/Qasba	*Sarkar*	*Suba/Vilayat*		
1572						
December	*jagir*		Kalpi		Shaham Khan	*AN*, III, p. 19
1573						
January	(assignment)	Zamania	(Ghazipur)		Qasim Muhrdar (same as Qasim Mushki)	Ibid., p. 22
,,	*hirasat-i qila*		Patan		Saiyed Ahmad Khan Barah	Ibid., p. 23; *TA*, II, p. 252
,,	(assignment)		Nagaur		Farrukh Khan	Badauni, II, p. 150
,,	*jagirdars*		Malwa		Qutbuddin Muhammad Shah Budagh Khan, Muttalib Khan	*AN*, III, pp. 23–4; Badauni, II, p. 147
,,	(assignment)	Dholqa	(Ahmadabad)		Shaikh Muhammad Bukhari	*AN*, III, p. 24
January–February	*jagirdar*		Gorakhpur		Payanda Muhammad Sultan	Bayazid, p. 314
,,	*jagirdar*		Ghazipur		Talib Sultan	Ibid.
,,	*jagirdar*	Bhadohi	(Allahabad)		Mirza Quli Sultan	Ibid.
,,	*jagirdar*	Dostpur	(Jaunpur)		Nadim Sultan	Ibid.
February	(assignment)		Gorakhpur		Payanda Muhammad	Ibid., p. 317
February	*jagirdar*	Qila'-i Zamania	(Ghazipur)		Qasim Mushki	Ibid., p. 318

(*contd.*)

Appendix I (*contd.*)

Date	Nomenclature	Locale			Name	Reference
		Pargana/Qasba	*Sarkar*	*Suba/Vilayat*		
1573						
February	*jagir*	Qila'-i Zamania	(Ghazipur)		Muhammad Khan	Bayazid, p. 318
February–March	*jagir*	Bhojpur Bahia-jit Ballia	(Rohtas) (Rohtas) (Gorakhpur)		Raja Gajpati	Ibid., p. 319
,,	*jagirdar*	Rae Bareli	(Manikpur)		Nauram Sultan Uzbek	Ibid., p. 322
,,	(assignment)		Qala'-i Surat		Shuja'at Khan	Ibid.
March–April	*tafwiz farmud*		Ahmadabad		'Aziz Koka	'Arif, p. 173; *AN*, III, p. 33; *TA*, II, p. 253
,,	*'anayat namūd*		Patan		Mir Muhammad Khan-i Kalan	*AN*, III, p. 33; Bayazid, p. 334
,,	*'anayat namūd*		Broach Baroda		Qutbuddin Khan	*AN*, III, p. 33; Bayazid, p. 334
,,	*alayat*	Sultanpur	Nandurbar (Nandurbar) Sarangpur Ujjain	*Vilayat-i* Malwa	Muzaffar Khan	'Arif, p. 173; *AN*, III, p. 33; *TA*, II, p. 253; Badauni, II, p. 149

(*contd.*)

Appendix I (*contd.*)

Date	Nomenclature	Locale			Name	Reference
		Pargana/Qasba	*Sarkar*	*Suba/Vilayat*		
1573 March–April	*jagir*		Qala'-i Surat		Qulij Khan	'Arif, p. 172; Bayazid, p. 333; *AN*, III, p. 31; *TA*, II, p. 249
,,	*hirasat*		Nagaur		Farrukh Khan	*AN*, III, p. 34
,,	*jaygir*	Sujat	(Jodhpur)		Rai Ram	Ibid.
,,	*hakim*	Merta	(Nagaur)		Farrukh Khan	*TA*, II, p. 253
,,	*jaygir*	Kant Gola	(Badaun)		Husain Khan	Badauni, II, p. 151
,,	*jagirdar*		Sambhal		Muinuddin Khan Farankhudi	Badauni, II, p. 153
,,	*sahib-i suba w jaygirdar*			Delhi	Muinuddin Ahamd Khan	Ibid., p. 154
,,	*wajah-i jaygir*	Nagarkot	(Bari Doab)		Raja Bir Bar	*AN*, III, p. 37; *TA*, II, p. 256
,,	*jagirdar*	Patiyali	(Kannauj)		Husain Khan	*AN*, III, p. 36
,,	*hakim*			Multan	Sa'id Khan Chaghta	Ibid., p. 38

(*contd.*)

Appendix I (*contd.*)

Date	Nomenclature	Locale			Name	Reference
		Pargana/Qasba	*Sarkar*	*Suba/Vilayat*		
June	*hakim*			Punjab / Lahore	Husain Quli Khan titled Khan-i Jahan	'Arif, p.163; *AN*, III, p. 40; *TA*, II, p.254
1573						
June	(assignment)		Multan		Sa'id Khan Chaghta	Arif, p. 163 Badauni, II, p. 165
June–August	*hakim*		*Qala'-i* Chunar		Hasan 'Ali Khan	Bayazid, p. 310
,,	*jagir*	Sanjauli	(Jaunpur)		Sa'adat Yar	Ibid., p. 312
July	*jaygir*	Idar	(Ahmadabad)		Mirza Muqeem	*AN*, III, p. 41
,,	*Qila' dārī*		Surat		Qulij Khan	Ibid., p. 42
,,	(assignment)		Broach		Qutbuddin Ahmad Khan	Ibid.; *TA*, p. II, 262; Badauni, II, p. 165
,,	*shiqdar*	Khambayat	(Ahmadabad)		Hasan Khan Karkaraq	*AN*, III, p. 42; *TA*, II, p. 261
September–October	(assignment)	Dholka Dandhuka	(Ahmadabad) (Ahmadabad)		Wazir Khan	*TA*, II, p. 273; Badauni, II, p. 170
,,	*hukumat*		Lahore		Husain Quli Khan titled Khan-i Jahan	*AN*, III, p. 43; *TA*, II, p. 264
,,	(assignment)			Punjab	Sa'id Khan Chaghta	*AN*, III, p. 43

(*contd.*)

Appendix I (*contd.*)

Date	Nomenclature	Locale			Name	Reference
		Pargana/Qasba	*Sarkar*	*Suba/Vilayat*		
October–November	*jagir*	(*Parganas*)		Punjab	Mirza Yusuf Khan Makhsus Khan	Ibid.
1573						
August	*jagir*	Kachiwara			Kunwar Man Singh	Ibid.
October–November	*hukumat*		Patan		Mir Muhammad Khan-i Kalan	Ibid., p. 64; *TA*, II, p. 273; Badauni, II, p. 170
,,	*wajah-i jagir*	Dholka Dandhuka	(Ahmadabad) (Ahmadabad)		Wazir Khan	*AN*, III, p. 64
,,	*hukumat*	Deesa	(Patan)		Shah 'Ali Langah	Ibid.; *TA*, II, p. 266
,,	*dar an sar zamin guzashtand*		Sirohi		Sadiq Khan	*AN*, III, p. 65
,,	*jagir*	Harba (Q)	Ajmer		Ram Das Kachwaha	*TA*, II, p. 274
November	*hukumat*		Sarangpur		Muzaffar Khan	*TA*, II, p. 276; Badauni, II, p. 171
1573	*hakim*		Dehli		Tayab Khan	*TA*, II, p. 266

(*contd.*)

Appendix I (*contd.*)

Date	Nomenclature	Locale			Name	Reference
		Pargana/Qasba	*Sarkar*	*Suba/Vilayat*		
1574						
March	*jaygir*		Saran		Hasan Khan Batani	*AN*, III, pp. 82–3
May–June	*hirasat*		Agra		Shahabuddin Ahmad Khan	Badauni, II, p. 175
,,	*jagirdar*	Chekur(Q)	(Manikpur)		Baba Khan Qaqshal	*TA*, II, p. 285
1574						
July–August	*jagir*	Kant Gola	(Badaun)		Husain Khan	Badauni, II, p. 179
,,	*hakim*	Bayana	(Agra)		Saiyed ‘Abdullah Khan Chaugan Begi	Ibid., p. 180
21 August	*jaygir*			Jaunpur (V)	Mun‘im Khan	*AN*, III, p. 103
,,	*wazarat*		Jaunpur Banaras Chunar etc.		Mirza Mirak Rizvi Ibrahim Sikriwal	‘Arif, p. 194; *AN*, III, p. 103; *TA*, II, p. 296; Badauni, II, p. 182
July–October	*jagir*	Jhusi Payag	(Allahabad)		Niyabat Khan	Badauni, II p. 289
,,	(assignment)		Patna Bihar		Mun‘im Khan	‘Arif, p.193
,,	*jagir*		Khitta-i Hajipur		Muhammad Quli Khan Barlas	Ibid.;, Bayazid, p. 341

(*contd.*)

Appendix I (*contd.*)

Date	Nomenclature	Locale			Name	Reference
		Pargana/Qasba	*Sarkar*	*Suba/Vilayat*		
July–October	(assignment)		Rohtas		Farhat Khan	'Arif, p. 194; Badauni, II, p. 182
August	*hakim*		Patna		Muhsin Khan	Bayazid, p. 347
,,	(assignment)		Ghoraghat		Majnun Khan Qaqshal Baba Khan Qaqshal	Ibid., p. 341
,,	*dadand*		Tirhut		Khan-i A'lam	Ibid.
,,	*inayat kardand*	Khalgaon	(Monghyr)		Wazir Khan-i Jamil	Ibid.
August	(assignment)		Sonargaon		Saiyed Khan Toghpai	Bayazid, p. 34
,,	(assignment)	Burdwan	(Sharifabad)		Qaya Khan	Ibid.
,,	*inayat kardand*		Satgoan		Tukhta Alabam	Ibid.
October	*muhafizat*		*Qala-i* Bhakkar		Mir Gesu	'Arif, p. 200 *TA*, II, p. 301
October–November	*jaygir*	Kant Gola	(Badaun)		Hussain Khan	*AN*, III, p. 110
1575						
January	(assignment)		Lucknow		Khwaja Amina titled Khwaja Jahan	Badauni, II, p. 186

(*contd.*)

Appendix I (*contd.*)

Date	Nomenclature	Locale			Name	Reference
		Pargana/Qasba	*Sarkar*	*Suba/Vilayat*		
January–March	*jagir*		*parganas*	(Bengal)	Mun'im Khan	Bayazid, p. 342, *AN*, III, p.116
,,	*ba tariq-i dar bast–i wajah-i juldui*		Chunar		Mun'im Khan	Bayazid, pp. 312, 341–2
,,	jagir	(*Parganas*)	Chunar		Bayazid Bayat	Ibid., p. 250
,,	(assignment)		Ghoraghat		Majnun Khan Qaqshal	'Arif, p. 204 *TA*, II, p. 303
,,	*hukumat*		Ahmadabad		Mirza Aziz Koka	'Arif, p. 204,
April–May	*tuyul*			Orissa	Daud Kararani	*AN*, III, p. 131
June	(assignment)		Patna Bihar		Mun'im Khan	Ibid., p. 133
1575						
June	*jagir*	Sasaram	(Rohtas)		Muzaffar Khan	Bayazid, p. 348
,,	*jagirdar*		Ghazipur		Talib Sultan	Ibid., p. 347
,,	*jagir*		Bihar		Tangar Quli Khan	Ibid., p. 347
16 July	*jaygir*	Merta	(Ajmer)		Kala S/o. Ram Rai	*AN*, III, p. 159
August–September	*hakim*			Punjab	Khan-i Jahan	*TA*, II, p. 316

(*contd.*)

Appendix I (*contd.*)

Date	Nomenclature	Locale			Name	Reference
		Pargana/Qasba	*Sarkar*	*Suba/Vilayat*		
June–October	*iyalat*	Thanesar	Sirhind		Malik Ashraf	*AN*, III, p. 142
September–October	*hakim*		Lahore		Bhagwan Das	*TA*, II, p. 315 Badauni, II, p. 214
October	*jagir*	Tajpur	Tirhut		Khwaja Muhammad Zakariya	Bayazid, p. 351
8 October	*assignment*		Ahmadabad		Aziz Koka titled Khan-i Azam	*TA*, II, p. 315
October–November	*tuyul*		Hajipur		Muhammad Quli Khan	*AN*, III, p. 136
,,	*hukumat*		Hajipur		Muzaffar Khan	'Arif, p. 210; *AN*, III, p. 136
,,	(assignment)		Hajipur		Mir Muhammad Shaukati	Ibid.
,,	*hakim*			Punjab	Khan-i Jahan	Badauni, II, p. 216
1575						
October–November	*mutasaraf shud*		*Qila'-i*		Baiyazid Bayat	Bayazid, p. 352
,,			Chunar			

(*contd.*)

Date	Nomenclature	Locale			Name	Reference
		Pargana/Qasba	*Sarkar*	*Suba/Vilayat*		
,,	*karori*		Jaunpur		Mirza Mirak	Bayazed, p. 352
,,	*hukumat*			Bangala	Khan-i Jahan	*TA*, II, p. 319; Badauni, II, p. 218
,,	*iyalat*		Bhakkar		Mir Saiyed Muhammad *Mir-i 'adl*	*AN*, III, p. 158
4 November	*jaygir*		Garaha		Rai Surjan	Ibid.
,,	*jaygir*		Garaha		Sadiq Khan	Ibid.
,,	*jaygir*		Chunar		Rai Surjan	Ibid.
November–December	*hakim*		Patan		Mir Muhammad Khan-i Kalan	'Arif, p. 206
1576						
March	*hukumat*		Surat		Qulij Khan	*TA*, II, p. 319
March–April	*hakim*		Patna		Muzaffar Khan	Badauni, II, p. 230
May–June	*hakim*	Sambhar	(Ajmer)		Raja Lon Karan	Ibid., p. 231
,,	*jaygirdar*	Arrah	(Rohtas)		Farhat Khan	*AN*, III, p. 169
,,	(assignment)		Ghazipur		Khan-i Jahan	Ibid., p. 170

(*contd.*)

Appendix I (*contd.*)

Date	Nomenclature	Locale			Name	Reference
		Pargana/Qasba	*Sarkar*	*Suba/Vilayat*		
August–September	(assignment)	Arrah	(Rohtas)		Farhat Khan	Badauni, II, p. 237
1576						
September–October	*iyalat*		Patan		Tarsun Khan	*AN*, III, p. 190
December	(assignment)		Ujjain		Bayazid Bayat	Bayazid, p. 353
December–January 1577	(assignment)		Rohtas		Shahbaz Khan	'Arif, p. 221
,,	(assignment)		Rohtas		Muhibb 'Ali Khan	Ibid., p. 222
,,	*jaygirdar*	Ishhar	Rohtas		Muhammad M'asum Kabuli	Ibid., pp. 222, 223
,,	(assignment)	Islampur Mohi	(Chittor)		Ghazi Khan	Badauni, II, p. 242
,,	(assignment)	Madaria	(Chittor)		'Abdur Rahman Beg	Ibid.
1577						
February–March	*hukumat*		Bhakkar		Mir Saiyed Muhammad, *Mir-i 'Adl*	Ibid., p. 245
,,	(assignment)	Siwi	(Bhakkar)		Mir Saiyed Abu'l Fazl	Ibid.
	(assignment)			Malwa	Shahabuddin Ahmad Khan	Ibid., pp. 241–2

(*contd.*)

Date	Nomenclature	Locale			Name	Reference
		Pargana/Qasba	*Sarkar*	*Suba/Vilayat*		
March–April	(assignment)		Sarangpur		Shahabuddin Ahmad Khan	Badauni, II, p. 353
,,	(assignment)		Ahmadabad		Shahabuddin Ahmad Khan	Ibid.
,,	(assignment)		Sarangpur		Bayazid Bayat	Bayazid, p. 353
,,	*jagir*		Sarangpur		Shuja'at Khan	Ibid.
April–May	*jaygir*		Broach Baroda		Qutbuddin Muhammad	Badauni, II, p. 250
,,	*faujdari*	Bareilly	(Badaun)		Deep Chand Manjhula	Ibid.
,,	*hakim*			Gujarat (V)	Wazir Khan	Ibid., p. 249
June–July	*iyalat*			Suba-i Ajmer	Dastam Khan	*AN*, III, p. 210
,,	*tuyul*		Ranthambhor		Dastam Khan	Ibid. –
August–September	*iyalat*			Multan	Saiyed Hamid	*AN*, III, p. 213
September	*thanedari*	Islampur Mohi	(Chittor)		Mujahid Beg	Ibid., III., p. 216
October–November	*iyalat*			Malwa	Shahabuddin Ahmad Khan	Ibid., III, pp. 217–18
,,	*iyalat*			Gujarat (V)	Shahabuddin Ahmad Khan	Ibid., III, p. 218
,,	(assignment)	Idar	(Ahmadabad)		Wazir Khan	Ibid.
,,	(assignments)			Malwa	Qasim Khan Tahir Khan	*AN*, III, p. 218

(*contd.*)

Date	Nomenclature	Locale			Name	Reference
		Pargana/Qasba	*Sarkar*	*Suba/Vilayat*		
					Naqib Khan	
					Qamar Khan	
					Firuz	
					Shaikh M'uazzam	
					Shaikh Junaid	
1577						
13 November	*muqarrar gasht*		Bihar		Shuja'at Khan	*AN*, III, p. 227
					Mir Mu'izzul Mulk	
November–December	*shafqat kardand*		Sarangpur		Shuja'at Khan	Arif, p. 233
,,	*hukumat*			Gujarat (V)	Qutbuddin Muhammad	Ibid.
					Shihab Khan	
,,	*shafqat kardand*		Ujjain		Shah Fakhruddin Khan	Ibid., p. 233
			Mandu		Shah Budagh Khan	
1578						
5 January	(assignment)		Hisar Firuza		Mehr 'Ali Khan Silduz	Ibid., p. 232
January	(assignment)	Thara/ Pathaura	(Bari Doab)		Chaman Quli the *Qush-begi*	'Arif, p. 235
March–April	*hukumat*			Punjab	Sa'id Khan	Badauni, II, p. 254

(*contd.*)

Appendix I (*contd.*)

Date	Nomenclature	Locale			Name	Reference
		Pargana/Qasba	*Sarkar*	*Suba/Vilayat*		
2 May	*hukumat*		Dehli		Muhibb 'Ali Khan	*AN*, III, p. 248; Badauni, II, p. 276
May	*hakim*			Gujarat	Wazir Khan	*TA*, II, p. 322
,,	(assignment)		Nandurbar		Baz Bahadur s/o Sharif Khan	Ibid.
1 December	(assignment)			Punjab	Raja Bhagwant Das Jagannath Raja Gopal Jag Mal Panwar	*AN*, III, p. 262
1579						
February–March	*hukumat*			Bangala	Muzaffar Khan	'Arif, p. 246
June–December	(assignment)		Sarangpur		Shuja'at Khan	Badauni, II, p. 284
September	(assignment)			Ajmer	Dastam Khan	*AN*, III, p. 326
September–October	*hakim*		Patan		Tarsun Muhammad Khan	Badauni, II, p. 274

(*contd.*)

Appendix I (*contd.*)

Date	Nomenclature	Locale			Name	Reference
		Pargana/Qasba	*Sarkar*	*Suba/Vilayat*		
September–October	*hukumat*		Jaunpur		M'asum Khan Farankhudi	Badauni, II, pp. 276, 282
1579		,,	*hakim*		Kalpi	Qasim 'Ail
Khan Baqqal	Ibid., II, p. 282	,,	*hakim*		Rohtas	Muhibb 'Ali
Khan	Ibid., II, p. 282					
,,	(assignment)		*Qila'-i* Patna		Bahar Khan Khasa Khail	Ibid., II, p. 283
,,	(assignment)			Malwa	Sharif Khan Atka	Ibid., II, p. 285
,,	*tuyuldari*		Jalesar		Khaldin Khan	AN, III, p. 292
,,	(assignment)		Jalesar		Mir Jamaluddin Husain Anju	
November–December	*tuyul*		Etawa		Zain Khan Koka	Ibid., III, p. 278
1580						
February–March	(assignment)		Khitta-i Jaunpur		Ma'sum Khan Farankhudi	Ibid., III., p. 281
,,	(assignment)		Ghazipur		Ma'sum Khan Farankhudi	Ibid., III., p. 281

(*contd.*)

Date	Nomenclature	Locale			Name	Reference
		Pargana/Qasba	*Sarkar*	*Suba/Vilayat*		
1580						
February–March	(assignment)		Khitta-i Jaunpur		Tarsun Muhammad Khan	*AN*, III, p. 281
,,	*iqta*			Orissa	M'asum Kabul-i	AN, III, p. 281
,,	*iqta*		Patna		M'asum Kabul-i	Ibid., p. 285
,,	*jaygirdar*	Sasaram	(Rohtas)		Sa'id Beg Bakhshi,	Ibid.
,,	(assignment)	Nanor	(Rohtas)		Sa'adat 'Ali	Ibid.
,,	*tuyul*	Dilwara	(Tajpur)		Haji Kolabi,	Ibid.
,,	(assignment)		Tirhut		Sa'id Khan Bakhshi, Bahadur s/o Sa'id Khan Durvesh 'Ali Sanjar	
,,	*jaygirdar*		Hajipur		Shaham	Ibid.
,,	*dashtand*	Arrah	(Rohtas)		*Mir* Muizul Mulk *Mir* Akbar 'Ali Samaji Khan	Ibid.
,,	*iqtadaran*	Khitta-i Baksar	(Rohtas)		Kamaluddin Husain Sistani, Saiyed Hasan Dud Raj	Ibid., p. 287
,,	*jagirdar*			Awadh	Tarsun Khan	Ibid.

(*contd.*)

Date	Nomenclature	Locale			Name	Reference
		Pargana/Qasba	*Sarkar*	*Suba/Vilayat*		
				Allahabad	M'asum Khan Farankhudi, Ghazi Khan Badakhshi, Rai Surjan & others	*AN*, III, p. 287
May	*hukumat*			Bangala	A'zam Koka titled Khan-i A'zam	Ibid., p. 308; Badauni, II, p. 285
1580						
January–June	(assignment)		Manikpur		As'ad Khan Turkman	*AN*, III, p. 309
January–July	(assignment)	(*Parganas*)		Malwa	Sharif Khan	Ibid., p. 314
August–September	*iqtadaran*			Ajmer	Payanda Muhammad Khan Saiyed Hashim Saiyed Qasim	Ibid., p. 318
,,	*iqta*		Patan		I'timad Khan Gujarati	Ibid.
,,	*tuyul*		Fathabad	(Bangala)	Murad Khan	Ibid., p. 320
September–October	(assignment)	Qila'-i Kant (Q)	(Rohtas)		Sa'adat 'Ali Payanda Rustam Rup Narayan Bumi	Ibid., p. 324

(*contd.*)

Appendix I (*contd.*)

Date	Nomenclature	Locale			Name	Reference
		Pargana/Qasba	*Sarkar*	*Suba/Vilayat*		
October–November	*jagir*		Sarangpur		Shaham Khan	*AN*, III, p. 325
,,	(assignment)		Hajipur		‘Aziz Koka	Ibid., p. 325
,,	(assignment)		Patna		Shahbaz Khan	Ibid.
,,	*intizam*			Ajmer	‘Abdur Rahim	Ibid., p. 327
,,	*Iqta*		Ranthambour		‘Abdur Rahim	Ibid.
,,	*bungah*	Boni	(Ranthambour)		Achla s/o Balabdhar	Ibid., p. 326
November–December	(assignment)		Kara		Ism’ail Quli Khan	Ibid., p. 328, Badauni, II, p. 289
1580						
,,	*hakim*		Kara		Iliyas	*AN*, III, p. 328
,,	*jaygir*	Jhusi Payag	(Allahabad)		Niyabat Khan	Ibid.
,,	*jaygir*		Awadh		Ma‘sum Khan Farankhudi	*AN*, III, p. 330
,,	(assignment)		Jaunpur		Tarsun Khan	Badauni, II, p. 289
,,	*iqtadar*		Sind Sagar Doab		Mirza Yusuf	*AN*, III, p. 336
,,	(assignment)	Sialkot	(Rachnao Doab)		Man Singh	Ibid.

(*contd.*)

Appendix I (*contd.*)

Date	Nomenclature	Locale: *Pargana/Qasba*	Locale: *Sarkar*	Locale: *Suba/Vilayat*	Name	Reference
November–December	(assignment)		Sind Sagar Doab		Man Singh	*AN*, III, p. 336
,,	(assignment)	Safadun	(Hisar Firuza)		Mullah Nuruddin Tarkhan	Badauni, III, p. 199
,, ,,	*gumashtagan-i* Man Singh	Nilab	(Sind Sagar Doab)		Zainuddin 'Ali and others	*AN*, III, p. 336
,,	(assignment)	Bhera	(Channat Doab)		Muhibb 'Ali Khan	Ibid., p. 324
		Rohtas	(Sind Sagar Doab)			

Appendix II

Frequency of Different Terms Used for Assignment (based upon Appendix I)

	jagir	*tuyul*	*iqta*	*bungah*	*hakim*	*shiqdar*	*faujdar*	*thanedar*	*diwan*	*gumashta*	*Other terms and vague expression*	*Total*
1556	4	--	--	--	3	--	--	--	--	--	16	23
1557	3	--	--	--	1	--	--	--	--	--	2	6
1558	5	--	--	--	--	--	--	--	--	--	2	7
1559	1	--	--	--	1	--	--	--	--	--	4	6
1560	9	--	--	--	6	--	--	--	1	--	10	26
1561	6	--	--	--	3	--	--	--	--	--	7	16
1562	7	--	--	--	2	1	--	--	--	--	--	10
1563	8	--	--	--	2	1	--	--	--	--	8	19
1564	3	--	--	--	6	--	--	--	--	--	2	11
1565	8	--	--	--	1	--	--	--	--	--	1	10
1566	1	--	--	--	--	1	1	--	--	--	8	11
1567	15	--	--	--	6	--	--	--	--	1	10	32
1568	6	--	--	--	4	--	--	--	--	--	5	15
1569	3	--	--	--	3	--	--	--	--	--	--	6

(contd.)

Appendix II (*contd.*)

	jagir	*tuyul*	*iqta*	*bungah*	*hakim*	*shiqdar*	*faujdar*	*thanedar*	*diwan*	*gumashta*	*Other terms and vague expression*	*Total*
1570	1	--	--	--	1	--	--	--	--	--	1	3
1571	2	--	--	--	2	--	--	--	--	--	--	4
1572	5	--	--	--	3	1	--	--	--	--	2	11
1573	22	--	--	--	9	1	--	--	--	--	17	49
1574	7	--	--	--	2	--	--	--	--	--	11	20
1575	10	2	--	--	7	--	--	--	--	--	10	29
1576	2	--	--	--	3	--	--	--	--	--	8	13
1577	2	1	--	--	3	--	1	1	--	--	15	23
1578		--	--	--	3	--	--	--	--	--	4	7
1579		2	--	--	5	--	--	--	--	--	5	12
1580	6	2	6	1	2	--	--	--	--	1	18	36

Appendix III

Transfer of Assignments during 1556–75

1. Assignments held by thirteen leading nobles at different points of time

Date		Locale
Mun'im Khan		
March	1556	Kabul-wa-Ghazni
December	1560	Hisar Firuza
April	1561	Hisar Firuza
March	1563	[*Pargana*] Hisar Firuza
		[*Pargana*] Etawah
		[*Pargana*] Khairabad
		Shahpur [Karli/ Bari Doab]
		Kalanaur [Karli/ Bari Doab]
		Jallandhar [Bet-Jallandhar Doab]
		Indri [Saharanpur]
January	1566	Jaunpur
		Banaras
		Ghazipur
June	1567	Jaunpur
		Banaras
		Ghazipur
		Chunar
June	1572	Saraon [Manikpur]
August	1574	Jaunpur
July–October	1574	Patna
		Bihar
January–March	1575	[*Parganas*] Bengal
January–March	1575	Chunar
June	1575	Patna
		Bihar
Ali 'Quli Khan		
March	1556	Sambhal
November	1556	Sambhal
March–September	1559	Lucknow

(*contd.*)

Appendix III (*contd.*)

Date		Locale
March–September	1559	Jaunpur
December	1560	Jaunpur
		Banaras
		Ghazipur
August	1561	Jaunpur
March	1565	Jaunpur
Sikandar Khan Uzbek		
March	1556	Agra
September–October	1556	Agra
December	1556	Sialkot [Rachnao Doab]
March	1565	Awadh
September	1572	Lucknow
'Abdullah Khan Uzbek		
March	1556	Kalpi
November	1556	Kalpi
December	1560	Kalpi
March	1561	Kalpi
August	1562	Mandu
July–August	1564	Malva-wa-Mandu
Qaya Khan Gung		
March	1556	Kol-wa-Jalali
September–October	1556	Etawa
November	1556	Agra
April–May	1560	Bahraich
March	1561	Handia
August	1562	[*Parganas*] Malwa
August	1574	Burdwan [Sharifabad]
Haidar Muhammad Khan		
March	1556	Bayana
September–October	1556	Bayana
May	1560	Kabul
Majnun Khan Qaqshal		
March	1556	Narnaul
May	1561	[*Parganas*] Jaunpur and the eastern *sarkasr* in general

(*contd.*)

Appendix III (*contd.*)

Date		Locale
March	1567	Mankipur
April–May	1567	Manikpur
June–August	1569	Kalinjar
August	1574	Ghoraghat
January–March	1575	Ghoraghat
Mahdi Qasim Khan		
November	1556	Delhi
August	1563	[*parganas*] Punjab
March	1565	[*parganas*] Punjab
March–July	1566	Garaha
June–December	1568	Lucknow
Muhammad Quli Khan Barlas		
March	1557	Multan
March	1557	Nagaur
August–September	1560	Multan
March	1563	Multan
March	1565	Multan
January–March	1567	Malwa
September	1567	Awadh
July–October	1574	Hajipur
Bahadur Khan Uzbek		
March	1557	Multan
March–September	1559	Dipalpur
January–March	1561	Etawa
January–March	1561	Banaras
Shahabuddin Ahmad Khan		
March	1560	Delhi
January–March	1566	Malwa
February–March	1568	Saronj (Chanderi)
February–March	1569	Saronj (Chanderi)
Mir Muhammad Khan-i Kalan		
March	1560	Lahore
August	1563	Punjab
March	1565	Punjab
March	1567	Punjab

(*contd.*)

Appendix III (*contd.*)

Date		Locale
August–September	1568	Sambhal
October–November	1570	Nagaur
		Ajmer
		Jodhpur
July–August	1572	Nagaur
		Ajmer
		Jodhpur
March–April	1573	Patan
October–November	1573	Patan
November–December	1575	Patan
Husain Quli Khan		
September	1563	Hajipur (Jodhpur)
September	1563	Danduana (Nagaur)
August–September	1568	Punjab
September	1570	Lahore
March–April	1571	Punjab
September–October	1573	Punjab
October–November	1575	Bangala

2. Nobles Holding *Sarkars* Multan, Etawah, Narnaul, Kalpi, and Sambhal as Assignments

Date	Nomenclature for Assignment or Assignee	Assignee	Reference
***Sarkar* Multan**			
March 1557	*jagir*	Muhammad Quli Khan Barlas	*AN*, II, p. 53
March 1557	(assignment)	Bahadur Khan Uzbek	Ibid.
Aug.–Sept. 1560	*jaygir*	Muhammad Qasim Nishapuri	*AN*, II, pp. 114–15
March 1563	*hakim*	Muhammad Quli Khan Barlas	*AN*, II, p. 187
Sept. 1564–March 1566	*hakim*	Muhammad Quli Khan Barlas	*AN*, II, p. 239

(*contd.*)

Appendix III (*contd.*)

Date	Nomenclature for Assignment or Assignee	Assignee	Reference
March–April 1571	*jaygir*	Muhibb 'Ali Khan	*TA*, II, p. 233
March–April 1571	*hakim*	Sa'id Khan Chaghta	Ibid.
March–April 1573	*hakim*	Sa'id Khan Chaghta	*AN*, III, p. 38
June 1573	(assignment)	Sa'id Khan Chaghta	'Arif, p. 163
Sept.–Oct. 1573	(assignment)	Sa'id Khan Chaghta	*AN*, III, p. 43
Sarkar **Etawah**			
Sept.–Oct. 1556	*hakim*	Qaya Khan Gung	Badauni, II, p. 13
1558	*jagir (pargana hatkant)*	Adham Khan	*AN*, II, p. 78
Aug.–Sept. 1560	*jaygir*	Bahadur Khan Uzbek	*AN*, II, p. 115
Jan.–March 1561	*(assignment)*	Bahadur Khan Uzbek	Bayazid, p. 244
March 1563	*jagir (parganas)*	Mun'im Khan	*AN*, II, p. 189
July–Aug. 1567	*(assignment)*	Shujaat Khan	*AN*, II, p. 289
Sarkar **Narnaul**			
March 1556	*jagir*	Majnun Khan Qaqshal	*AN*, II, p. 20
August 1563	*jagir (pargana)*	Khanzada	*TA*, II, p. 166
August 1563	*shiqdar*	Gesu Khan	Arif, p. 73
September 1563	*maqarrar shud*	Shujaat Khan	*AN*, II, p. 199
Sarkar **Kalpi**			
March 1556	*ba-sardari*	'Abdullah Khan Uzbek	*AN*, II, p. 14
Sep.–Oct. 1556	(assignment)	'Abdullah Khan Uzbek	Badauni, II, p. 13
November 1556	*ikhtisas, bakhshidand*	'Abdullah Khan Uzbek	*AN*, III, p. 45
1560	*hukumat*	'Abdullah Khan Uzbek	Badauni, III, p. 6
March 1561	*jaygir*	Abdullah Khan Uzbek	*AN*, II, p. 138
August 1561	*hakim*	Abdullah Khan Uzbek	Badauni, II, p. 49
December 1572	*jaygir*	Shaham Khan	*AN*, III, p. 19
Sarkar **Sambhal**			
March 1556	*nizam-i sarkar*	'Ali Quli Khan Uzbek	*AN*, II, p. 14
November 1566	(assignment)	'Ali Quli Khan Uzbek	'Arif, p. 52
March–July 1566	*jaygir* (*pargana* Azampur)	Ibrahim Husain Mirza	Badauni, II, p. 85
Jan.–March 1567	*bakharch-i maishat* (*pargana* Azampur)	Muhammad Sultan Mirza	*AN*, II, p. 279

(*contd.*)

Appendix III (*contd.*)

Date	Nomenclature for Assignment or Assignee	Assignee	Reference
Jan.–March 1567	*jaygir*	Ibrahim Husain Mirza and brothers	*AN*, II, pp. 279-80
Jan.–March 1567	*jaygir* (*pargana* Nihtaur)	Ulugh Mirza and Shah Mirza	Badauni, II, p. 91
Aug.- Sep. 1568	*jaygir*	Mir Muhammad Khan-i Kalan	*AN*, III, pp. 332-3
March–April 1573	*jaygirdār*	Moinuddin Khan Farankhudi	Badauni, II, p. 153

2

Mughal Court Politics during Bairam Khan's Regency

THE PERIOD OF BAIRAM KHAN'S *wikalat* or regency (1556–60) represents a very significant phase in the history of the Mughal Empire, inasmuch as it saw the defeat of a formidable attempt to overthrow it, and the consolidation of power, opening the path to its future expansion. The nature of Bairam Khan's power during this time, the way it was exercised, and factors which led to his rise and contributed to his fall have excited the interest of many historians. The prevailing interpretation seems to be that, from his appointment in January 1556, Bairam Khan, seizing the opportunity given to him by the critical position of the Mughals and the minority of Akbar, steadily went on extending his power, eliminating rivals, disregarding the wishes of the king, and behaving with intolerable arrogance, until the young king and the bulk of the nobility could suffer it no more and united to overthrow the tyrant.[1]

[1] This is broadly the point of view put forward by V.A. Smith in a passage captioned 'Causes of the Fall of Bairam Khan' (V.A. Smith, *Akbar the Great Mughal,* Delhi, 1962, p. 32). A.L. Srivastava generally follows the same line of argument, deviating from Smith's view only to the extent that he puts real blame on 'unworthy flatterers' surrounding Bairam Khan, who, he says, 'indulged in arrogant talk, gave him wrong advice and drove him into rebellion' (A.L. Srivastava, *Akbar the Great,* vol. 1, Agra, 1967, p. 40). Qazi Mukhtar Ahmad refers to Bairam Khan's 'womanish jealousy'

This rather simple interpretation is bolstered by bringing in certain other factors to explain Bairam Khan's role: The execution of Tardi Beg, the justifiability of which on moral grounds has been the subject of scholarly debate, is said to have irreparably embittered all the other nobles, so that they simply bided their time for four years before their hostility came into the open.[2] Another view, which, unknown to contemporaries, has won wide acceptance among modern scholars, is that Bairam Khan provoked Sunni opposition to his regime by reckless favours heaped on Shiites. Finally, R.P. Tripathi has suggested yet another reason: Bairam Khan, presumably as an Irani, excited the jealousy of all the Turkish nobles.[3]

While much that has been said on the subject of Bairam Khan's regency in modern works can hardly be disputed, it does seem that at least three factors advanced to supplement the main interpretation

---

and 'intellectual bankruptcy' while trying to elaborate the above views (cf. Qazi Mukhtar Ahmad, 'Was Bairam Khan a Rebel?', *Islamic Culture,* January 1947, pp. 58, 63).

[2] A.L. Srivastava, supporting the contention of V.A. Smith, characterizes Tardi Beg's execution as 'just and necessary' (A.L. Srivastava, *Akbar the Great,* vol. I, p. 27). Von Noer, on the other hand, denounces Bairam Khan's action as one taken with 'unconcerned barbarity' to remove someone 'whom he believed likely to endanger his position' (*The Emperor Akbar*, tr. A.S. Beveridge, 1890, p. 79). Qazi Mukhtar Ahmad ('Was Bairam Khan a Rebel?' *Islamic Culture*, 1947, p. 59) endorses this view and declares: 'The murder of Tardi Beg was no less than a bomb-shell but it was a timebomb which exploded later on' ('The Execution of Tardi Beg Khan', *Indian Historical Quarterly,* June 1952, p. 152). S.K. Ray ('The Execution of Tardi Beg Khan', *Indian Historical Quarterly,* June, 1952, p. 152) broadly supports the second view.

[3] Cf. V.A. Smith, *Akbar the Great Mughal*, p. 32. 'His appointment of Shaikh Gadai as *Sadr-us-Sudur* excited the sectarian animosity of all the Sunnis at court, who complained, and not without reason, that Bairam Khan showed excessive favour to the adherents of his own Shia sect.' R.P. Tripathi, while supporting this thesis, describes 'the Turkish nobles in general and the foster-parents of Akbar in particular' as the most formidable opponents of the Regent. Cf. R.P. Tripathi, *Rise and Fall of the Mughal Empire*, vol. I, Allahabad, 1956, p. 179.

lack adequate supporting evidence. As far as the main statement is concerned, in it too certain qualifications would seem desirable. For example, it is questionable whether Bairam Khan's power increased as steadily, without any checks, as is suggested; or that Bairam Khan was overthrown simply because he became too powerful, it having not been enquired into if he was not compelled to increase his power precisely in order to forestall his fall. There is also a further aspect to be studied, *viz.*, whether political and military events outside the king's personal attachments and the factional groupings within the Mughal nobility influenced vicissitudes in the fortunes of Bairam Khan.

These considerations suggest that a detailed enquiry, strictly following contemporary evidence and tracing developments in a chronological order, may be useful in clarifying the various historical problems concerning Bairam Khan's regency. My purpose here is to attempt such an enquiry, correlating the various events and checking existing views against the statements of sources, and on this basis to offer a fresh appraisal.

The period of Bairam Khan's regency broadly falls into four parts and these have been studied here separately. The first phase covered the period from Akbar's accession to just before the Battle of Panipat (January–October 1556), when Bairam Khan's leadership was acknowledged by all nobles facing a grave threat to their common interests. During the second phase, which saw the Second Battle of Panipat and closed with the arrival of the ladies of the court from Kabul (April 1557), Bairam Khan's control over the state apparatus was complete and he attempted to create a personal following. In the third phase, which extended till the middle of 1559, Bairam Khan's influence and powers diminished progressively. The final phase, which began with an attempt on the part of the regent to regain control over the state apparatus, witnessed the renewal of factional struggle at the court in an accentuated form, leading to Bairam Khan's dismissal.

I

The first phase began with Humayun's sudden death in January 1556, at which point the Mughal position in India was far from secure.

About this time Mubariz Khan Sur ('Adil Shah) and his famous general, Hemu, were making frenzied efforts to rally the Afghans of eastern India for a final showdown with the Mughals. The strength of the forces commanded by Hemu was formidable. According to Abul Fazl, on coming to know of Humayun's death, the Afghans decided to launch an offensive against the Mughal positions without further delay as they wanted to take full advantage of the situation.[4] The Mughals, on the other hand, were handicapped by the fact of Akbar being a minor. A regent who would rule in the name of the king had to be found and Bairam Khan was the obvious choice. But the *de facto* exercise of sovereign authority by one of the nobles was nevertheless bound to complicate the mutual relations of nobles, and was hence fraught with a serious threat to the stability of administration.

Under the circumstances, Bairam Khan's appointment as *wakil* was not contested by any of the great nobles. Tardi Beg, Munim Beg, Khizr Khwaja Khan, Khwaja Jalal-ud-din Mahmud, and Khwaja Muazzam,[5] each of whom could claim *wikalat* on the basis of his long record of service, blood relationship, or past association with Akbar, accepted Bairam Khan's appointment as a matter of course. Even the hot-tempered and ambitious Shah Abul Ma'ali raised no objection.[6]

[4] Abul Fazl, *Akbar-nama,* vol. II, pp. 27–8. Ahmad Yaagar, *Tarikh-i Shahi,* ed. Hidayat Husain, Calcutta, 1939, pp. 349–50. According to Abul Fazl's estimate, the total strength of the Afghan forces came up to 50,000 cavalry, 1000 elephants, 51 cannons, and 50 falconets.

[5] For the biographies of these nobles, cf. Shaikh Farid Bhakkari, *Zakhirat al-Khwanin,* vol. I, ed. Moinul Haq, Karachi, 1961, pp. 24, 209; Shah Nawaz Khan, *Ma'asir-ul Umara,* ed. Ashraf Ali, Bibliotheca Indica Series, vol. I, pp. 466–71, 615–22, 635–45; *Haft-Risalah-i Taqawim al-Baldan,* MS., Buhar Collection, National Library, Calcutta (a remarkably rich and accurate *tadhkira* of the nobles of Babur and Humayun, compiled sometime in the eighteenth century), ff. 98b,131b, 139a, 140b, I56b.

[6] Cf. *Zakhirat al-Khwanin,* vol. I, p. 77. Shaikh Farid Bhakkari maintains that Shah Abul Ma'ali wanted to take power into his own hands after Humayun's death. But this statement is not corroborated by any of the contemporary authorities. Abul Fazl and Abul Baqi Nahavandi, while giving reasons for the arrest of Shah Abul Ma'ali at Akbar's coronation,

His elevation was tacitly approved by all sections of the Mughal nobility. On Humayun's death, Tardi Beg Khan, the commandant of Delhi, voluntarily transferred custody of Mirza Kamran's son, Mirza Abul Qasim, to Bairam Khan.[7] Had he had any reservations regarding Bairam Khan's assumption of *wikalat*, there would have been no reason why he should have thus sent Mirza Abul Qasim to Kalanaur, thereby losing the advantage of having with him a prince of royal blood whom he could have utilized, if needed, as a pawn to further his own interests. Similarly, Mun'im Beg's prompt compliance with Bairam Khan's instructions to imprison Shah Abul Ma'ali's brother, Shah Hashim, at Kabul,[8] goes to show that his initial reaction to Bairam Khan's rise to *wikalat* was not on the whole unfavourable.

It is, however, probable that senior nobles already enjoying high posts or key positions wanted to share power and influence with Bairam Khan and were not prepared to accept his absolute power. Bairam Khan, on the other hand, was determined from the very beginning to exercise power with a firm hand. He seems to have

---

do not accuse him either of claiming sovereignty or of contesting for *wikalat*. His actual crime was that when invited to attend the post-coronation festivities, he made excuses pretending that he had not yet finished mourning. He agreed to attend the court only after getting an assurance that he would be treated with the same honour and distinction as was shown him during Humayun's lifetime (*Akbar-nama*, vol. II, p. 16; Abdul Baqi Nahavandi, *Ma'asir-i Rahimi*, ed. Hidayat Husain, Bibliotheca Indica Series, vol. I, p. 642).

[7] *Akbar-nama*, vol. I, p. 365; Nizamuddin Ahmad, *Tabaqat-i Akbari*, ed. B. De, Bibliotheca Indica Series, vol. II, p. 128; *Tarikh-i Alfi*, MS., India Office, Ethe, 112, f. 589b; Faizi Sirhindi, *Akbar-nama*, MS., British Library, Or. 169, f. 7a. For Tardi Beg's inimical relations with Bairam Khan, see Bayazid Bayat, *Tarikh-i Humayun w Akbar*, ed. Hidayat Husain, Bibliotheca Indica, pp. 220–1; *Akbar-nama*, vol. I, p. 344. Cf. *Tarikh-i Dilkusha*, MS., Cambridge, King's, 71, ff. 530b–531a. Inayat-ul-lah Kamboh maintains that Tardi Beg Khan was also a claimant to *wikalat*. He makes this statement while enumerating the causes of Tardi Beg's execution. This was obviously a later story.

[8] *Akbar-nama*, vol. II, p. 15; Bayazid Bayat, *Tarikh-i Humayun w Akbar*, ed. Hidayat Husain, Calcutta, 1941, p. 196.

been conscious of the fact that sooner or later this would bring him in conflict with the leading nobles. The pattern of subsequent events suggests that Bairam Khan, after becoming *wakil-us-saltanat*, started taking measures to eliminate from effective positions all those from whom he expected a challenge to his authority. On Akbar's accession, Shah Abul Ma'ali was dismissed and imprisoned. This evoked no retaliation as Shah Abul Ma'ali was universally unpopular because of his quick temper and presumptuous ways.[9] A few days later Bapus Beg, the *faujdar* of Lahore, was removed from his post and dispatched to Kabul with a small contingent on the pretext of reinforcing Mun'im Beg.[10] Another important noble, Tulak Khan Quchin, was also obliged to leave Hindustan and take up service under Mun'im Khan.[11] Khwaja Sultan 'Ali as well was apparently relieved of his responsibilities as *wazir* on Bairam Khan's assumption of *wikalat.* Although Khwaja Sultan 'Ali still continued as a functionary of the central government, his status was no longer that of a *wazir.* The affairs of the *diwani* (financial department) were subsequently supervised by the *wakil* himself. This represented the reversal of a measure introduced into the structure of the central government during the last ten years of

[9] *Akbar-nama,* vol. II, pp. 16-17. For the career of Shah Abul Ma'ali, see *Akbar-nama,* vol. I, pp. 311, 334, 350–1, 355, 367; Badauni, *Muntakhab-ut-Tawarikh,* vol. II, pp. 9–10; *Zakhirat al-Khawanin,* vol. I, pp. 77–9; *Maasir-i Rahimi,* vol. I, p. 610; *Maasir-ul Umara*, vol. III, pp. 557–60.

[10] Cf. Sidi 'Ali Reis, *Travels and Adventures of a Turkish Admiral*, trans. A. Vamberey, London, 1899, pp. 59–66. Bapus Beg and four other officers were sent with troops to Kabul within a few days of Akbar's accession. They carried to Munim Beg the news of Shah Abul Ma'ali's arrest. This party reached Kabul towards the beginning of Jumada I, 963H, i.e. the third week of March 1556.

[11] Cf. *Akbar-nama,* vol. II, p. 16 and Bayazid Bayat, *Tarikh-i Humayun w Akbar,* ed. Hidayat Husain, p. 207. Tulak Khan Quchin was present at the court on the occasion of Akbar's accession (February 1556). He was the person who overpowered Shah Abul Ma'ali in the court. He must have come to Kabul sometime before May 1556, for we find him present there at the time of Mirza Sulaiman's attack on Kabul.

Humayun's reign.[12] Lastly, it is worth noting that within a few days of Akbar's coronation Shams ud din Muhammad Atka, Khwaja Jalal-ud-din Mahmud, Muhammad Quli Khan Barlas, Mirza Khizr Khan Hazara—in short, almost all those important nobles whose presence in the camp could have proved embarrassing to Bairam Khan—were sent away to Kabul 'to bring their highnesses, the Begums'.[13]

Towards Mun'im Khan, the governor of Kabul, and 'Ali Quli Khan Uzbek, the commander of the Mughal forces in Awadh, Bairam Khan adopted an attitude of great politeness and favour with a view to enlisting their goodwill and co-operation, so that, in the eventuality of a showdown between him and the other nobles, these might at least be neutralized.[14] Bairam Khan was not altogether unsuccessful in this effort. 'Ali Quli Khan became a close ally, while Mun'im Khan, not known to be a friend of his, also co-operated. However, Bairam Khan could not take Mun'im Khan's loyalty for granted. Indeed, there could be no certainty that the understanding between Bairam Khan and Mun'im Khan would not be undermined by the influence of disgruntled nobles who, relieved of their posts by Bairam Khan, had now converged upon Kabul. In these circumstances it suited Bairam Khan's purpose that Mun'im Khan should be so tied down to Kabul that he might be prevented from exercising any influence at the court. Mirza Sulaiman's attack upon Kabul of May 1556, therefore, must have come as a godsend to Bairam Khan. It interrupted Mun'im Khan's

[12] *Akbar-nama,* vol. II, pp. 5, 15; *Tarikh-i Alfi,* f. 600a; Faizi Sirhindi, f. 8a. See also Iqtidar Alam Khan, 'Wizarat under Humayun', *Medieval India Quarterly,* vol. V, no. 1.

[13] *Akbar-nama,* vol. II, p. 17.

[14] Both of them were raised to the position of *khan.* Significantly, these two nobles alone were so honoured on the occasion of Akbar's accession. Others were rewarded only after the Battle of Panipat. Bayazid Bayat, *Tarikh-i Humayun w Akbar,* ed. Hidayat Husain, p. 195; *Akbar-nama,* vol. II, p. 45; Faizi Sirhindi, *Akbar-nama,* MS. British Library, Or.169, f. 7a. Cf. Kewal Ram, *Tazkirat-ul- Umara,* MS., Habib Ganj Collection, Maulana Azad Library, Aligarh, f. 114b, Munim Khan's son Ghani Khan was also made a *khan.*

contacts with the court for the next four months,[15] during which time Bairam Khan strengthened his grip over the administration. Bairam Khan's tardiness in sending help to Mun'im Khan during Mirza Sulaiman's attack could not have been entirely due to the difficulties of the Mughal position in Hindustan.[16]

The tensions within the Mughal nobility had already started to tell upon the stability of the administration by the time the Afghans launched their offensive in October 1556. The uncertainties roused by Bairam Khan's measures, discussed above, further undermined efforts of the Mughal officers to resist the Afghan advance towards Delhi. It is evident from Abul Fazl's account that on the eve of the battle of Tughluqabad the Mughal officers were totally lacking in unity of purpose. While the majority of the officers wanted to postpone a clash until the arrival of contingents from the Punjab and Sambhal, Tardi Beg Khan hastened to offer battle.[17] The latter possibly feared that,

[15] Abul Fazl places the attack in the beginning of the first Divine Year (commencing on 10 March 1556) in the middle of spring. Bayazid also mentions spring (*naunah*). News of the attack reached the imperial camp while it was at Jallundhar, where it had arrived towards the end of May 1556. From the account of Sidi Ali Reis it is evident that Mirza Sulaiman had not yet entered the confines of Kabul about the middle of April 1556. Since the siege lasted for about four months and was definitely over before the battle of Tughluqabad, which was fought on 6 October 1556, it is clear that Mirza Sulaiman's attack must have commenced sometime before 6 June 1556. These circumstances obviously suggest that the attack took place in May. *Akbar-nama,* vol. II, pp. 21, 22, 31, 54; Sidi Ali Reis, *Travels and Adventures of a Turkish Admiral,* p. 66; Bayazid Bayat, *Tarikh-i Humayun w Akbar,* ed. Hidayat Husain, pp. 197, 210; *Tarikh-i Alfi,* f. 591b.

[16] Cf. *Akbar-nama,* vol. II, p. 24. On coming to know of Mirza Sulaiman's attack on Kabul, Akbar expressed himself in favour of sending reinforcements to Mun'im Khan, but 'certain people' intervened to stop it. They maintained that the nobles earlier sent to escort the royal ladies would be able to cope with the task. They also referred to the 'pressing circumstances in India', but there is no evidence that at this time any large-scale campaign was in progress.

[17] *Akbar-nama,* vol. II, p. 29. 'The cowards out of fear' and 'the lion-hearted ones out of caution' were not in favour of a battle.

once Bairam Khan reached the area, he too would be removed from his charge and, like the others, would be sent off on some insignificant assignment. There was also present in the army Pir Muhammad Khan, who had been sent by Bairam Khan, possibly with a secret brief, to thwart Tardi Beg's efforts at achieving a decisive victory over the Afghans in the absence of the Regent.[18] These circumstances combined to bring about the Mughal defeat at Tughluqabad.

The Mughal defeat at Tughluqabad disturbed the balance of forces within the nobility by weakening the position of Tardi Beg Khan. Following this battle, Tardi Beg Khan and his followers came to the imperial camp in the Punjab as virtual fugitives, having lost their *jagirs* in the Doab and Mewat to the Afghans.[19] This tilted the balance finally in Bairam Khan's favour. He now got the opportunity to remove from his path the last remaining hurdle to a free exercise of his powers as regent. About 22 October 1556, without obtaining the king's sanction, Bairam Khan had Tardi Beg executed on the charge of 'knowingly and treacherously' bringing about the defeat by fleeing from the field of battle.[20] In laying this charge he was supported by 'Ali Quli Khan and Pir Muhammad Khan.

[18] Cf. *Akbar-nama,* vol. II, pp. 29, 30. Abul Fazl alludes to such a possibility. It is also noted that Pir Muhammad was the first to flee the battlefield.

[19] Prominently mentioned among Tardi Beg's followers were Khwaja Sultan 'Ali, Mir Asghar Munshi, Khanjer Beg, Baltu Beg, Majnun Khan Qaqshal, Haider Muhammad Khan *Akhta Begi,* Qasim Mukhlis, 'Ali Dost *Bar Begi,* Haidar *Bakhshi* (cf. *Akbar-nama,* vol. I, p. 344, vol. II, pp. 20, 29). Apparently, most of these nobles held *jagirs* in those parts of the Doab and Mewat that were looked after by Tardi Beg Khan from Delhi. Following the Mughal defeat at Tughluqabad, this entire region passed into the hands of the Afghans.

[20] Cf. *Akbar-nama,* vol. II, p. 32. *Tarikh-i Haji 'Arif Qandahari,* Aligarh transcript of Rampur MS., p. 45; Bayazid Bayat, *Tarikh-i Humayun w Akbar,* ed. Hidayat Husain, p. 220; *Tarikh-i Alfi,* India Office, Ethe 12, MS. f. 591b; *Tarikh-i Firishta,* vol. I, Nawal Kishore, p. 245. Badauni's statement (vol. II, p. 14) that Bairam Khan obtained from Akbar a 'sort of permission' to execute Tardi Beg, probably refers to the *post facto* approval of the action. Ahmad Yadgar's version that Tardi Beg was executed on

II

Tardi Beg's execution roused considerable indignation among the Mughal nobles in Hindustan, but it was not expressed in a violent manner. The Mughals were faced with a grave menace which did not permit them to risk an open rift within their ranks. Probably, Bairam Khan relied on this factor while deciding to execute Tardi Beg. Moreover, some people of influence who could have taken a lead in protesting against the execution were persuaded through various favours to support the regent's action. Among those thus bought over was Maham Anaga.[21] A few devoted adherents of Tardi Beg who obstinately refused to be silenced and came out openly against the regent were put to death.[22] Several others, like Khwaja Sultan 'Ali, Mir Asghar Munshi, and Khanjer Beg, were imprisoned.[23] Moreover, the

---

the orders of the king himself (*Tarikh-i Shahi,* pp. 354-5) is unacceptable as it is contradicted by all the contemporary authorities. See also S.K. Ray, 'The Execution of Tardi Beg', *Journal of Indian History,* June 1952, p. 154. Cf. *Maasir-i Rahimi,* vol. I, pp. 649–50. There is a curious passage which may be construed as alluding to differences between Bairam Khan and Tardi Beg on religious grounds. A literal translation of this passage would run as follows: '(some unnamed persons) who regarded the bigoted adherence to the faith of this betrayer of faith as one of the requisites of their religion were parties to the attempt to overthrow Bairam Khan.' Apparently, it was on the basis of this obscure statement that the author of *Maasir-ul Umara* (vol. I, p. 470) asserts that religious bigotry was an additional factor determining their mutual relations. Blochmann (*Ain-i Akbari,* trans., vol. I, Calcutta, 1927, p. 335) has accepted this version uncritically.

[21] *Tarikh-i Alfi*, India Office, Ethe 12, MS. f. 552a; cf. *Tarikh-i Shahi*, p. 355. Ahmad Yadgar also alludes to this fact.

[22] *Tarikh-i Haji Arif Qandahari* (Aligarh transcript of Rampur MS.), p. 45.

[23] Among the persons so punished were Khwaja Sultan 'Ali and Mir Asghar Munshi. The statement in *Maasir-ul Umara* (vol. I, p. 66) accepted by Blochmann *(Ain-i Akbari,* trans. vol. I, p. 408) that these two officers, along with Pir Muhammad Khan, were hostile towards Tardi Beg (a hostility

news of Tardi Beg's execution was not made public officially until a month after the Battle of Panipat. Special care was taken to conceal it from the nobles at Kabul,[24] among whom were not a few close friends and relatives of the fallen noble.[25] Through such measures Bairam Khan was able to keep the nobility under control despite the resentments to which his actions might have given rise.

Indeed, for the time being at any rate, Bairam Khan was able to establish a unity of command, probably unachievable had a rival like Tardi Beg been present. This certainly contributed to the splendid victory at Panipat. The commanders of the Mughal troops in this

---

further ascribed by Blochmann to their Khurasani origin) is apparently based on a misunderstanding of a passage in the *Akbar-nama,* (vol. II, p. 29). Only Pir Muhammad Khan is there said to have been hostile to Tardi Beg. As Abul Fazl (ibid., vol. II, p. 32) puts it, they were imprisoned because they were suspected of bribery and treachery. According to the *Tarikh-i Alfi* (f. 552a) and Badauni (vol. II, p. 14), Bairam Khan suspected them of treachery. Mutamad Khan (*Iqbalnama-i Jahangir* [1620], Nawal Kishore, p. 133) is still more explicit: the imprisoned nobles, he says, were staunch supporters of Tardi Beg.

[24] Cf. Bayazid Bayat, *Tarikh-i Humayun w Akbar*, pp. 213, 218, 221; and *Akbar-nama,* vol. II, pp. 31–2, 38, 412. When the royal messenger carrying the news of the Mughal victory at Panipat reached Kabul, Mun'im Khan and his subordinates were still ignorant of Tardi Beg's execution. Apparently, this messenger also did not disclose the news to Mun'im Khan, who came to know about it a month later through a letter from Bairam Khan himself. This goes to suggest that the official announcement of the event was withheld till then. No doubt the fact of executions and subsequent arrests must have become known in Hindustan and different versions of the episode were bound to have been in circulation. These rumours reached Kabul as well, but officers there were so ignorant of the trend of developments at the court that they probably did not give them much credence.

[25] Muqim Khan (later Shuja'at Khan), a nephew of Tardi Beg, was at Kabul about this time. He had been left there to look after Tardi Beg's interests. Another relative of Tardi Beg present at Kabul was Baltu Beg. He probably came to Kabul some time before Mirza Sulaiman's attack in May 1557. Cf. *Akbar-nama,* vol. I, 354; Bayazid Bayat, *Tarikh-i Humayun w Akbar*, p. 224; and *Tabaqat-i Akbari,* vol. II, p. 148.

battle were almost all personal allies and friends of Bairam Khan.[26] Bairam Khan utilized this occasion given him by the victory to reward and promote his own friends among the nobles, thus creating an independent following for himself. Titles and *jagirs* in the Doab were bestowed upon Bairam Khan's known friends and adherents like 'Abdulla Khan Uzbek, Sikandar Khan Uzbek, 'Ali Quli Khan Uzbek, Qiya Khan Gung, and Pir Muhammad Khan, further cementing his bonds with them.[27] It was mainly with the assistance of these nobles that Bairam Khan sought to pacify the regions occupied as a result of success at Panipat. In all the expeditions sent in different directions after the Battle of Panipat, these men played a key role.[28] Khizr Khwaja Khan was perhaps the only senior noble not belonging to

[26] Sikandar Khan Uzbek, 'Abdullah Khan Uzbek, 'Ali Quli Khan Uzbek, Husain Quli Khan, and Shah Quli Khan Mahram were the commanders of the wings of the army at Panipat. The first three belonged to one family: Abdullah Khan was a stepbrother of Ali Quli Khan's father (*Akbar-nama,* vol. I, p. 142; Bayazid Bayat, *Tarikh-i Humayun w Akbar*, p. 87). The exact nature of the relationship between them and Sikandar Khan is not known. Their subsequent careers, however, show that they were a well-knit family of nobles who always acted in unison (cf. *Akbar-nama,* vol. II, pp. 221–99, for the account of the revolt of the Uzbek officers during 1565–7). For instances of co-operation between Bairam Khan and the Uzbek nobles, see Badauni, vol. II, p. 14; *Akbar-nama,* vol. II, pp. 45, 69, 82, 97, 105–6, 114; cf. also *Tarikh-i Firishta,* vol. I, pp. 247–8; Khafi Khan, *Muntakhab al-Lubab,* ed. Ashraf Ali, Bibliotheca Indica Series, vol. I, pp. 138–9, 145. The other two, Husain Quli and Shah Quli Khan Mahram, were also Bairam Khan's personal servants and close adherents who stood by him to the last. Cf. *Akbar-nama,* vol. II, pp. 33, 104; *Zakhirat al-Khwanin,* vol. I, pp. 181, 209.

[27] 'Ali Quli Khan Uzbek, entitled Khan-i Zaman and assigned the *sarkar* of Sambhal and other *parganas* of the Doab; 'Abdullah Khan Uzbek, titled Shuja'at Khan and appointed to the *sarkar* of Kalpi; Sikandar Khan, titled Khan-i 'Alam and appointed, soon after, to Sialkot and asked to assist Khizr Khwaja Khan in operations against Sikandar Sur; Maulana Pir Muhammad, entitled Nasir ul-Mulk and attached to the person of the king, perhaps in the capacity of the *wakil* of the regent; Qaya Khan appointed to Agra. Cf. *Akbar-nama,* vol. II, pp. 45, 47, 30.

[28] After the Battle of Panipat, 'Ali Quli Khan Uzbek, Qiya Khan, 'Abdullah Khan Uzbek, Pir Muhammad Khan, and Muhammad Qasim Nishapuri led

the close circle of Bairam Khan's adherents who was trusted with an important command at this time.[29] He was stationed at the head of the Mughal forces in the Punjab on the eve of the Battle of Panipat. But even he was not left free to act according to his own judgement. The real initiative was throughout in the hands of Haji Muhammad Khan Sistani, a personal servant of Bairam Khan and not an officer of high rank.[30] Further, as soon as the military operations in the Punjab grew in intensity as a result of Sikandar Sur's coming out into the open, Bairam Khan hastened to send off there Sikandar Khan Uzbek,[31] a high-ranking officer belonging to the circle of his adherents, thus further limiting the powers of Khizr Khwaja Khan. Some time later 'Ali Quli Khan's younger brother Bahadur Khan was appointed to Multan, and from there Muhammad Quli Khan Barlas' *jagir* was transferred to Nagaur while the latter was still in Kabul.[32] This must have further strengthened Bairam Khan's control over Mughal officers in the Punjab.

At the level of the central government as well, authority passed completely into Bairam Khan's hands after the arrest and dismissal of Khwaja Sultan 'Ali and Mir Asghar Munshi in October 1556.[33]

---

expeditions into the regions of Sambhal, Agra, Kalpi, Alwar, and Ajmer, respectively. Cf. *Akbar-nama,* vol. II, pp. 33, 45–6.

[29] He was a descendant of the Mughal rulers of Kashgar. His status as a noble was very high as he was related to the royal family and held the title of *Amir ul-Umara.* Cf. *Zakhirat al-Khwanin,* vol. I, p. 209; *Maasir ul-Umara,* vol. I, pp. 613–15; *Haft Risalah-i Taqwim-al-Baldan,* f. 246b.

[30] *Akbar-nama,* vol. II, p. 47. Another trusted man of Bairam Khan present in the Punjab about this time was Shah Quli Naranji. For the fact that Haji Muhammad Khan and Shah Quli Naranji were ex-servants of Bairam Khan and fully trusted by him, see Bayazid Bayat, *Tarikh-i Humayun w Akbar*, pp. 186; *Zakhirat al-Khwanin,* vol. I, p. 231; *Massir-ul Umara,* vol. I, pp. 548–51.

[31] He was stationed at Sialkot: cf. *Akbar-nama,* vol. II, p. 47.

[32] *Akbar-nama,* vol. II, p. 54. For the fact that Muhammad Quli Khan was earlier sent to Kabul to escort the royal ladies from there, *vide supra.*

[33] From the account of Badauni (vol. II, p. 14) it is apparent that these two were working in one or other capacity in the central administration

A variety of jobs in the central government were now performed by Bairam Khan's personal *wakil,* Pir Muhammad Khan, who became a key figure in the administration.[34] Two other persons managing the central government, Khwaja Amin-ud-din, the *bakhshi,*[35] and Shaikh Gadai, the *sadr,*[36] were also favourites of Bairam Khan.

Bairam Khan was thus able to achieve full control over the state apparatus during the six months following Tardi Beg's execution. To

---

until October 1556. For the fact that Khwaja Sultan 'Ali continued as *wazir* down to Bairam Khan's rise to *wikalat, vide supra;* see also Iqtidar Alam Khan, 'Wizarat under Humayun', *Medieval India Quarterly,* vol. V, no. 1, p. 7

[34] For Pir Muhammad Khan's antecedents, cf. *Zakhirat al-Khwanin,* vol. I, pp. 101–3*; Maasir ul-Umara,* vol. III, pp. 182–6; *Akbar-nama,* vol. II, p. 29. Following the Battle of Panipat he was assigned to attend upon the king.

[35] For the antecedents of Khwaja Amin-ud-din Mahmud, see *Maasir ul-Umara,* vol. I, pp. 630. Cf. *Akbar-nama,* vol. II, p. 96. He was one of those three trusted servants of Bairam Khan who were sent by the latter in 1560 to allay Akbar's misgivings regarding the attitude of the regent.

[36] Shaikh Gadai was appointed *sadar,* apparently replacing Maulana 'Abdul Baqi in that capacity, soon after Bairam Khan's assumption of *wikalat* (*Akbar-nama,* vol. II, p. 20; *Maasir ul-Umara,* vol. II, p. 29), and not in III R.Y., as is maintained by V.A. Smith and other modern scholars. Gadai is also painted as a staunch Shiite and his appointment is supposed to have given 'extreme offence to the orthodox Sunni courtiers' (V. Smith, *Akbar the Great Mughal,* Delhi, 1962, p. 31; R.P. Tripathi, *Rise and fall of the Mughal Empire,* vol. I, Allahabad, 1956, p. 179; S.R. Sharma, *The Religious Policy of the Mughal Emperors,* Bombay, 1962, p. 18; A.L. Srivastava, *Akbar the Great,* vol. I, Agra, 1967, p. 41). This is nowhere corroborated by contemporary historians. On the other hand the way Badauni (vol. III, p. 76) approvingly refers to his accomplishments in religious sciences suggests that Gadai's religious views were not in the least offensive to the former. Apparently, this whole misunderstanding originated from certain statements in *Maasir-i Rahimi* (vol. I, pp. 649–50), *Dhakhirat al-Khwanin* (vol. I, p. 62), *Muntakhab al-Lubab* (vol. I, p. 138), and *Maasir-i Rahimi* (vol. I, p. 470, trans. vol. I, p. 63) hinting at Bairam Khan's inclination towards Shiite beliefs.

secure his position he took blatant measures to prevent his possible rivals from gaining access to the king. He saw to it that Mun'im Khan and Khwaja Jalal-ud-din Mahmud, both then in the Kabul region, abandoned all intentions of coming to the court.[37] He also had it seen to that none of the nobles who had close contact with the young king were allowed to stay in the imperial camp for any considerable time.[38]

This development must have been viewed with alarm by all those who were not prepared to tolerate the exercise of power by the regent as *de facto* sovereign. There are grounds to believe that this problem was discussed amongst the royal ladies and the senior nobles present at Kabul before the former's departure for Hindustan. It also seems that as a result of these discussions a definite line of action to curb the powers of the regent was evolved. Developments at the court after the arrival of the ladies from Kabul go to strengthen this impression.[39]

The ground was thus prepared for a serious challenge to Bairam Khan's authority within six months of the two great symbolic events marking his ascendancy, the execution of Tardi Beg and the Battle of Panipat.

III

Apparently one of the measures agreed upon among the royal ladies, Mun'im Khan, and other nobles for weaning away the young king

[37] Cf. Bayazid Bayat, *Tarikh-i Humayun w Akbar*, p. 220. The manner in which the news of Tardi Beg's execution was conveyed to Mun'im Khan about three months after the actual happening goes to suggest that Bairam Khan wanted to induce the former, then on his way to Hindustan, to return to Kabul by thus scaring him. For Bairam Khan's anxiety to keep Khwaja Jalal-ud-din away from the court, see *Akbar-nama,* vol. II, pp. 70–1, 78. According to Abul Fazl, Khwaja Jalal-ud-din decided to stay back in Ghazni as Bairam Khan was all-powerful in Hindustan.

[38] Cf. *Akbar-nama,* vol. II, pp. 55, 66, 95. Atka Khan was sent away to Bhira soon after his arrival from Kabul in April 1557 and he remained there for the rest of the period of Bairam Khan's regency.

[39] *Infra.*

from the influence of Bairam Khan was to marry him to a daughter of Mirza Abdulla Mughal, son-in-law of Mun'im Khan.[40] It is worth noting that as soon as Hamida Banu Begam and other ladies joined Akbar at Mankot, the proposal for such a match was mooted and, much to Bairam Khan's annoyance, the marriage took place with great pomp and show. This was the first setback suffered by Bairam Khan.[41]

Following the arrival of the royal ladies from Kabul in April 1557, events followed in succession that gradually led the Mughal imperial camp to the point of a crisis. It is significant that organized opposition to Bairam Khan became possible only after the arrival of Hamida Banu Begam and other royal ladies at the imperial camp from Kabul. Before this even Maham Anaga, who later became a moving spirit behind the opposition to the regent, was on cordial terms with him. She had been in the imperial camp, and not at Kabul, and in October 1556 she had supported Bairam Khan's execution of Tardi Beg Khan.[42] But now with the arrival of the royal ladies from Kabul, her attitude changed. This suggests that Hamida Banu Begam played a far more important role in ousting Bairam Khan than is usually believed.[43]

Certain incidents marked this new situation. An attempt was made on Bairam Khan's life soon after the arrival of the ladies. This roused Bairam Khan's suspicions, which were mainly directed against

[40] Bayazid Bayat, *Tarikh-i Humayun w Akbar*, p. 177.

[41] *Akbar-nama*, vol. II, p. 57. Abul Fazl nowhere gives the name of the person who put forward the proposal for this match. But on the basis of circumstantial evidence it is clear that the prime mover was Hamida Banu Begam. It would hardly have been possible for anyone else to carry through this proposal in the teeth of Bairam Khan's opposition.

[42] *Tarikh-i Alfi*, f. 592a.

[43] Cf. R.P. Tripathi, 'Akbar and Maham Anaga', *Journal of Indian History*, vol. I, 1922, pp. 329–32. He maintains that the ladies were simply the tools of young Akbar, who himself wanted to shake off the regent. But the fact that Hamida Banu Begam and Maham Anaga started opposing Bairam Khan as far back as April–August 1557, when Akbar was still very young (hardly fifteen), suggests that the role played by these ladies was essentially independent of any deliberate inspiration from Akbar.

Atka Khan, Adham Khan, Maham Anaga, and others who enjoyed a high degree of influence at the court owing to their close association with Akbar. He tried to meet the situation firmly. The distribution of royal elephants amongst the men of his trust, a stern warning to Maham Anaga and Atka Khan and the appointment of the latter to the distant outpost of Bhira, were some of the steps he took soon after the fall of Mankot (4 July 1557).[44] The arrangement of Bairam Khan's marriage with Akbar's cousin, Salima Sultan Begam, during this time, and the co-operation that he received from Maham Anaga in the matter, indicate that the above measures were not wholly fruitless.[45] Apparently, the opponents of the regent were forced to abandon the attitude of open defiance and hostility towards him which they had tended to adopt in the beginning. One factor that must have contributed in bringing about such a change was obviously the significant victories recently achieved in the Doab and Bundelkhand under such close friends and adherents of Bairam Khan as 'Ali Quli Khan and Qiya Khan Gung.[46]

Through his marriage with the princess, Bairam Khan reasserted his unique position among the nobles. It would, however, be wrong to suppose that it ensured Bairam Khan's continued hegemony for any considerable period. The fact that for no ostensible purpose the imperial camp remained in the Punjab for about a year after the fall of Mankot goes to suggest that, throughout this period, the central authority remained paralysed and confused as a result of ongoing tussle between Bairam Khan and the sections of the nobility opposed to him.[47] A way out of that impasse could be found only through a

[44] *Akbar-nama,* vol. II, pp. 60–2; *Maasir-i Rahimi,* vol. I, p. 657. It is difficult to accept Abul Fazl's view that the rushing of elephants upon Bairam Khan at Mankot was purely an accident. At least Bairam Khan himself was convinced that it was the result of a conspiracy to kill him.

[45] *Akbar-nama,* vol. II, pp. 64–5.

[46] *Tarikh-i Haji 'Arif Qandahari,* p. 48; *Akbar-nama,* vol. II, pp. 56, 57.

[47] Mankot was occupied on 7 *Ramzan* 964 H., i.e. 4 July 1557. The camp reached Lahore on 12 *Shawwal* 964 H., i.e. 8 August 1557. It left

working arrangement between the regent and his opponents regarding the routine functioning of the central government. It was on this crucial matter that Bairam Khan had to give substantial concessions by agreeing to share with other leading nobles some of his power. It was agreed round April 1558 that from that time on Bairam Khan as *wakil* would not place any proposal before the king for orders without obtaining the prior consent of the leading nobles, who were expected to meet in an assembly twice every week.[48] This was not an agreement merely on paper; that it was a real compromise between contending groups of nobles is borne out by the fashion in which the central administration worked subsequently. For instance, from then on Bairam Khan's authority at the centre diminished progressively and ultimately, late in 1558, there came about a situation when even his personal *wakil*, or agent, Pir Muhammad, was encouraged to work in open disregard of his wishes. His known supporters were singled out for harassment and persecution by the organs of the very central authority over which he was supposed to preside.[49]

IV

It was to retrieve this situation that Bairam Khan attempted what was almost a *coup d'état.* This took place in the second half of 1559. He dismissed and exiled Pir Muhammad Khan, appointing in his place Haji Muhammad Khan Sistani as his personal *wakil.* Following this change, central authority once again passed into Bairam Khan's effective control. In the new scheme of things at the centre Shaikh Gadai emerged as the key figure, who was now allocated certain functions concerning political and financial affairs in addition to

---

Lahore for Delhi on 12 *Safar* 965, i.e. 7 December 1557, reaching Delhi five months later, on 20 *Jumad* I, 965, H., i.e. 14 April 1558. Cf. *Akbar-nama,* vol. II, pp. 59, 61, 64–5.

[48] *Akbar-nama,* vol. II, p. 67.

[49] Cf. *Akbar-nama,* vol. II, p. 69: the measures taken against 'Ali Quli Khan in 1558 and Bairam Khan's inability to protect him were a clear indication of the direction in which the situation was moving.

his routine work as *sadr*.[50] Simultaneously, a number of low-ranking officers from amongst Bairam Khan's servants were given sudden promotions, possibly with the aim of bolstering the fast waning prestige of the regent among the nobility.[51] These steps were buttressed by a grand design of fresh military campaigns in the east and in Malwa, as well as in south-eastern Rajputana.[52]

These measures brought forth a sharp reaction from the other side. Following upon Akbar's initial estrangement from Bairam Khan at Mankot, the oppositional elements worked systematically, and with considerable success, to make the chasm between the two unbridgeable. The campaign of ridicule and vilification against Bairam Khan's friends grew in intensity with the passage of time.[53] They were depicted before Akbar as incompetent and disloyal and were held responsible for the misdeeds of Khan-i Khanan.[54] As Bairam Khan's isolation from the king and large sections of the nobility increased, his behaviour grew more and more impulsive.[55] He apparently added to the number of his enemies, unnecessarily provoking the hostility

[50] *Akbar-nama,* vol. II, pp. 86–7. Cf. *Massir ul-Umara,* vol. II, p. 540. Gadai used to put his seal on the back of the court orders.

[51] In one of the royal *farmans* addressed to Bairam Khan, following his dismissal, he was accused of giving undue promotions to his own servants and disregarding the claims of old and loyal nobles (*Akbar-nama,* vol. II, p. 106). Farid Bhakkari, quoting an earlier source, tells us that twenty-five persons were promoted by Bairam Khan to the position of *khans* holding ranks of 5000 (*Zakhirat al-Khwanin,* vol. I, p. 17; see also *Maasir-i Rahimi,* vol. II, p. 60).

[52] *Akbar-nama,* vol. II, pp. 82, 87, 89.

[53] They were now ridiculed and denigrated publicly. 'A dog has assumed the status of a sweet seller' was a jibe on Haji Muhammad Khan Sistani's appointment in the central government which received wide publicity. A verse ridiculing Shaikh Gadai composed by Mir Saiyed Rasuli was written on the walls of his house (Badauni, *Muntakhab ut-Tawarikh,* vol. II, p. 29).

[54] Apart from Shaikh Gadai and Haji Muhammad Khan Sistani, the main targets of criticism were Qiya Khan Gung, Shah Quli Khan Naranji, and Muhammad Tahir. Cf. *Akbar-nama,* vol. II, pp. 106–7.

[55] This is evident from the way he executed a royal elephant driver in 1559. Cf. *Akbar-nama,* vol. II, p. 92.

of various sections of the nobility by his authoritarian and indiscreet ways. Although there were not a few Chaghtai nobles among his own supporters,[56] with the passage of time his behaviour tended to create the impression that he was seeking to drive out all Chaghtais from positions of importance. This gave Bairam Khan's opponents a good opportunity to brand him as an enemy of the Chaghtais and to mobilize against him a considerable section of the Chaghtai clan, who were numerically still the single biggest group among high nobles.[57] This naturally paved the way for his fall.

Modern scholars almost unanimously introduce another source of the mounting opposition to Bairam Khan, namely, his supposed grant of favours to Shiites during his last days, thus causing great annoyance to Sunnis. While it appears that Bairam Khan held Shiite beliefs, no contemporary account whatsoever, nor any historian of the Mughal

[56] Some of the Chaghtai nobles, such as Qiya Khan Gung and Mihr Ali Sildoz, stood by Bairam Khan to the last. There were certain others among the followers of Bairam Khan who were, most probably, Turanis, e.g. Tarsun Muhammad Khan, Qasim Khan Nishapuri, and Husain Khan Tukerya. In addition to these there were the Uzbek nobles, apparently, a mixed lot of Shias and Sunnis; some of them like 'Ali Quli Khan Uzbek and his brother Bahadur Khan Uzbek were for all practical purposes Khurasanis as they were brought up in Persia. But there were others like 'Abdullah Khan Uzbek and Sikandar Khan Uzbek who spent their entire careers in the service of the Timurids and, apparently, had no special links with Khurasan. Cf. *Tarikh-i Haji 'Arif Qandahari,* p. 51; Bayazid Bayat, *Tarikh-i Humayun w Akbar*, p. 36; *Akbar-nama,* vol. 11, pp. 48, 113; *Tabaqat-i Akbari,* vol. II, p. 445; Badauni, vol. II, pp. 25–6, 32, 38, 41; *Zakhirat al-Khawanin* , vol. I, p. 211; *Maasir-i Rahimi,* vol. II, p. 60; *Muntakhab al-Lubab*, vol. I, p. 138; *Maasir ul-Umara*, vol. I, pp. 471–5, 551–4; ibid., vol II, pp. 503–5; ibid., vol. III, pp. 54–6; Blochmann, trans., *Ain-i Akbari,* vol. I, pp. 364, 366, 379, 402, 481, 484.

[57] Cf. *Akbar-nama,* vol. II, p. 117. Before surrendering to Akbar at Bajwara, Bairam Khan sent a message to the king saying he was apprehensive about the attitude of the Chaghtai nobles and would be willing to come out of the fort only if Munim Khan would personally assure him safety. It is obvious from this that by 1560 a very large section of the Chaghtai nobles had turned against Bairam Khan.

period, has suggested that he distributed his favours on religious grounds.[58] His chief favourite among the theologians, Shaikh Gadai, was undoubtedly a Sunni, and not a Shiite, as is so often asserted, without any authority going beyond Smith.[59]

It appears that in adopting measures to regain full control over the central administration Bairam Khan depended entirely on the support of his adherents who held important commands in various parts of the empire. He appears to have almost forgotten the necessity of gaining the confidence of the young king. He perhaps thought that it would be easy to tackle the king once he was able to regain complete control over the administration. But in doing so he gravely underrated the shrewdness of his ward as well as the loyalty and devotion of the Mughal nobility to the person of the king. As soon as Akbar left

[58] For Bairam Khan's Shiite beliefs, cf. *Maasir-i Rahimi*, vol. I, pp. 649–50; *Zakhirat ul-Khwanin*, vol. I, p. 62; *Maasir-ul Umara*, vol. I, p. 470; trans. vol. I, p. 63. Compare, Khafi Khan, *Muntakhab ul-Lubab*, vol. I, pp. 138, 147–8. It is asserted that Bairam Khan was very liberal in his religious outlook and was in the habit of mixing with all the sects. The fact that some of the Turani nobles, the majority of whom must have been Sunnis, remained Bairam Khan's supporters throughout the period of regency goes to reinforce this contention. One of these nobles was Husain Khan Turkerya, a nephew of Mahdi Qasim Khan, about whom Badauni (vol. II, p. 87) categorically says that he was a Sunni. Khafi Khan (*Muntakhab al-Lubab*, vol. I, pp. 147–8) has reproduced a letter purported to have been written by Bairam Khan to Akbar which might suggest that some of the bigoted Sunni theologians wanted to give the whole controversy a religious tinge. But the heroic overtones of the letter, which tend to dramatize the whole situation, suggest that it is in most part a piece of Khafi Khan's own imagination. Also *vide supra*, note 56, on Bairam Khan's Chaghtai and Turk adherents.

[59] There is no evidence to show that Gadai was a Shiite. On the other hand, the way in which Badauni (*Muntakhab-ut-Tawarikh*, vol. III, p. 76) praises Gadai's learning in matters of religion suggests that he found nothing repugnant in the latter's beliefs. Moreover, it is known that Gadai's father, Shaikh Jamali, a follower of the Soharwardi order, was definitely a Sunni. These circumstances indicate that Shaikh Gadai himself was a Sunni. Cf. *Akbar ul-Akhyar*, ed. Muhammad 'Abdul-Ahad, Delhi, pp. 227–9; *Maasir-ul Umara*, vol. II, pp. 539–41.

Agra in March 1560 and announced the dismissal of Bairam Khan, the latter's following among the nobles built so laboriously by him during the preceding four years melted away.[60] Even some of the most trusted lieutenants of Bairam Khan either deserted him or adopted an attitude of neutrality. Whatever following he continued to command up to the battle of Mechiwara was solely on the plea that he was fighting to free the king from the influence of his opponents.[61] But once Akbar took to the field himself, even this following vanished and the only section that remained with him was those of his sympathizers among the local chiefs of the Punjab Hills. The very fact that he was obliged to take shelter with a small *zamindar* of the Punjab was an open admission of the total collapse of his power.

V

From the above study it emerges that throughout the period of regency the political power essentially rested with the dominant sec-

[60] *Akbar-nama,* vol. II, p. 95. Cf. 'Ala-ud-daula Qazvini, *Nafais ul-Maasir,* MS. Br. Library, Or. 1761, f. 45b. 'As soon as the King left Agra all the nobles, even Bairam Khan's own servants, some with his permission, and others without his permission, hastened to join the King.'

[61] In this connection the attitude of the Uzbek officers may be cited as an example. These nobles had all along been supporting Bairam Khan (*supra*). Even at this occasion their sympathies were with him. To wean them away from Bairam Khan's influence, Bahadur Khan Uzbek was appointed *wakil* about this time, but even then they were not reconciled and remained hostile towards the royalists (*Akbar-nama,* vol. II, pp. 99–100, 114). However, even this powerful section of the nobility whose loyalty to the Mughal king was, as it later turned out, only skin deep, could not dare to side with Bairam Khan openly (cf. *Akbar-nama,* vol. II, p. 97; *Tarikh-i Firishta,* vol. I, p. 248). After his dismissal, Bairam Khan toyed, for some time, with the idea of invading Bengal with the help of Uzbek nobles and establish himself there as an independent king. He even set out for the east with this objective but later he suddenly changed his mind. It is possible that he was discouraged by the reluctance of the Uzbek nobles. Cf. *Akbar-nama,* vol. II, p. 97; *Maasir-i Rahimi*, vol. II, pp. 41–4. Bairam Khan in his communications to Akbar hammered the point that some people had poisoned the king's ears against him and expressed his wish to meet the king personally.

tions of the nobility. Bairam Khan was able to exercise his powers as a regent only insofar as it was condoned by broad sections of the Mughal officers and state functionaries. The nobles accepted his authority only in a limited sense. They were not prepared to allow him to function as *de facto* sovereign. Although Bairam Khan tried very hard to strengthen his hold over the state apparatus by curbing the nobility, except for the brief period of six months following Tardi Beg's execution, when the nobility's own interests demanded unity of command, the position of Regent was never anywhere near absolute supremacy. He had to depend all along to maintain his authority on the support of one or the other section of the nobility. There was, apparently, hardly any chance of creating a stable and independent following for himself: his attempt to do so added to his problems. On the one hand it alienated a large section of the nobility who felt jealous on account of the sudden rise of comparatively junior and low-ranking officers, and on the other newly created *amirs* further complicated the matters by their inefficiency and lack of moderation. Some of Bairam Khan's own creatures, having attained the position of *amirs,* were also emboldened to act occasionally against his wishes. At the same time their spontaneous responses to the factors effecting their position as a class could not have been very different from those of the older nobles.

The struggle between Bairam Khan and his opponents at the court was basically a struggle between the central authority as represented by the regent, whose powers rested on principles not very well defined, and the rest of the nobles. The king during this period was simply a figurehead whose whims and fancies led him frequently into becoming a tool in the hands of elements working against the regent. While Bairam Khan apparently endeavoured to establish a unified command and weld the two main elements constituting the Mughal nobility (the Chaghtais and the Khurasanis) into one whole, the bulk of the nobility looked askance at all such attempts on his part and took these as deliberate assaults on their freedom of action in their own commands and charges. Indeed, Bairam Khan's measures did imply a certain amount of curtailment of the nobles' powers and freedom of action. Even such nobles as were close to Bairam Khan often found themselves pitted against the central authority.

Bairam Khan's dilemma was that on the one hand he wanted to curtail the independence and autonomy of the nobles and on the other hand he had to depend for his power and authority on one or the other section of the nobility. There was hardly any escape from this obvious contradiction in his position. It was not possible to introduce any new element into the Mughal nobility to counterbalance the existing factions at that early stage when the process of the re-establishment of the empire in India was not complete. On no account was it feasible to recruit Afghan chiefs in the nobility in any appreciable number, for they were the real contenders for power against the Mughals. The only other element that could have been considered in this respect were the Rajput chiefs and other *zamindars*. The keen interest displayed by Bairam Khan in cultivating relations with the local chiefs is worth remembering. 'Abdul Baqi Nahavandi in fact credits Bairam Khan with laying down the policy of recruiting Rajputs into the Mughal nobility.[62]

It is possible that Bairam Khan thought in terms of using the recruits from amongst the Rajput chiefs to counterbalance the influence of the existing factions. But even had he wanted to recruit Rajputs, the process would have taken a long time to materialize whereas the problem he faced demanded an immediate solution. The only way out for him was either to placate his opponents by giving them sweeping concessions one after another, which only whetted their appetites, or adopt a stern attitude towards them. A recourse to the first alternative led to the compromise of April 1558, which practically paralysed the central authority. When to retrieve this situation Bairam Khan made a frontal attack upon his opponents, he found himself in complete isolation, which led to his overthrow.

The crisis leading to Bairam Khan's exit was perhaps the first round of the struggle between the central authority and forces operating

[62] *Ma'asir-i Rahimi*, vol. II, p. 59.

in the opposite direction within the Mughal polity. It resulted in the victory for the latter trend. This would perhaps explain why Akbar had to face such enormous difficulties in his relations with the nobility between 1562 and 1567 after his full assumption of sovereign powers.

3

The Nobility under Akbar and the Development of His Religious Policy, 1560–1580

THE SIGNIFICANT CHANGES that were introduced in the organization of Mughal government and the accompanying shifts in Akbar's administrative and religious policies during the period 1560–80 have remained for long a favourite subject of study. The existing interpretation of these changes seems largely to run parallel to Abul Fazl's line of argument which seeks to explain the growth of institutions and policies in terms of the unfolding of Akbar's personality. Abul Fazl often tries to ignore, or brush aside as the outcome of 'evil advice', all those measures or decisions which appear to him inconsistent with Akbar's policy during the last twenty-five years of his reign.[1] The impression created by Abul

[1] A glaring example of such an attitude is Abul Fazl's attempt to create an impression that the *mahzar* (1579) recognized Akbar as an arbitrator not only between the orthodox schools of Muslim jurisprudence but also between different religions and sects. It is significant that he fails to give the text of the document, which, according to Badauni, was drafted by Shaikh Mubarik, and is reproduced both in the *Tabaqat-i Akbari* and the *Muntakhab-ut-Tawarikh*. Cf. *Akbar-nama*, vol. III, pp. 269–70.

Fazl is reinforced by a similar tendency in Badauni, who, from an opposite point of view, quite frequently mixes up his comments on some of Akbar's enlightened measures of the later period with events of the earlier phase when there was hardly any ground for him to find fault with Akbar from a doctrinal angle. Under the influence of these interpretations modern historians also tend to disregard facts that are inconsistent with Abul Fazl's theory of Akbar's gradual 'unveiling' of himself as 'the superman', through the introduction, one after another, of policies based on the principles of *sulh-i kul* and universal kingship. This has often resulted in reducing discussion of Akbar's religious policy and his relations with the Rajputs largely to speculation based on selected facts that have been highlighted by Abul Fazl and Badauni.

It may further be pointed out that the whole problem of the nobility under Akbar is generally sought to be understood in terms of their relations with the king—no doubt an important aspect but not the sole one; and the exclusive attention given to this has served to hide from view many other equally important factors, such as the pattern of racial and religious alignments within the nobility, tribal or clan ties among groups of nobles, their relations with other sections of the people, etc., the interactions of which determined to a large extent changes in the role and standing of the nobility.

I suggest here a reappraisal of Akbar's early policies by raising certain points which tell against the accepted interpretation. The views I put forward are purely tentative and by no means based on an exhaustive analysis of the available evidence. My purpose will be served if it succeeds in stimulating fresh thinking about some of the well-known generalizations so often repeated in textbooks.

A significant aspect of the transformation that came about in the nature and functioning of the institutions of the Mughal Empire in the sixteenth century was the evolution of a homogeneous nobility out of the multiracial and religiously heterogeneous elements brought together by Akbar. An analysis of the list of nobles who accompanied Humayun to Hindustan in 1555 shows that the nobility inherited by Akbar consisted chiefly of two racial groups,[2] the Persians and the Turanis; and of the two the Turanis enjoyed the predominant position. The nobility left behind by Humayun had thus essentially a Turani complexion. Persian nobles—with the exception of Bairam Khan, Mirza Nijat, and Mirza Hasan—were simply exalted scribes who could exercise but little influence on state policies.[3] Excluding a few (hardly three or four) persons of Persian origin who were promoted,[4] the composition of the nobility remained unaltered during the regime of Bairam Khan. After his fall the situation gradually changed. As is apparent from the accompanying tables, two new elements of local origin entered the imperial service between 1560 and 1575. These new elements were the Rajput chiefs and the Indian Muslims (mostly Shaikhzadas, the majority of whom belonged to families living on *madad-i maash* grants or enjoying *zamindari* rights). At the same time, there was a marked increase in the relative strength of Persians, especially in the higher grades.[5] The net result of this process was the gradual fading away of the Turani complexion of the nobility as well as the erosion of the Chaghtai traditions and customs of

[2] See Appendix I. For this analysis the list of nobles accompanying Humayun in 1555 as given by Abul Fazl is taken as the sample, with the modification that the following six persons then known to be minor attendants or officials at Humayun's court have been excluded: Baqi Beg, *yatish begi*, Khwaja Abdus Samad, Mir Saiyed 'Ali, Khwaja Ataullah, *diwan-i khak*, Mir Shihab Nishapuri, Khwaja Aminuddin Mahmud. Cf. *Akbar-nama*, vol. I, p. 342.

[3] Cf. Appendix I. Turanis were 52.9 per cent of the total. But if it is kept in mind that a number of Turani nobles including Mun'im Beg were left behind in the Kabul tract, there is every reason to believe that the actual percentage was much higher.

[4] I have noticed only four such persons: Haji Muhammad Khan Sistani, Wali Beg, Shihabuddin Ahmad Khan, and Khwaja Jahan.

[5] Cf. Appendix I. The figure for the absolute number of nobles for the period 1565–75 is arrived at by putting together the names contained in Abul Fazl's lists for various campaigns and expeditions of these years. Although this figure cannot be treated as conclusive, still, for a tentative study of this kind it can be accepted as a reasonably good sample.

state organization,[6] thus indirectly facilitating Akbar's quest for an alternative theory of kingship in the subsequent years.

The Persian nobles seem to have improved their position in the period 1562–7,[7] mainly by earning promotions in the course of military operations during the revolts of sections of the nobility. It may be noted that except for the temporary desertion by Asaf Khan in 1565–6, none of the revolts which took place in this period were staged by Persians, or for that matter by any other non-Turani section of the nobles.[8] Even the rebellion of the Uzbek officers led by 'Ali Quli Khan, who himself had a Persian background, was in reality the rebellion of the whole clan of the Uzbek nobles serving under Akbar, amongst whom, but for 'Ali Quli Khan and his brother, all the leading figures—like 'Abdullah Khan, Ibrahim Khan, and Sikandar

[6] Commenting on Mirza Sulaiman's arrival at the court in 1575, Badauni observes: 'At this time (the Emperor) revived the old *tora-i chaghtai*. For some time, in order to exhibit it to Mirza Sulaiman, they spread royal tables in *diwankhana* and the *tawachis* entertained the soldiers. But when the Mirza departed, all these (revived customs) departed too.' (*Muntakhab-ut-Tawarikh*, vol. II, p. 216.) The English translation (vol. II, p. 220) of this passage is inaccurate and misleading.

[7] Cf. Appendix I. Although their strength in absolute numbers fell from 31.37 per cent in 1555 to 27.27 per cent in 1565–75, this does not necessarily prove a decline in their position. This fall in percentage was more the result of the sharp rise in the total number of nobles with the expansion of the empire. There was a corresponding fall in the absolute strength of the Turanis as well. What is more important is the fact that in the higher grades the Iranis had come to equal the Turanis and their percentage was also considerably higher (38.58 per cent). This clearly suggests the rapid promotion of Persian nobles during the period.

[8] There were six major rebellions between 1562 and 1567:

(a) Revolt by Mirza Sharfuddin, 1562–3.
(b) Shah Abul Maali's revolt, 1564.
(c) 'Abdullah Khan's revolt, 1564.
(d) 'Ali Quli Khan's revolt, 1565–7.
(e) Asaf Khan's desertion, 1565–6.
(f) The revolt by the Mirzas, 1566.

Khan—were Turanis.[9] It is also significant that during the operations against the Uzbek officers, Mun'im Khan, the most senior Chaghtai noble of the realm, endeavoured to secure a peaceful settlement, whereas a group of senior Khurasani officers, such as Khwaja Jahan, Asaf Khan, Muiz ul-Mulk, and Mir Ghiasuddin, appeared to be quite apathetic if not actually hostile towards the efforts aimed at reconciliation.[10]

Another piece of information sheds some light on the attitudes of the Turanis and Khurasanis during this period. Abul Fazl notes that a large section of the Turani nobles participating in the operations against Mirza Sharfuddin and Shah Abul Maali in 1563–4 were quite lukewarm, while Persian officers like Husain Quli Khan, Ismail Quli Khan, and others who were directing the operations, as well as other Persians serving under them, were steadfast and unsparing in their support of the royal cause.[11] On no occasion after 1567, not even in 1580–1,[12] was such undivided support of the Persian nobles

[9] 'Abdullah Khan was a close relative (perhaps a stepbrother) of Babur's well-known noble, Qasim Husain Khan Uzbek (maternal grandson of Sultan Husain Mirza of Herat), and an uncle of 'Ali Quli. He served under Humayun in 1536. Cf. *Akbar-nama*, vol. I, p. 142; Gulbadan, *Humayun-nama*, p. 17. Sikandar Khan, a former servant of Mirza Kamran, remained in the Mughal service from the early years of the reign of Humayun and was not one of those who joined Humayun's service in Persia. Cf. Mirza Haider Doghlat, *Tarikh-i Rashidi*, tr. Denison Ross, London, 1895, p. 474. Ibrahim Khan was the seniormost of the Uzbek officers. 'Ali Quli Khan treated him just like an uncle. For his biography, see *Maathir ul-Umara*, vol. I, pp. 75–7. Cf. *Tarikh-i Alfi*, MS India Office Ethe 12, f. 620a.

[10] For the attitudes of these officers, see *Akbar-nama*, vol. II, pp. 261–2, 268–9; *Tazkira-i Humayun w Akbar*, pp. 288, 290; *Tabaqat-i Akbari*, vol. II, p. 187; *Tarikh-i Alfi*, f. 620a. From a reference in Bayazid's account it appears that at the time of Asaf Khan's selection as the commander of the royal army that was sent against 'Ali Quli Khan in 1565, there arose a controversy which had racial overtones. In the heat of the argument Khwaja Jahan is reported to have remarked: 'Even a single hair of Asaf Khan is more useful than the whole of the Chaghtai clan.'

[11] *Akbar-nama*, vol. II, p. 200.

[12] Appendix IV. In 1580–1, while 32 Persians supported the imperial side, 12 actually joined the rebels and 3 remained neutral.

available to Akbar in his struggle with recalcitrant sections of the nobility. These facts put together indicate clearly that the trend visible in the fortunes of the Persians, from the table for 1565–75, is not unreal or accidental, and also confirm the suggestion that the rise in their numbers in the higher grades actually took place between 1562 and 1567.

There can be no doubt that the recruitment of Rajputs into Mughal service commenced soon after Akbar's assumption of the direction of the state. The same was perhaps the case with the Shaikhzadas. The presence of important clans of the Rajputs and the Shaikhzadas in Mughal service can be traced as far back as 1561.[13] Apparently during this period Akbar was anxious to win recruits from these sections by placating and befriending them in various ways. One of his measures towards this goal was matrimonial relations with the Rajput chiefs. It is possible that an attempt to establish similar relations was made with the Shaikhzadas of Delhi and Agra, though it seems to have proved abortive.[14] The abolition of pilgrimage tax in 1562, and of the *jiziah* in 1564,[15] were steps of a similar nature dictated principally by the exigencies of state policy rather than considerations of religious tolerance or intellectual influences of any kind.

It is interesting to note that soon after the suppression of the Uzbek rebellion Akbar's attitude towards the Rajputs changed radically. He now adopted a vigorous policy to reduce them into submission by force. There was a corresponding shift in religious policy too, shown

[13] Cf. *Akbar-nama*, vol. II, pp. 155, 180. The most important section of the Shaikhzadas taken into service was composed of the Saiyads of Barha. They were in service as far back as 1561. The list of *Ain-i Akbari* contains the following nine names from the Barhas: Saiyad Mahmud (No. 75), Saiyad Ahmad (No. 91), Saiyad Qasim (No. 105), Saiyad Hashim (No. 143), Saiyad Raju (No. 168), Saiyad Jamaluddin (No. 217), Saiyad Chaju (No. 221), Saiyad Bayazid (No. 295), Saiyad Lad (No. 409). Numbers within brackets are those given by Blochmann (*Ain-i Akbari*, tr. Blochmann, Calcutta, 1867–77). With the exception of the last two, all belonged to the categories of *mansabdars* of 500 and above.

[14] *Muntakhab-ut-Tawarikh*, vol. II, pp. 61–2.

[15] *Akbar-nama*, vol. II, pp. 190, 203–4.

by efforts at placating orthodox Muslim sentiments. The appeal of such a policy was, apparently, directed towards the Persians, the Turanis, and the newly recruited Indian Muslims, all of whom were possibly regarded as equally bigoted in their devotion to Islam. The public manifestation of Akbar's attitude during the siege of Chittor (1568) is in this connection quite instructive. The fall of Chittor was proclaimed by him as the victory of Islam over infidels. A *fathnama* issued on 9 March 1568 conveying the news of his victory at Chittor to the officers of the Punjab is so full of intolerant professions and sentiments, and is couched in such aggressive language, that it could compete favourably with similar documents issued by the most orthodox among the Muslim rulers of India.[16] There is some other evidence as well which reinforces the impression conveyed by this document. For example, there exists a *farman* of Akbar, presumably of this period, which directs Qazi 'Abdul Samad, the *muhtasib* of Bilgram, and other officials of the town 'to prevent the Hindus of that *pargana* from practising idol-worship and take such other steps as might help in eradicating the manifestations of heresy and deviation from that *pargana*.'[17] The reimposition of *jiziah* in 1575

[16] Cf. Abul Qasim Namakin, *Munshiat-i Namakin*, Aligarh MS, ff. 26a–32a. 'As directed by the word of God', Akbar claims, 'we, as far as it is within our power, remain busy in *jihad* and owing to the kindness of the supreme Lord, who is the promoter of our victories, we have succeeded in occupying a number of forts and towns belonging to the infidels and have established Islam there. With the help of our bloodthirsty sword we have erased the signs of infidelity from their minds and have destroyed temples in those places and also all over Hindustan.'

[17] *Sharaif-i Usmani*, MS, Department of History, AMU Aligarh (a local history of Bilgram compiled in the eighteenth century, containing a large number of documents), f. 144a. The date is illegible. From certain other documents reproduced in the same book (ff. 56a and 58a) it appears that Qazi 'Abdul Samad was alive during 1571–92. Obviously, there is a greater likelihood of its being issued in the 1570s rather than in the 1580s or 1590s, when, according to the unanimous testimony of our authorities, Akbar was drifting away from orthodox Islam.

was the logical culmination of this policy.[18] Apparently, it was by and large successful in attaining the object that Akbar had in mind: it is noteworthy that all the important Rajput chiefs, with the exception of the Kachwahas, joined Akbar's service after the fall of Chittor and not before it.[19] This would suggest that the factors which induced the Rajputs to join Mughal service were anything but their appreciation of Akbar's attitude towards non-Muslims.

It would appear from the breakdown of the total figure of nobles for 1565–75, 1580, and 1575–95 under different racial categories

[18] Cf. *Muntakhab-ut-Tawarikh*, vol. II, p. 210. 'During the same period (983H) (the Emperor) directed Shaikh 'Abdun Nabi and Makhdum ul-Mulk to investigate and reimpose *jiziah* on Hindus. *Farmans* to this effect were sent on all sides. But this order soon disappeared like a painting on water.' Lowe's translation of the passage (Calcutta, 1924, vol. II, p. 213) is misleading. He has dropped the word *jiziah.*

[19] This point is amply borne out by the following chronology of Akbar's relations with the Rajput chiefs:

Raja Ram Chand of Bhatta attacked	1561
Kachwahas joined service, gave daughter in marriage Jan.–Feb.	1562
Mirtha reduced	Jan.–Feb. 1562
Raja Ram Chand sent Tan Sen	1562
Abortive expedition against Jodhpur	1563
Military measures against the Ujjainia Chief, Gajpati of Achna down to	1567
Chittor occupied	February 1568
Ranthambhor reduced	May 1569
Kalinjar surrendered by he ruler of Bhatta	August 1569
Chandra Sen, Jodhpur, joined service	November 1570
Kalyan Mal, Bikaner, joined service, gave niece in marriage	November 1570
Har Rai, joined service and gave niece in marriage	November 1570
Raja Gajpati Ujjainia of Achna joined service	1567–73
Jai Chand of Nagarkot disgraced and expedition sent against his state	Feb.–March 1573

Cf. *Akbar-nama*, vol. II, pp. 155, 182–3, 197–8, 335–40, 340–1, 358; *Muntakhab-ut-Tawarikh*, vol. II, pp. 49, 50, 63, 161–2,179–80.

that Indian Muslims who entered the Mughal service in the early 1560s improved their positions particularly during 1575–80.[20] It is significant that during the rebellion of 1580–1 Indian Muslims and Rajputs as a body sided with the king while the Turanis, and to a lesser degree the Persians as well, were divided over it.[21] This clearly shows that during the years preceding the revolt the Indian nobles must have been specially cultivated to make them steadfast supporters of the central authority in a conflict that arose around certain issues vitally affecting the position of the nobility.

The emergence of Indian Muslims as an important section of the nobility was also important in so far as it must have contributed towards creating wider support for the empire amongst the Muslim communities in India. Apparently the reorganization of the Department of *Sadarat* during the 1570s was motivated by Akbar's desire to gain and preserve the sympathies of still further sections of the Muslim upper class in North India. Shaikh Abdun Nabi, after his appointment as *Sadr* in 1564–5, was given wide powers and considerable resources were placed at his disposal for the purpose of obliging 'deserving people'. According to Badauni, 'If the bounty of all former kings of Hind were thrown into one scale and the liberality of this age into the other, yet this would preponderate'.[22] It is evident even from Badauni's bitter denunciation of the policy of resuming excessive land from grants carrying more than 100 *bighas* of land (1575) that this measure was not so much aimed at curbing the theologians, as has been generally thought, but was motivated by the desire to extend state patronage to a larger number of influential and leading Indian Muslims, and without maintaining any particular distinction between 'the learned' and 'the illiterate'.[23] Similarly, Akbar's well-known order (of 1578) directing all the *madad-i maash* grants in a *pargana* to be concentrated in a few select villages, and

[20] Appendix I.
[21] Appendix IV.
[22] *Muntakhab-ut-Tawarikh*, vol. II, p. 71; tr., II, p. 70.
[23] *Muntakhab-ut-Tawarikh*, vol. II, p. 205.

making it obligatory on the part of grantees to reside in the villages of their grants, has been criticized by Badauni for the hardships it imposed on the grantees. But as the original text of the *farman*, now discovered, shows, the intention was to protect the grantees against *jagirdars* and due care was taken to ensure that the grantees' interests were not adversely affected.[24]

In this discussion a reference to the much debated *mahzar* of 1579 will not be without interest. It is obvious that the *mahzar* reproduced by Badauni and Nizamuddin was the outcome of Akbar's eagerness to win recognition as the sole head of the orthodox Muslims of India and not of the whole world.[25] This policy had little in common with the concept of 'universal kingship' that won official recognition later. In the *mahzar* the king's title as head of the orthodox Muslims (*Amir ul-Muminin* and *Sultan-i Islam*) rests on the sanction given by the leading *Ulama* of the realm, while, according to the theory that developed later, kingship is recognized as a divine attribute: it is communicated by God to kings without intermediate assistance.[26] It is, therefore, natural that Abul Fazl, an exponent of the later theory, should have thought it fit not to reproduce the text of the *mahzar*, but to treat it rather casually. He does not disclose the fact, pointedly mentioned by Badauni, that the chief architect of the document was

[24] *Akbar-nama*, vol. III, p. 240; *Muntakhab-ut-Tawarikh*, vol. II, p. 254. The original *farman* is preserved in the UP Records Office, Allahabad (No. 24). Cf. Irfan Habib, *The Agrarian System of Mughal India*, p. 302 n. 21.

[25] *Tabaqat-i Akbari*, vol. II, pp. 345-6; *Muntakhab-ut-Tawarikh*, vol. II, p. 272. Cf. Nurul Hasan, 'The "Mahzar" of Akbar's Reign', *Journal of U.P. Historical Society*, vol. XVI, pt I, p. 126, where it is maintained that although the titles used are *Sultan-i 'Adil and Amir ul-Muminin*, the 'intention of the signatories was clearly to call Akbar a *Khalifa*.' It may well be that the use of the word *khalifa* was avoided because the intention was to proclaim Akbar as the head of the Muslims of India and not of the whole world. The very opening lines of the *mahzar* make it quite clear that it was exclusively concerned with conditions in India.

[26] Abul Fazl, *Ain-i Akbari*, vol. I, ed. Sayed Ahmad Khan, p. 3; tr. Blochmann, pp. 1, 3.

his own father, whose works, even when quite minor, are referred to by him in the most laudatory terms. Moreover, the summary of this document as given by him is inaccurate and tendentious. It tends to create the impression that the *mahzar* declared the king's role to be that of an arbitrator, not only between the orthodox schools of Muslim law, but also between the various religions and sects (*Keshha w mazhabha*). There is also no reference in Abul Fazl's account to the titles of *Sultan-i Islam* and *Amir ul-Muminin* used for the king in the *mahzar.*[27] It is obvious that Abul Fazl found it rather embarrassing to handle the *mahzar,* which would seem to have been the final and by far the most blatant of Akbar's measures to placate and win over orthodox Muslim opinion in India. Hence the full significance of the *mahzar* can be appreciated only if it is viewed against the background of Akbar's general attitude of promoting and befriending Indian Muslims. It was in line with a series of other measures by which Akbar strove to show that he shared the religious beliefs and sentiments of his Muslim subjects. His devotion to the tomb at Ajmer,[28] his relations with Salim Chishti,[29] his hostility towards the Mahadavis (who were so unpopular with the orthodox sections),[30] and his attempt to deliver

[27] *Akbar-nama*, vol. III, pp. 269–70.

[28] Apparently Akbar's interest in Ajmer was very great between 1568 and 1579. During this period he visited Ajmer almost every year. But his veneration for Khwaja Moin Chishti seems to have disappeared rather abruptly after his last visit in September 1579. The year following, in July, he avoided going there on the occasion of the annual *urs* and deputed his son, Daniyal, to officiate for him. While mentioning this fact Abul Fazl specifically states that he no longer believed in visiting tombs. Cf. *Nafais ul-Maathir*, MS Br. Museum, f. 53 a & b; Shaikh Mustafa Gujarati, *Majalis* (Haiderabad), p. 58; *Akbar-nama*, vol. II, pp. 276, 317; *Muntakhab-ut-Tawarikh*, vol. II, pp. 49, 105, 108, 124, 132, 139, 170, 172, 185, 198, 226, 272.

[29] It appears that relatives of Shaikh Salim Chishti were greatly benefited in terms of wealth and status by the Shaikh's close relations with Akbar. Cf. *Muntakhab-ut-Tawarikh*, vol. II, p.109.

[30] Cf. *Nafais ul-Maathir*, MS, British Library, ff. 62 a & b. Allauddaulah, the earliest authority on Akbar's reign, quotes a proclamation issued by Akbar before setting out from Ajmer to invade Gujarat in which it was stated that the emperor considered it necessary to subjugate Gujarat in view of the fact

the Friday sermon[31]—all make a definite pattern and show Akbar's great anxiety to conciliate the Muslim orthodoxy.

This phase in Akbar's policy ended around 1580. Apparently, the attempt to project Akbar's image as *Sultan-i Islam* proved abortive.[32] The revolt of 1580–1 showed that it failed to create the desired impression upon the Turani and Persian nobles, who took a major part in it,[33] and who were feeling agitated over the introduction of *dagh*, a new mode of revenue collection, and such other administrative reforms as affected their income and power. The dismissal of Shaikh 'Abdun Nabi and Makhdum ul-Mulk (December 1579) and the abolition of the *jiziah* for the second time (1580),[34] in the tense political atmosphere of the eastern part of the empire, indicate a sudden collapse of the policy pursued so vigorously during the preceding thirteen years.

The turning point might well have come immediately after the *mahzar*. This document not only failed to strengthen Akbar's hands but was responsible for reopening a very sensitive issue by seeking to

---

that a number of the Afghans in that region deviating from true Islam had accepted Mahadavism and were tyrannizing the orthodox people. According to Ghausi Shattari, Shaikh Muhammad of Nahrwala, a Bohra theologian of orthodox views, had taken a vow not to put on a turban so long as heresy was not eradicated from the Bohra community. When Akbar reached Nahrwala he promised the Shaikh that he would do his best to suppress the Mahadavis and he himself put the turban on the Shaikh's head. A reference to this event is made by 'Abdul Haq Dehlvi and also in some of the Mahadavi sources. Cf. *Gulzar-i Abrar*, MS, John Rylands Library, f. 207b; *Akhbar ul-Akhyar*, Delhi, 1322H., p. 28; Mahmud Shirani, *Faiz-i 'Am* (A summary of a *mathnavi*, written in 1141 H.), *Oriental College Magazine*, 1940, p. 48.

[31] *Muntakhab-ut-Tawarikh*, vol. II, p. 268; *Tabaqat-i Akbari*, vol. II, p. 344.

[32] I should like to thank Dr Azizuddin for pointing out that the expression '*Badshah-i Islam*' does not occur in the text; the title used is *Sultan-i Islam*. See his article in *Professor K.S. Gupta Commemoration Volume*, ed. Chandra Shekhar, Udaipur, 2007.

[33] Appendix IV.

[34] *Akbar-nama*, vol. II, p. 278; *Muntakhab-ut-Tawarikh*, vol. II, p. 276. Cf. *Tabaqat-i Akbari*, vol. II, p. 347.

provide a theological justification for his sovereignty. It is noteworthy that a *fatwa* of *kufr* against Akbar appeared only after the signing of the *mahzar*.[35] It is understandable that Akbar soon realized his mistake in issuing the *mahzar* and took a decision to put it in cold storage.

But if the policy behind the *mahzar* ended in a debacle, this very failure liberated Akbar from the fetters of a mental attitude seeking justification for his royal authority within a religious framework. Subsequently, there was, more or less, a smooth unfolding of Akbar's enlightened religious policy based on his philosophy of *sulh-i kul*. The ground for this was partly prepared by Akbar's success in putting down the rebellion of 1580–1, and partly by the experience acquired during the twenty years preceding 1580, when the alternative had been given a full and fair trial.

[35] *Muntakhab-ut-Tawarikh*, vol. II, p. 276.

APPENDIX I

Period		Total No. of Nobles	Turanis	Persians	Indian Muslims	Rajputs and Other Hindus	Unspecified
1555		51	27 (52.9%)	16 (31.37%)	–		8 (15.68%)
1565–75	500 and above	96	38 (39.58%)	37 (38.54%)	9 (9.37%)	8 (8.33%)	4 (4.16%)
	Absolute number	176	67 (38.06%)	48 (27.27%)	25 (14.2%)	18 (10.22%)	18 (10.22%)
1580		272	66 (24.26%)	47 (17.27%)	44 (16.17%)	43 (15.83%)	72 (26.47%)
1575–95	1000 and above	87	32 (36.78%)	24 (27.58%)	14 (16.09%)	14 (16.09%)	3 (3.44%)
	500 and above	184	64 (34.78%)	47 (25.54%)	34 (18.48%)	30 (16.30%)	9 (4.89%)

APPENDIX II

1565–1575

Mansab	Turanis	Persians	Indian Muslims	Rajputs and other Hindus	Others	Total
3000–5000	15	15	2	4	–	36
1000–2500	14	17	5	3	4	43
500–900	9	5	2	1	–	17
Mansab not known	29	11	16	10	14	80
Total	67	48	25	18	18	176

APPENDIX III

Racial Composition during 1575–1595 based on the List of *Ain-i Akbari*

Mansab	Total No.	Turanis	Persians	Indian Muslims	Rajputs	Other Hindus	Others
5000	15	7	6		2		
4500	2		2				
4000	6	2	2		2		
3500	2		2				
3000	11	8	3				
2500	5	2		2	1		
2000	17	4	3	5	3	1	1
1500	7	2		3	2		
1250	1				1		
1000	21	7	6	4	2		2
900	34	13	9	8	3		1
800	2	1		1			
700	22	12	3	3	2	1	1
600	4	1	3				
500	35	5	8	8	9	1	4
Total	184	64	47	34	27	3	9

Appendix IV

Rebellion of 1580–1

	Turanis	Persians	Muslims	Rajputs, other Hindus, officials and *zamindars*	Unspecified	Total
On the side of the rebellion	33	12	3	6 All *zamindars* of the east	22	76
On the imperial side	28	32	41	37	50	188
Neutral	5	3				8
Total	66	47	44	43	72	272

4

The *Tazkirat ul-Muluk* by Rafi'uddin Ibrahim Shirazi

As a Source on the History of Akbar's Reign

THE *TAZKIRAT UL-MULUK,* a chronicle dealing primarily with the history of the 'Adil Shahi kingdom of Bijapur, was compiled in 1017–20 AH/1608–12 AD by Rafi'uddin Ibrahim Shirazi, then a high official in the service of Ibrahim 'Adil Shah (987–1035 AH/1579–1626 AD). Rafi'uddin Ibrahim was born in Persia around 947 AH/1540–1 AD He came to India in 967 AH/1559–60 AD as a trader.[1] During the subsequent four or five years, in connection with his business, he travelled across Gujarat, Malwa, and the Gangetic plains. Around 972 AH/1564–5 AD he settled in the Deccan and five years later took up service under 'Ali 'Adil Shah (965–87 AH/1557–79 AD) of Bijapur as a *khawan-salar.*[2] In the service

[1] C.A. Storey, *Persian Literature: A Bio-Bibliographical Survey,* vol. I, pt I, London, 1970, pp. 742–3; Charles Rieu, *Catalogue of Persian Manuscripts in the British Museum,* vol. II, 1879 AD, p. 316 (*b*); Hermann Ethe, *Catalogue of Persian Manuscripts of the Library of India Office,* vol. I, 1903, pp. 1538–9.

[2] *Tazkirat ul-Muluk,* Br. Library, Add. 23,883, ff. 107b, 195b. In his chapter (*fasl*) on Akbar, which he completed during 1018 AH/1609–10 AD, at one place Rafi'uddin Ibrahim claims that, at the time of writing, forty-six

of the rulers of Bijapur he rose to the position of a high-ranking official. Ibrahim 'Adil Shah (987–1035 AH/1579–1626 AD) made him Commandant of the fort of Bijapur and Master of the Mint.[3] That he was still alive in 1028 AH/1618–19 AD is evident from a contemporary treatise by a Mughal *mansabdar* at Lahore which makes reference to his reputation as a man of wide learning.[4]

The *Tazkirat ul-Muluk* comprises ten chapters (*fasls*), each of which is divided into a number of sections carrying different subheadings. While Chapters I–V and VII–VIII deal with the history of the Bijapur kingdom, the remaining three chapters contain notices on the kings of Gujarat (Chapter VI), the first two Timurid rulers of India (Chapter IX), and the history of Akbar's reign (Chapter X). A considerable portion of Rafi'uddin Ibrahim's narrative on the developments of Akbar's reign consists of the events to which he was an eyewitness during his stay in North India between 1560 and 1564 AD.

The *Tazkirat ul-Muluk* has been used as source material primarily for the history of Bijapur; and frequently also in researches on the early history of the Bahmani empire. But somehow the portions dealing with Akbar's reign have not been analysed or even been properly noticed. It would, therefore, be useful to assess its veracity and relevance as source material for the history of Akbar's reign.

Here I attempt to bring out the significance of its evidence by identifying those sections that appear to be based on the author's personal observation or on reliable information accessible to him. While trying to do so, some of the more interesting passages of the text have been reproduced in English for the benefit of scholars without direct access to the extant manuscripts. For present purposes the British

---

years had elapsed since he came to the Deccan from North India. From this, one may infer that he came to the Deccan in 972 AH/1564–5 AD. In the same passage, he says that he took up service 'in the Department of *Diwani*' five or six years after coming to the Deccan, i.e. in 977 or 978 AH/1575–6 AD.

[3] *Tazkirat ul-Muluk,* f. 152a.

[4] Mirza Kamran, *Mirza-nama,* text and English translation published by Hidayat Hosain in *The Journal of the Asiatic Society of Bengal,* 1913.

Library manuscript, written in *nastaliq* and transcribed by a certain Khiman Singh in 1832 AD has been used.[5]

Rafi'uddin Ibrahim came to Delhi from Gujarat in *Zil Hij* 967 AH/ August–September 1560,[6] when the tussle between Bairam Khan and the nobles who were responsible for persuading Akbar to announce his dismissal was at its peak. In the first half of August 1560 Bairam Khan was still at large, mobilizing his supporters in the Punjab for a showdown with the royalists, which finally came around 23 August 1560,[7] when he was defeated at the hands of Shamsuddin Muhammad Atka near Philaur (Distt Jullunder). Rafi'uddin Ibrahim appears to have been in Delhi during these crucial days before proceeding to Sagar some time in 968 AH/22 September 1560–10 September 1561 AD.[8] No definite information is, however, available about his whereabouts during the next year; possibly he was at Sagar till he came to 'Ali Quli Khan's camp near Hajipur towards the middle of 1561.[9] For the ensuing year or so he was in 'Ali Quli Khan-i Zaman's camp. During this time he was an eyewitness to skirmishes between 'Ali Quli Khan-i Zaman and Jalal Shah, the Afghan ruler of Bengal, to the eventual agreement and exchange of presents between them and to 'Ali Quli Khan-i Zaman's operations against the Ujjainia chief of Jagdishpur.[10] These events described by Rafi'uddin Ibrahim are not referred to in any other chronicle. But the details and timings of various other episodes recorded by him seem plausible in the light of

[5] Charles Rieu, *Catalogue of Persian Manuscripts in the British Museum,* vol. II, p. 316 (*b*).

[6] *Tazkirat ul-Muluk*, f. 189a.

[7] Abul Fazl, *Akbar-nama,* vol. II, p. 112.

[8] Either Sagar, District Headquarter in Madhya Pradesh or Sagar in Gulbarga District of Karnataka. It is more likely to be a reference to the last mentioned place which was famous for a particular kind of cloth (*sila-i saghari*). Cf. Tek Chand *Bahar, Bahar-i 'Ajam,* Nawal Kishore, 1916, p. 74.

[9] *Tazkirat ul-Muluk,* ff. 165a, 187b. Rafi'uddin Ibrahim says he visited Shaham Khan's tomb at Jaunpur two years after his death in 967 AH.

[10] *Tazkirat ul-Muluk,* ff. 189b–194b.

circumstantial evidence furnished by other sources, thereby indirectly validating his account of the skirmishes mentioned above.

After the conclusion of 'Ali Quli Khan-i Zaman's campaign against the Ujjainia chief, Rafi'uddin Ibrahim came to Jaunpur, reaching it some time in 969 AH/September 1561–August 1562.[11] From there he went to Agra. He says he was present at Agra on the occasion of the reception given by Akbar to Shah Tahmasp's envoy Mirza Saiyed Beg during the 7th RY/5 *Rajab* 969–15 *Rajab* 970 AH/March 1562–March 1563.[12] In any case, he subsequently returned to the east and was present at 'Ali Quli Khan-i Zaman's camp at Sasaram in the first half of 972 AH/August 1564–July 1565.[13] It was apparently sometime in the first half of 1565 that Rafi'uddin Ibrahim came to Agra en route to Gujarat and the Deccan.[14]

The information furnished by Rafi'uddin Ibrahim in his chapter on Akbar's reign can be divided into three broad categories: (a) reports

[11] *Tazkirat ul-Muluk,* f. 187b. Rafi'uddin Ibrahim hints that he visited Jaunpur in 969 AH/September 1561–August 1562 AD. In another context, he says that when he first came to the east, he went directly to 'Ali Quli Khan-i Zaman's camp near Hajipur. From there he followed him to Jagdishpur and spent the whole of the rainy season in its neighbourhood. Thus the obvious inference would be that he came to Jaunpur with 'Ali Quli Khan-i Zaman some time after September–October 1561 but before August 1562.

[12] Cf. *Tazkirat ul-Muluk,* ff. 173b–174a; *Akbar-nama,* vol. II, 170; Nizamuddin Ahmad, *Tabaqat-i Akbari,* vol. II, p. 158.

[13] *Tazkirat ul-Muluk,* f. 195a. The news of Taj Khan Kararani's death was received by Rafi'uddin Ibrahim a few days before his leaving 'Ali Quli Khan-i Zaman's camp in the vicinity of Sasaram. The date of Taj Khan Kararani's death is not recorded by any of the contemporary and near-contemporary sources I consulted. Charles Stewart (*History of Bengal,* Calcutta, 1910, p. 173) places it in 972 AH/9 August 1564–28 July 1565 AD. This date is, however, corroborated by another statement of Rafi'uddin Ibrahim. Writing in 1018 AH he says that forty-six years had elapsed since he was with 'Ali Quli Khan-i Zaman near Rohtas.

[14] *Supra.* It has been established above (see fn. 13) that Shirazi left 'Ali Quli Khan-i Zaman's camp near Sasaram and proceeded to the Deccan in 972 AH/August 1564–July 1565. Cf. *Tazkirat ul-Muluk*, f. 195a. On this occasion, he passed through Agra.

of the events to which he was eyewitness; (b) information based on bazaar gossip heard by him at Delhi, Agra, Jaunpur, and Sasaram both about past events and current developments during 1560–4; and (c) information received by him at Bijapur about developments in North India over 1565–1605. It goes without saying that the information in category (a) deserves special attention here. At the same time, some of the information in categories (b) and (c) is also worth noticing. For instance the information he furnished on Akbar's religious policy and on some of his measures of a reformatory nature significantly corroborates, modifies, or elaborates many of the statements of Abul Fazl, Badauni, and other authorities. This should, therefore, be treated as evidence of considerable significance. Thus, before we turn to a more detailed survey of information in category (a), it would be useful to offer brief comments on the significance of Rafi'uddin Ibrahim's section on Akbar's religious policy which is based mainly on the information in categories (b) and (c).

II

The section in the *Tazkirat ul-Muluk* on Akbar's religious policy is entitled *'zikr-i taghaiyur-i miliat-i Akbar Padshah waqt-i Ke dar sultanat mustaqil shuda bud* ('An account of change in Akbar Padshah's religion after he was firmly settled in government').[15] One of the early measures of Akbar reported in this section is an order prohibiting not only the enslavement of prisoners of war but the slave trade as such. This measure is also recorded by Haji 'Arif Qandahari and Abul Fazl, with the latter placing it in the 7th RY/11 March 1562–10 March 1563.[16] S.R. Sharma has interpreted Abul Fazl's evidence on this measure as suggesting simply an attempt on Akbar's part to prevent forcible conversions of prisoners of war.[17] He has, apparently,

[15] *Tazkirat ul-Muluk,* ff. 231a–232b.

[16] *Tarikh-i Akbari,* ed. Imtiaz Ali Arshi, Rampur, 1962, p. 39: *Akbarnama,* vol. II, p. 246.

[17] S.R. Sharma, *The Religious Policy of the Mughal Emperors,* 1941, p. 25.

ignored Abul Fazl's characterization of this measure as a step aimed at restricting slave-trade. The details given by Rafi'uddin Ibrahim on this measure, however, strongly support 'Arif Qandabari's and Abul Fazl's versions. According to him, prior to the introduction of this measure, every year, about two lakh persons captured in the course of military operations were exported from the Mughal Empire as slaves. It was pointed out to Akbar by one of his Hindu wives that if slaves continued to be exported on such a large scale there would, after a time, be a shortage of manpower in the empire. This argument appealed to Akbar and he promulgated a ban on the sale and purchase of slaves. An anecdote narrated by Rafi'uddin Ibrahim suggests a rigorous enforcement of this order at Agra in 1565. 'During those days', he writes, 'I set out from Agra for Gujarat. I had a companion. He sold a slave (at Agra). On coming to know about this (transaction) the *Kotwal* of the city arrested the (original) owner of the slave and carried him to the gate of the fort where his ears were pierced with a pin so that it should serve as a warning to other men.'[18]

It may be suggested that this measure must at least partly have been dictated by a shortage of manpower experienced by the authorities at Agra during this time. If one accepts Rafi'uddin Ibrahim's evidence, during this time (1564–5), about 3000 *qalandars* and other able-bodied persons living on charity at Agra were rounded up and put to work on the construction of Agra fort. They were placed under the supervision of 300 experts of the decorative arts who made them work from morning till sunset and for this labour they were paid 'a daily wage of one Akbari *tanka* which is equal to 10 *tanks* of Lar'.'[19]

[18] *Tazkirat ul-Muluk*, ff. 231b–232a.

[19] *Tazkirat ul-Muluk*, f. 231a and b; cf. *Akbar-nama*, vol. II, pp. 245, 247; *Ain-i Akbari*, vol. I, Lucknow: Nawal Kishore, 1893, pp. 117–18 under '*dast-i muzd.*' According to Abul Fazl, the reconstruction of Agra fort began in the 10th RY/ March 1565–March 1566. The rate of daily wage mentioned by Rafi'uddin Ibrahim corresponds to the lowest wage of an unskilled worker mentioned in *Ain-i Akbari*, i.e. 2 *dams* per day, which would be equal to one copper *tanka* per day.

Akbar's anxiety to discourage the slave-trade at this stage was not dictated by any legal or moral objection to the institution of slavery. Plugging the draining away of productive labour from his empire was perhaps the main consideration. Akbar certainly did not plan to abolish slavery. He also had no scruples about the state exporting slaves to Central Asia in return for horses, provided those sold as slaves were either children or persons otherwise incapable of productive labour. This is borne out by Rafi'uddin Ibrahim's statement: 'It was reported to the king that the number of beggars (*gada*) in this city (Agra) has become very large. He ordered them to be rounded up. From amongst them, about 4000 persons of tender age were selected who were sent to Qandahar and Kabul and were exchanged for 5000 or 6000 horses. During his reign, Akbar *Padhsah* twice exchanged beggars for horses in this manner.'[20] This is partly corroborated by Badauni, who alleges that on Akbar's orders *'Shaikhs'* belonging to a particular order of *qalandars* were exchanged in Bhakkar and Qandahar for Turkish horses.[21]

The general characterization by Rafi'uddin Ibrahim of Akbar's religious policy is basically the same as that by Badauni. 'Deviating from the religion of his forefathers', writes Rafi'uddin Ibrahim,

> he [Akbar] started worshipping idols and also adopted the dress and eating habits of idol worshippers. He openly dissuaded people from following the religion of Muhammad (peace be on him). If he came to know of anyone performing [regular] *namaz*, he would make it a point to ridicule him. During *Ramazan*, if a person were not chewing the betel leaf [*paan*], he [Akbar] would suspect him of observing a fast and would humiliate that person [by] excluding him from the [royal] company in future. He persisted in oppressing the *'Ulama,* some of whom were expelled; others fled out of fear. The *khatibs* and *aimma* were abandoned. He prohibited Muslim congregations. The mosques were converted into storehouses and inns. Every day, at daybreak and sunset, he would stand facing the sun and worship in the Brahmanic fashion, a practice called by the Brahmans

[20] *Tazkirat ul-Muluk,* f. 213b.

[21] 'Abdul Qadar Badauni, *Muntakhab ut-Tawarikh,* vol. II, p. 299.

> *sandhiya.* He [Akbar] nursed a grievance against the Holy Prophet on account of His being the last of the prophets. He thought that had the Holy Prophet not made such a claim, he [Akbar] could have claimed the position of Prophet for himself without opposition. For about forty years, he endeavoured to establish a religion of his own [*millat-i khud*] and [eventually] succeeded in establishing one. That religion is still in vogue. Sultan Salim was not attracted to this religion during his father's lifetime. But after his [Akbar's] death, [Sultan Salim] has conformed to the same religion. [It] is in vogue to this date which is the 1018th year since *hijrat.*[22]

S.R. Sharma has referred to this assessment in passing. He brushes it aside as a view based on rumours about Akbar's apostasy having reached the Deccan and argues that if there had been any substance in the rumours, Prince Salim, while in revolt, could have found his father's apostasy a very powerful weapon against him. 'But neither Jahangir nor his historians use this argument to justify his rebellion.'[23] One might, however, suggest that S.R. Sharma has not given sufficient attention to Rafi'uddin Ibrahim's evidence on this count, else the significance of Rafi'uddin Ibrahim's observation about the change that came in Salim's outlook after ascending the throne could not have been missed by him. Again, in another context Rafi'uddin Ibrahim pointedly refers to *farmans* issued by Salim during his rebellion in which the following proclamation was made:

> At the instigation of some mischievous persons, my father has abolished the arrangements for the maintenance of *khatibs, mu'azzins*, and *imams* in the mosques and has prohibited the performance of *namaz* in congregations. He has converted many of the mosques into storehouses and stables. It was improper on his part to have acted in this manner. They [the recipients of the *farmans*] should resume paying stipends for the maintenance of the mosques, the *khatibs,* the *mu'azzins*, and the *imams* and should induce the people to offer prayers. Anyone showing reluctance in this respect will be duly punished.

[22] *Tazkirat ul- Muluk,* ff. 231b-232a.
[23] *The Religious Policy of the Mughal Emperors*, Bombay, 1962, pp. 47–8.

According to Rafi'uddin Ibrahim, when one of these *farmans* was brought to Akbar's notice at Burhanpur, he remarked: 'Sultan Salim has tried to protect me. He has held other people responsible for my actions.'[24] This evidence altogether demolishes S.R. Sharma's arguments refuting Badauni's testimony regarding Akbar's deviation from Islam and his policy of withdrawing financial support from Muslim religious institutions. On the other hand, this conforms with similar evidence marshalled by M. Athar 'Ali in a paper, 'Akbar and Islam.'[25]

III

Rafi'uddin Ibrahim's evidence on Akbar's reign based on personal observation (falling under category 'a') is of two types. On the one hand are scattered pieces of information providing incidental but significant insights into social and economic conditions, as well as political developments in the early years of Akbar's reign. On the other hand there are included in the *Tazkirat ul-Muluk* a number of sections entirely devoted to hitherto unnoticed developments on the eastern frontier of the Mughal Empire during 1560–4.

The scattered information of this category covers a variety of subjects ranging from measures of weight current in North India and Iran; the exchange value of different currencies; the existence of a library at Burhanpur containing a thousand books; the location and features of the fort of Rohtas; monuments and landmarks indicating the layout of the townships of Delhi, Jaunpur, and Sasaram; the proposal by one of Bairam Khan's adherents in July 1560 to set up Mirza Hakim against Akbar; delightfully amusing anecdotes depicting Akbar's youthful misadventures and pranks, and his unconventional behaviour which caused much worry and embarrassment to his senior

[24] *Tazkirat ul-Muluk,* f. 224b.

[25] Presented at the Indian History Congress, Calicut, 1976, published in *Islamic Society and Culture: Essays in Honour of Professor Aziz Ahmad,* ed. Milton Israel and N.K Wagle, New Delhi, 1983/1993.

nobles. The following passage should give an idea of the kind of random information available on Akbar in the *Tazkirat ul-Muluk*:

> From Gujarat, I came to Agra in connection with my business and got busy making transactions [*dad o sitad*]. [While at Agra] I resolved to see the king of that place. It so happened that around this time Saiyed Beg, son of M'asum Beg, a relation of Shah Tahmasp, had come there as an ambassador. For his reception they had erected a pavilion in the royal gardens where festivities were being held. The people of the town would go off there for their entertainment. Following their example, I became desirous of going [there too] to witness the display. While I was standing inside the enclosure [of the pavilion], all of a sudden there arose a clamour of 'Cheers for the King' (*badshah salamat*). From this circumstance, I concluded that the king had arrived. I looked to my left and my right but could not find anyone with the appearance of a king. As I turned around I saw, standing there, a young man of about twenty years. He supported his head on one of his hands, which rested on the shoulder of a companion. I guessed he was the king. But the men continued to stand around rubbing shoulders with each other. No one [bothered] with observing etiquette—of showing respect [to the king]. I took position at a short distance and observed what was happening. I was greatly surprised and asked (those present): 'Is the custom of showing respect not observed at this court? No one has paid respects to the king.' They replied: 'As compared to other realms the tradition of showing respect and observing etiquette is much more elaborate here. But this king is an exceedingly informal person. He often comes out of his private apartment in ordinary dress and mixes with the people around him, making no distinction between friends and strangers. In this situation, how is it possible [for men] to observe etiquette all the time?' On another occasion I saw him [Akbar] flying a kite from the roof of his apartment. [On that occasion] he was wearing a *lungi* and his head was not covered.'[26]

However, the most significant part of Rafi'uddin Ibrahim's account of Akbar's reign is that which relates to the developments on the eastern frontier of the Mughal Empire during 1560–5. This is a record of hitherto unnoticed developments to which the author was

[26] *Tazkirat ul-Muluk,* ff.173b–174b.

an eyewitness. It comprises five separate sections with the following headings:

- (I) 'An Account of the Death of Sikandar Afghan and Khan-i Zaman's Invasion of Ujjainiya Territory' (ff. 188b–189b)
- (II) 'An Account of the Bengal King, Jalal Shah's Invasion of Taj Khan Kararani's *Vilayat,* Hajipur' (ff. 189b–196b)
- (III) 'An Account of Khan-i Zaman's invasion of the *Vilayat-i Ujjainia* for Reducing the Fort of Jagdishpur' (ff. 192b–196b)
- (IV) 'An Account of Khan-i Zaman and the Arrival of the Royal Officers for Taking Possession of His Territory and Their Frustration' (ff. 196b–198b)
- (V) 'An Account of Khan-i Zaman's Proceeding Against the Fort of Rohtas and Occupation of that *Vilayat*' (ff. 194a–196b).

One of the episodes relating to the developments on the eastern frontier recorded by Shirazi was an attack upon Jaunpur by Sikandar Sur. According to Abul Fazl, Sikandar Sur, after he surrendered to Akbar at Mankot in May 1557, was allowed to go to Kharid and Bihar, which were assigned to him as *jagirs*, and there he died two years later (i.e. in 1559).[27] Badauni, on the other hand, holds that Akbar temporarily gave Jaunpur to Sikandar Sur on the understanding that after Bihar and Bengal were annexed he would be given a suitable assignment there. Badauni also alludes vaguely to some kind of struggle between 'Ali Quli Khan and Sikandar Sur over Jaunpur and to Sikandar Sur's going over to the Afghans of the east.[28] This version is corroborated by Rafi'uddin Ibrahim, who records that in *Zil Hij* 967 AH/August–September 1560, Sikandar Sur had come to attack 'Ali Quli Khan at Jaunpur. In this struggle the Afghans were defeated, and Sikandar Sur was killed in the battle. The news of this victory

[27] *Akbar-nama,* vol. II, p. 59.

[28] *Muntakhab ut-Tawarikh,* vol. II, pp. 18–19.

reached Delhi towards October–November 1560.[29] This timing of Sikandar Sur's death is supported by Abul Fazl, who vaguely places it two years after his surrender to Akbar at Mankot in May 1557.[30]

Sometime in the first half of 1561, the Afghan ruler of Bangal, Giyasuddin Abul Muzaffar Jalal Shah,[31] marched against Taj Khan Kararani who, at this time, was controlling a considerable territory in Bihar from his seat of power at Hajipur.[32]

'Ali Quli Khan, the Mughal commander of Jaunpur went to Taj Khan Kararani's help. He encamped with his army on the Ganges

[29] Rafi'uddin Ibrahim says he heard about Sikandar Sur's attack on Jaunpur after reaching Delhi in Zil Hij 967 AH/August–September 1560 AD. Forty days later, he came to know about Khan-i Zaman's victory. From this evidence, it might be deduced that this news reached Delhi roughly towards October–November 1560.

[30] *Akbar-nama,* vol. II, pp. 58–9.

[31] Jalal Shah's father Muhammad Khan Sur was a trusted noble of Islam Shah Sur. After Islam Shah's death, Muhammad Khan proclaimed himself king at Gaur. In 962 AH/November 1554–November 1555 AD, Muhammad Khan Sur was killed in a battle with Mubariz Shah Sur's general Hemu at Chapparghatta (near Kalpi). He was succeeded by his son Jalalud-din Bahadur Shah who defeated and killed Mubariz Khan Sur (Adili) at Fathpur (four miles west of Surajgarh) in May 1557 AD. In 1560 or 1561, Bahadur Shah died and he was succeeded by his brother Jalaluddin who ascended the throne at Gaur with the title Ghyasuddin Abul Muzaffar Jalal Shah. According to the author of *Riaz us-Salatin,* Jalal Shah ruled for five years. The only known reference in a contemporary source to Jalal Shah's moves and activities after his ascending the throne is a remark by Abul Fazl that ' Taj Khan and his brother were some times at strife with Jalaluddin and some times were on friendly terms with him.' Cf. *Akbar-nama,* vol. II, pp. 58, 325; *Muntakhab ut-Tawarikh,* vol. I, pp. 430–1 and vol. II, p. 18; Ghulam Husain, *Riyaz-us-Salatin: A History of Bengal,* tr. Abdus Salam, reprint, Delhi, 1975, p. 149; J.N. Sarkar', *History of Bengal,* Patna, 1973, p. 180 and n. 1.

[32] For Taj Khan Kararani's success in establishing himself at Hajipur after displacing the Kakkar chiefs from there, see *Tarikh-i Khan Jahani,* vol. I, ed. by S.M. Imamuddin, Dacca, 1960, pp. 409–13. See also Abul Fazl, *Akbar-nama,* vol. II, p. 325, who informs us that sometimes Taj Khan was on friendly terms with the Afghan ruler of Gaur, Jalal Shah, and sometimes at strife with him.

opposite Jalal Shah's army. The two armies remained face to face for several months. During this time Rafi'uddin Ibrahim and a few other Irani merchants travelling with him came to 'Ali Quli Khan's camp to sell their goods. They stayed at 'Ali Quli Khan's camp for the next few months. This episode is described by Rafi'uddin Ibrahim:

> 'Some persons hailing from my native town were accompanying me [at this time]. They had with them a number of exquisitely decorated items [*nuskha-i chand nafis mazin*] [for sale]. They were eager to go to Khan-i Zaman. As I also had with me a few items, I thought it appropriate to accompany them. We left for our destination. On the way, with every passing day we met a large number of people proceeding towards Agra. They said to us, 'What pressing necessity forces you to proceed towards this frontier in the present unsettled conditions resulting from war and insurrection? The army that expelled Humayun from Hind has appeared on the frontier once again. They [the Mughals] still remember that event [Humayun's defeat] with awe and fear. Khan-i Zaman sought help from Akbar Padshah, who issued orders that nobles on the frontier should go to Khan-i Zaman's help. [But] out of fear the nobles remained in their places and avoided going [there]. The wealthy in Agra, the capital where Akbar Padshah was staying, have become panicky. They have transferred, and are transferring, their wealth, cash as well as kind and [every] rare or precious article in their possession to Kabul. The whole of Akbar's empire has fallen into confusion. No one feels confident of completing even a single day's work in safety.' On the way, many reproached us for undertaking our journey. [However], placing our trust in the creator of the universe, we continued our journey towards Khan-i Zaman's camp. We were relieved to find [Khan-i Zaman's] army in an excellent state. All our fears were dispelled. My companions sold their items and the other articles that they had with them to Khan-i Zaman and the other nobles.
>
> 'Every day we would go to the river bank as recreation and witness skirmishes on the river between the two armies. That brave and gallant solider, Khan-i Zaman remained encamped there, [all the time] planning to cross the river with his army. As the rains approached, Khan-i Zaman sent an envoy to Jalal Shah [with a message]: "By thus remaining encamped on the bank of the river you are daily causing men to be killed. Don't you fear God? Either allow me to cross over to that side or you come over this side and [to facilitate your crossing] I am prepared to give you

passage so that we might test in one battle whom God is going to favour with victory." Jalal Shah replied: "My elders have asked me to prevent, as far as possible, the enemy from crossing the river. They have also advised me to desist from crossing the river to engage the enemy."

Khan-i Zaman [thereupon] sent the following retort: "This is the language of cowards. If I am a man, I shall cross over to that side of the river and shall establish a foothold [there].'"[33]

In the ensuing passage Rafi'uddin Ibrahim goes on to describe the Mughals' success in gaining a foothold over the other side of the river and consequently the grievous losses inflicted upon the Bengal army. 'Finally, Taj Khan Kararani realized that if the situation were allowed to drift, the Mughals would entirely overpower [Jalal Shah] and occupy [the territory] up to Gaur, his seat of power, which would leave him at their mercy. He first repaired his own quarrel with Jalal Shah and then arranged a peace between him and Khan-i Zaman.' 'Taj Khan,' writes Rafi'uddin Ibrahim,

> made a *peshkash* of 30,000 *huns* in cash and kind from his own establishment.[34] He had also forwarded the *peshkash* of Jalal Shah. [On that occasion], we [went and] stood at the door of (Khan-i Zaman's) tent to amuse ourselves.
>
> 'The items which we saw being carried into the enclosure were as follows:
>
> (a) One *quzfan*[35] of gold.
> (b) Nine *quzfans* of silver, each weighing one Akbari *man*.
> (c) One hundred bundles of *qimash-i sufaid bangali, malmal-i shahi, chautar, sandil khasa-i bangali,* each packet containing one hundred and fifty (pieces of) fine linen.[36]

[33] *Tazkirat ul-Muluk*, ff. 189b–192b.

[34] Here it is significant that Rafi'uddin Ibrahim is describing the amount in the Bijapuri currency.

[35] It was not possible to ascertain the meaning of this term. From the manner it is used here by the author, it seems to denote a container for carrying gold and silver.

[36] Out of the four varieties of cloth mentioned in this list, two, *chautar* and *khaas-i bangali,* are mentioned by European travellers of the seventeenth

(d) One hundred packets of aromatic roots *(aqaqir),* which in Persia are called *dam-i karam,* and pepper, cloves, cinnamon, dry ginger, etc.

(e) Twenty-five packets of *sandal,* aloe-wood, musk, ambergris, and camphor.

(f) One trunk and a scabbard reportedly containing a dagger, and a belt for sword, [both] studded with gems.

(g) One casket containing (various) articles studded with gems.

(h) A rosary of pearls.

(i) A few more chests containing costly presents which we were not able to see.

Regarding the presents sent by Khan-i Zaman we heard the following details:

(a) Three *raqas* of Arabian horses which comprised twenty-seven heads.

(b) Five strings [*qitar*][37] of camels loaded with fine linen and silk and brocade [*qimash-ha-i abreshmi wa zarbaft*].

(c) A number of camels and mules carrying rugs made of skin [*qalicha-i dawal*] and cushions of props made of felt.

(d) Aristocratic furnishings [*farash-ha-i malukana*].

(e) A few heads of Turkish, Indian, and Abyssinian slaves, and many other excellent but rare presents.

Having ensured his peace with Jalal Shah, 'Ali Quli Khan-i Zaman moved against Jagdishpur,[38] the seat of power of the powerful Ujjainia *zamindars* who controlled the tract between the Ganges and the Son. On this expedition he was accompanied by several Afghan chiefs of Bihar such as Nusrat Khan, Darya Khan Lodi, and Mubarak

---

century as being produced in different centres in Bengal. See *Studies in Indian Textile Industry, Calico Museum of Textile*, Ahmedabad, 1966, p. 62 (John Irwin's 'A Glossary of Textile Terms').

[37] Steingass, *Persian–English Dictionary*. The term *qitar* is explained as 'strings of camel (in poetry often)'.

[38] Jagdishpur in Shahabad District of Bihar, around this time, the seat of power of Ujjainiya *zamindars*. See my note on Ujjainiyas in Iqtidar Alam Khan, *The Political Biography of a Mughal Noble*, New Delhi, 1973, p. 109, nn. 4–5.

Khan Kakkar. In order to facilitate his military operations against the Ujjainis, 'Ali Quli Khan undertook the clearing of the forest around Jagdishpur on a massive scale. The Ujjainiyas, on the other hand, tried to thwart his advance towards Jagdishpur by laying traps and digging trenches in the forest. This account of the campaign by Rafi'uddin Ibrahim is perhaps one of the few descriptions available to us of jungle warfare conducted by the Mughals against a local chief.[39]

'From Hajipur', writes Rafi'uddin Ibrahim,

> Khan-i Zaman came to the neighbourhood of Jagdishpur and encamped there. A dense forest surrounds that fort. [Khan-i Zaman] began clearing the forest. As it was the rainy season, [Khan-i Zaman] ordered that to build their shelters the officers, troops, and *rayat* should use the wood and grass that were abundantly available. For his own use too, instead of pitching tents, he had apartments constructed, which he fortified. In this manner he founded a township, and since it was located within the territory of the infidels, he called it Islampur. Within a few days, the officers, troops, and *rayat* constructed houses. They also created a market. Around that township they built fortifications and a moat. That town still survives. They employed 5000 to 6000 *payadas* for clearing the forest, and 300 Mughal horsemen were deputed to supervise them. Twenty elephants were used for carrying away the trees felled inside the forest so that the path was cleared [for the army to advance]. It was the rainy season. We were in Khan-i Zaman's party. We had also built hutments for ourselves. Every day we would go into the forest [to watch the progress in the forest clearing operation]. They were working very hard. Taj Khan Kararani had sent his brother with a large number of horsemen and *payadas* wielding axes [*tabars*] to cut the forest . . . When Sulaiman arrived in Khan-i Zaman's camp, Nusrat Khan, [the younger] brother of Fath Khan, as he was not on good terms with him, thought it fit to leave that place. He fled with his contingent. This contributed to further aggravating their mutual hostility.
>
> In short during all the four months of the rainy season, the Mughals cleared the forest and [tried] to construct a road, while the garrison of the fort [of Jagdishpur] dug new trenches to thwart their path. They dug wells on the road and covered them with grass. In the meanwhile, the Raja

[39] *Tazkirat ul-Muluk*, ff. 192b–194b.

who controlled Jagdishpur died. He was survived by a seventeen-year-old son. The passing away of that cursed infidel proved to be a boon for the Mughals. The infidels became disheartened and helpless. Still, they did not relinquish their struggle. After the rains were over and the path [of the army] had been cleared, Khan-i Zaman himself mounted [a horse] and [his] troops moved forward to offer battle. They came to the centre of the forest and started making forays in every direction till they reached the spot where the enemy had dug pits. While fighting, many notable persons fell into the traps and were killed. From behind the thickets of trees, they [the Ujjainiya troops] fired *tufangs* [at the Mughals]. About three hundred were killed. Out of these, twelve were *amirs*. The first [to be killed] was Mirza Yadgar, an uncle of Khan-i Zaman. Among others killed were Haider Quli Khan Turkman and Khanjar Beg Sultan.

While this fighting was going on, the Raja tried to transfer his family and treasures from Jagdishpur 'to the hilly tract.' 'Ali Quli Khan-i Zaman's officers stationed at Buxar intercepted the boats carrying the Raja's wife and children and took them prisoners. Subsequently, the Raja was forced to start negotiations with 'Ali Quli Khan-i Zaman. He came to the Mughal camp for this purpose but could not arrive at a settlement, with the result that hostilities were resumed. Finally, the Khan declared: 'There is no scope for delay. Tomorrow there will be a royal battle and the fort is bound to be captured.' Next day, eight or nine thousand *payadas* carrying heaps of grass and wood, and sweepers [*jarodaran*] carrying mattocks [*tabarha-i khak*] on their shoulders, walked in front of the army. Wherever they detected a trench they filled it with heaps of grass and wood, and levelled the ground. In this manner three or four trenches were filled. [Only] a few of the insignificant ones were killed. That night out of caution they remained on the same ground. Next day the remaining trenches were filled and they came close to the fort. As night approached, they took their positions and kept up the fight. Next day the garrison of the town came out and fought doggedly. There were a large number of casualties on both sides. As night fell everyone returned to his place. After midnight, the usual signs of activity inside the fort were no longer visible. The besiegers made enquiries as to the reason for this unusual calm. It was discovered that the garrison had slipped out of the fort after having started many fires there.

Next morning 'Ali Quli Khan-i Zaman occupied the fort.

Yet another, hitherto unknown, episode recorded by Rafi'uddin Ibrahim is 'Ali Quli Khan-i Zaman's attack on Rohtas. It was in order to punish Fath Khan, the chief of Rohtas, for his withdrawal of support to the Mughals at a crucial juncture of their campaign against the Ujjainia chief, that 'Ali Quli Khan-i Zaman and Taj Khan Kararani's brother Sulaiman Kararani jointly proceeded against him in 1564–5.[40] On this occasion, once again, Rafi'uddin Ibrahim was accompanying 'Ali Quli Khan-i Zaman. To conduct the siege operations 'Ali Quli Khan-i Zaman had established his camp at a ruined fort in the neighbourhood of Rohtas. While the siege of Rohtas was in progress, news of Taj Khan Kararani's death reached the Mughal camp, and Sulaiman Kararani was obliged to proceed to Hajipur in order to take charge of his brother's territory. Some time after Taj Khan Kararani's death Jalal Shah, the Afghan ruler of Bengal, marched out from Gaur with the intention of going to Fath Khan's rescue, but he died on the way. Taking advantage of this situation, Sulaiman Kararani occupied Gaur, and, with the connivance of 'Ali Quli Khan-i Zaman, declared himself ruler of Bengal and Bihar.[41]

IV

The evidence highlighted here consists of only a part of the reliable information furnished by Rafi'uddin Ibrahim on the history of Akbar's reign. One set of evidence deliberately excluded from this discussion pertains to Akbar's relations with the Deccan states. This is because Rafi'uddin Ibrahim focused his study on the history of the Deccan states, rather than on Mughal expansion towards the south.

While concluding this discussion, it is necessary to point out that in certain portions Rafi'uddin Ibrahim's evidence on Mughal history is blatantly unreliable. As a matter of fact, his narrative in

[40] *Supra*, fn 13, where it is established that Rafi'uddin Ibrahim was in 'Ali Quli Khan-i Zaman's camp at Sasaram. On this occasion, according to Rafi'uddin Ibrahim, 'Ali Quli Khan-i Zaman was leading an expedition against the chief of Rohtas.

[41] *Tazkirat ul-Muluk*, ff. 194b–196b.

Chapters IX and X consists of a curious mixture of specific data verifiable from other sources and obviously incorrect statements that should be rejected. It seems very probable that Rafi'uddin Ibrahim had with him some kind of rough notes or memoranda which he had prepared during his stay in North India between 1560 and 1564, and to the extent that he is writing with reference to these notes his account is accurate and detailed. His description of the presents received by 'Ali Quli Khan-i Zaman from Jalal Shah, and his details of the military operations in the Ujjainia territory, for example, show great accuracy. But when he resorts to writing from memory, he often states things that are patently false. As such, in these portions his dates, the sequence of events that he suggests, as also his identification of men and places, are not very reliable. Therefore, this negative feature of Rafi'uddin Ibrahim's evidence on the history of Akbar's reign must always be borne in mind while assessing the merits of his book as source material for the history of the Mughals.

5

Akbar's Personality Traits and World Outlook

Akbar's contribution to the establishment of Mughal authority in Hindustan on a firm basis has engaged the attention of modern historians for a long time. Some of the researches on Akbar, however, have tended to focus on the factors contributing to the rise of his policy of religious tolerance based on the principles of *sulh-i kul*, or 'Absolute Peace'. Akbar's 'religious policy' is often viewed in these studies as being linked to his transformation of the nobility into a composite ruling group including within its ranks a fairly large number of Shi'as and Rajputs. There has been far less concentration on the nature of Akbar's personal world outlook and of the ideological influences that went into shaping it and his religious policy over the last twenty-five years of his reign. Athar Ali has re-examined this aspect,[1] which in turn has given rise to several significant questions bearing on the basic character and motivations of Akbar's 'religious policy'. Perhaps the two most relevant questions are, first, to what extent did Akbar's personal world outlook influence his religious policy? And, second, what was the response of the different

[1] Athar Ali, 'Akbar and Islam', in *Islamic Society and Culture: Essays in Honour of Professor Aziz Ahmad*, ed. Milton Israel and N.K. Wagle, New Delhi, 1983.

sections of his subjects to his religious views and, more importantly, to the measures he adopted. These questions assume special significance in view of the contemporary testimony of Badauni and the Jesuits suggesting that, from 1581 onwards, Akbar ceased to be a Muslim. Shaikh Ahmad Sirhindi's insistence that Akbar's tolerant attitude towards non-Muslims stemmed basically from his hostility to Islam further underlines the significance of his personal beliefs for a proper assessment of Akbar's policy of religious tolerance.[2]

While focusing on the two questions identified above, I here attempt to trace the development of Akbar's worldview from his accession in 1556 to his death in 1605. To the extent permitted by new evidence that I will present, I shall also suggest a reconsideration of some of the positions taken by Athar Ali.

II

Textbook explanations for Akbar's natural inclination towards religious tolerance, in terms of his being influenced by the broad-mindedness of his parents and teachers of Sunni and Shi'a persuasions who had no use for sectarian bigotry, undoubtedly appeal to common sense. But it may be pointed out that the supposition of some of these textbook writers that Akbar's mother, Hamida Bano Begam, was a Shi'a,[3] has no basis. On the contrary her brother, Mu'azzam Beg, became involved, in 1546, in the Sunni bigots' assassination of Humayun's *wazir*, Khwaja Sultan Rushdi, an Iranian and Shi'a. This strongly suggests that he and possibly the other members of the family,

[2] For a thorough examination of Badauni's and Shaikh Ahmad Sirhindi's assessment of Akbar, in addition to Irfan Habib's memorable piece, 'The Political Role of Shaikh Ahmad Sirhindi and Shah Waliullah' (*Proceedings of the Indian History Congress*, Aligarh, 1960, 23rd Session), reference may also be made to Athar Abbas Rizvi's pioneering work, *Muslim Revivalist Movements in Northern India in the Sixteenth and Seventeenth Centuries* (Agra, 1964) and his later study, *Religious and Intellectual History of Muslims in Akbar's Reign* (New Delhi, 1975).

[3] Cf. Ishwari Prasad, *The Mughal Empire*, Allahabad, 1976, p. 346.

including Hamida Bano, were Sunnis.[4] It cannot, however, be denied that Akbar's tutors, including the two Irani Shi'as Bairam Khan and Mir 'Abdul Latif Qazvini, and the Sunni Turani Mun'im Khan, were largely above sectarian prejudices. About Mir 'Abdul Latif Qazvini, it is asserted by Abul Fazl that for his rejection of sectarian prejudices he was condemned by bigots of both the sects.[5] So far as Bairam Khan is concerned, notwithstanding what some of the eighteenth-century Persian chroniclers—like Khafi Khan and Shah Nawaz Khan—write of his sectarian partiality (*ta'assub*), contemporary evidence presents him as a person who, seemingly, did not attach much significance to the Shi'a–Sunni divide.[6] On the other hand Mun'im Khan counted among his closest friends 'Ali Quli Khan, who was well known for his Shi'a beliefs.[7] It is therefore reasonable to imagine that the contribution of these early teachers and counsellors to Akbar's natural inclination for religious tolerance was not inconsiderable. In any discussion of influences that made Akbar's mind receptive to ideas promoting religious tolerance, one must also take into consideration the cultural ethos of the Timurids down to Humayun's time. Timur is reported to have respected all religions alike. This climate of religious tolerance appears to have by and large persisted in the Timurid polity down till the time Akbar came to the throne.[8] The Timurid

[4] Abul Fazl, *Akbar-nama*, vol. I, Calcutta, 1877, p. 254, and Bayazid Bayat, *Tarikh-i Humayun-wa-Akbar*, p. 74. For an interpretation of this evidence, see Iqtidar Alam Khan, 'Wizarat under Humayun (1545–1555)', *Medieval India Quarterly*, vol. V, no.1, Aligarh, 1963, p. 76.

[5] *Akbar-nama*, vol. II, p. 20.

[6] For a discussion of this evidence, see Iqtidar Alam Khan, 'Mughal Court Politics During Bairam Khan's Regency', *Medieval India—A Miscellany*, vol. I, Aligarh/Bombay, 1969 (reproduced herein as Chapter 2). Attention is invited to fns. 20, 36, 56, and 59.

[7] Mun'im Khan's close relations with 'Ali Quli Khan Uzbek and Bairam Khan are discussed in Iqtidar Alam Khan, *The Political Biography of a Mughal Noble: Mun'im Khan Khan-i Khanan 1497–1575*, New Delhi, 1973, pp. 59, 85n.3.

[8] For the continuing influence of *Yasa-i Chingezi* in the Timurid polity down to Humayun's reign, see ibid., Introduction, pp. ix–xiv.

cultural ethos perhaps had something to do with the considerable influence that the *Yasa-i Chingezi* continued to exercise on the minds of successive Timurid rulers (with the doubtful exception of Abu Sa'id Mirza) down to Akbar's time. According to 'Alauddin 'Ata Juwaini, the *Yasa-i Chingezi* required the ruler 'to consider all sects as one and not to distinguish them from one another.' It was in pursuance of this principle that Chingiz Khan, in Juwaini's words, 'eschewed bigotry and preference of one faith to another, placing some above others.'[9] The climate of religious tolerance promoted within the Timurid polity by the influence of the *Yasa-i Chingezi* is also highlighted by the absence of persecution of Shi'as in the Timurid principalities.

The increasing presence of Shi'a Iranis in the nobility after Humayun's return from Iran (1545),[10] without giving rise to Shi'a–Sunni tensions in any appreciable measure, is eloquent testimony to the Mughal Empire in India being, from the beginning, a very different type of state from the sultanates it replaced in many parts of the Indian subcontinent. It is worth noting that, before the induction of a large number of Irani Shi'as in Humayun's service, in no other state ruled by a Muslim dynasty did Shi'as and Sunnis coexist within the nobility in such remarkable amity. The Safavid Empire, where the rulers—claiming to be the *imams* of the Islamic community the world over—severely repressed elements suspected of Sunni leanings, was no exception. Thus it might be safely suggested that the influence of the *Yasa-i Chingezi,* to the extent it survived in the Timurid polity till the middle of the sixteenth century, was an important element in Akbar's cultural heritage, inducing him to be broad-minded towards other religious beliefs. Akbar's intolerant attitude towards the Shi'as and Mahadavis during the 1560s may conversely be explained as a partial consequence of the erosion of the influence of the original Mongol tradition with the passage of time.

[9] *Tarikh-i Jahan-gusha*, ed. Mirza Muhammad, vol. I, London, 1912, pp. 18–19 (tr. J.A. Boyle, vol. I, Manchester, 1958, p. 26).

[10] Afzal Husain, 'Growth of Irani Elements in Akbar's Nobility', *Proceedings of the Indian History Congress*, 1975, 36th Session, pp. 166–79.

For a proper appreciation of the way Akbar's world outlook gradually evolved and of his becoming, from around 1581, strongly committed to the principles of *sulh-i kul*, it is also important to keep in view some of the traits of his personality recorded by contemporary observers.

According to Montserrat, Akbar had 'a somewhat morose disposition' to which he attributes the latter's excessive interest in 'various games'.[11] That Akbar's extraordinary interest, during his early years, in hunting and elephant fights verged upon obsession is borne out even by Abul Fazl. Abul Fazl obviously finds it embarrassing to report Akbar senselessly and repeatedly endangering his life in hunts, or while witnessing elephant fights, or tackling elephants in musth; he devotes a whole chapter in the *Akbar-nama* to Akbar's 'inclination for elephants'. At another place, noticing Akbar recklessly endangering his life by mounting a musth elephant in 1561, Abul Fazl quotes a not very bright saying of Akbar from this period, suggesting that he thus risked his life deliberately: if he had displeased God in any manner, 'may that elephant finish us, for we cannot support the burden of life under God's displeasure.'[12] This, incidentally, also points to Akbar being vaguely dissatisfied and apologetic about his own conduct in society as well as in religious matters at this time.

The resulting psychological strain appears to have contributed to occasional fits of depression and melancholy that he is reported to have suffered down to 1578. The last fit of this nature is reported from 1578; it came in the midst of a hunting expedition. On this occasion Akbar fell unconscious for a brief period and, according to Abul Fazl, it appeared as if he were dying.[13] That these fits, which were characterized by Abul Fazl and by Akbar himself as spiritual experiences, recurred down to 1578 and are not reported from the subsequent period—when Akbar had developed a new worldview

[11] Antonio Montserrat, *Commentary on His Journey to the Court of Akbar*, tr. by J.S. Hoyland and annotated by S.N. Banerjee, Calcutta, 1922, p. 197.

[12] *Akbar-nama*, vol. II, p. 152.

[13] *Akbar-nama*, vol. III, pp. 14, 241–2.

identified with *sulh-i kul*—goes to suggest that these had something to do with the mental tensions of the earlier phase of his life.

The dichotomies of Akbar's religious beliefs and intellectual commitments during the 1570s are illustrated by the perplexing questions that he is reported to have posed to Muslim religious divines during the first phase of discussions in the '*Ibadat Khana* (1575–8). These uncertainties and dichotomies were partly also fed by Akbar's general inquisitiveness and questioning temperament as well as by his eagerness to conform to an accepted code of ethical and legal behaviour, a trait of personality that he seems to have inherited from his father. Two scientific experiments made by Akbar in the 1570s illustrate his questioning temperament in general. 'Arif Qandahari mentions his not very successful attempt at cross-breeding a male deer with a *barbari* goat. This experiment produced a non-productive hybrid deer.[14] The other experiment, involving six newborn infants, was aimed at testing the theory of *zuban-i qudrat*, or natural language, a notion having its origin, possibly, in the speculative philosophy of classical Greece. The notion of *zuban-i qudrat* certainly had no validity in the Islamic theological tradition.[15]

During the same period Akbar seems to have been exposed for the first time to philosophical discourses (*sukhnan-i hikmat*) strongly disapproved by post-Ghazali Islamic theology. Among the people who introduced him to an Islamized version of Greek philosophy in the early 1570s, Shaikh Mubarak and his sons, Faizi and Abul Fazl, were the most prominent. Akbar admits in one of his sayings to

[14] Arif Qandahari, *Tarikh-i Akbari*, ed. Imtiaz Ali Arshi, Rampur, 1962, pp. 42–3.

[15] *Akbar-nama,* vol. III, p. 393. According to Abul Fazl, the experiment was started in the 24th RY/11 March 1579–10 March 1580, by confining a few newborn children in a house specially built for the purpose in total seclusion; nurses appointed to look after them had orders not to speak in their hearing. It was concluded with Akbar's visit to that house on 9 August 1582. All the children used in this experiment failed to pick up any language, proving Akbar's contention that 'speech came to every tribe from hearing'.

finding these discourses so enchanting (*dil-awez, dilruba*) that it was difficult for him to keep away from them.[16] It was in consequence of his growing interest in philosophy, and his raising questions about religion in general, that the process of re-examining important aspects of Islamic theology and jurisprudence (*fiqh*) began in the *Ibadat Khana* around 1578. The ball was set rolling, according to Badauni, by Shaikh Mubarak when he raised a question regarding the position of *Imam-i 'Adil* vis-à-vis the *Mujtahid.* It was this discussion which led to the signing of a *mahzar* (1579) by leading theologians that recognized Akbar as the *Sultan-i Islam.*

One knows from unimpeachable evidence, including some of Akbar's own sayings recorded after 1581, that in his early years he was not only a practising Muslim but also had a very intolerant attitude towards Hindus. He regretfully admits having forced many Hindus, during those early years, to convert to Islam.[17] Akbar was then looked upon by orthodox Muslim elements as a pious Muslim committed to defending Islam against infidelity. Rizqullah Mushtaqi, a well-known Shaikhzada of Delhi, writing around 1580, says Akbar was sent by God to protect Islam from being suppressed by Hemu.[18] In one of his passing remarks, Badauni suggests that during the early years of his reign Akbar was under the influence of the Naqshbandiya order.[19]

However, it seems that his attitude towards Hindu religious rites and forms of worship was no longer contemptuous and hostile after 1562, when he married the daughters and nieces of a number of Rajput chieftains. Badauni says that during Akbar's early youth (*'unfuwan-i shabab*) he used to perform *hom*, a form of fire worship,

[16] *Ain-i Akbari*, vol. III, Nawal Kishore, 1893, pp. 182–3.

[17] See Akbar's sayings, *Ain-i Akbari,* vol. III, p. 181; also *Zubdatut Tawarikh*, tr. H.M. Elliot and John Dowson, *History of India as Told by its Own Historians*, vol. VI, reprint, Allahabad, 1964, p. 189, where Shaikh Nurul Haq says that, until AH 986/1578 AD, Akbar used to strictly observe the daily five prayers.

[18] *Waqi 'at-i Mushtaqi,* MS, Br. Library, Or. 1929, f. 94a.

[19] Abdul Qadir Badauni, *Muntakhab ut-Tawarikh*, vol. III, p. 74.

in the company of his Hindu wives.[20] Akbar was perceived by many of his contemporaries in these years as being not averse to performing Hindu rites, his Islamic orientation notwithstanding. This impression is reinforced by measures like the announcement of the abolition of Pilgrimage Tax (1563) and *jiziyah* (1564) or the establishment of an *in'am* grant for the support of a temple at Vrindavan (1565).[21]

However, during the same period he had a manifestly repressive attitude towards Muslim sects condemned by the orthodox as heretical. Iranian nobles, mostly Shi'as, were encouraged and used against discontented Turanis throughout the 1560s.[22] But at the same time their freedom to profess and practise their faith were sought to be restricted. A glaring example of this was the exhumation, in 1567, of Mir Murtaza Sharifi Shirazi's remains from the vicinity (*jawar*) of Amir Khusrau's tomb in Delhi at the suggestion of Shaikh 'Abdun Nabi. The argument was that a 'heretic' could not be allowed to remain buried so close to the grave of a renowned Sunni saint. This was no doubt an extreme action: even Badauni has criticized it as a very unjust act.[23] Akbar's *farman* to 'Abdus Samad, the *muhtasib* of *pargana* Bilgram, around 1572, directing him to 'help in eradicating heresy and deviation from the *pargana*', is an indication that

[20] *Muntakhab ut-Tawarikh*, vol. II, p. 261. Lowe's comment that *hom* was a substitute for *soma* juice offered by Parsees (*Muntakhab ut-Tawarikh*, tr. Calcutta, 1924, p. 269, fn. 1) is obviously a slip. Badauni's reference here is to a Hindu ritual. For a more viable explanation, see John T. Platts, *A Dictionary of Urdu, Classical Hindi and English*, rpnt, New Delhi, 1977, p. 1242. This term is explained as denoting 'an oblation with clarified butter, a burnt offering, a sacrifice', etc.

[21] See *Akbar-nama*, vol. II, pp. 190, 203–4; Tarapada Mukherjee and Irfan Habib, 'Akbar and the Temples of Mathura and its Environs', 48th Session, *Proceedings of the Indian History Congress*, Goa, 1987, pp. 235, 237.

[22] For the improvement in the position of Irani nobles during the 1560s, see Iqtidar Alam Khan, 'The Nobility under Akbar and the Development of His Religious Policy', *Journal of the Royal Asiatic Society*, 1968, p. 31, fn. 7 (reproduced herein as Chapter 3); and idem, *The Political Biography of a Mughal Noble*, pp. xvi–xvii.

[23] *Muntakhab ut-Tawarikh*, vol. III, p. 321.

the restrictive attitude towards Sh'ism continued to persist till the early 1570s.[24]

Akbar's hostility to the Mahadavis was still more pronounced. This was maintained down to 1573, when he is reported to have suppressed them severely in Gujarat. It was in the course of this suppression that the leading Mahadavi divine, Miyan Mustafa Bandagi, was arrested and brought to the court in chains.[25]

Akbar came increasingly under the influence of pantheistic *sufi* doctrines, roughly from 1571, and this caused a momentous turn in the development of his worldview. It paved the way for his eventual rejection of what he regarded as the Islam professed by traditional divines (*faqihan-i taqlidi*) in favour of a new and entirely different concept of Islam. This Islam transcended the limits demarcating the different religions (*kesh'ha*), and its essence, according to Akbar, lay not in reciting the articles of faith nor in getting circumcised, but in one's readiness and capacity to fight against overpowering worldly desires or urges (*nafs-i ammara*). Akbar was exposed to these ideas way back in the 1560s, when he first came into contact with the Chishti *khanqahs* at Ajmer and Sikri. His contacts, still earlier, with Shaikh Ghaus Gawalyari could also have provided him with an opportunity to become familiar with the pantheistic doctrines of *fana* and *wahdat ul-wujud*. Already by 1573 Akbar had come to regard Shaikh Mu'inuddin Chishti as his spiritual preceptor. In one of his conversations with Miyan Mustafa Bandagi, Akbar is reported to have declared: 'Hazarat Khwaja Mu'inuddin Chishti is my preceptor . . . Anyone who says that he was misguided [*gumrah*] is an infidel. I shall kill the person

[24] *Shara'if-i 'Usmani* MS., Department of History, Aligarh, ff. 26a–32a. Also see Iqtidar Alam Khan, 'The Nobility under Akbar and the Development of His Religious Policy', fn. 17.

[25] Ala'uddaulah Qazvini, *Nafa'is u'l-Ma'asir*, MS., Br. Library, ff.62 a&b; Ghausi Shattari, *Gulzar-i Akbar*, MS., John Rylands Library, f. 207b. Also see a detailed examination of the evidence in Athar Abbas Rizvi, *Muslim Revivalist Movements in Northern India in the Sixteenth and Seventeenth Centuries*, Agra, 1965, pp. 116–18.

saying this with my own hands.'[26] This is confirmed by Badauni's testimony to the effect that by 1577 Akbar was regularly practising the spiritual exercises prescribed in the Chishti *silsilah*. Sometime after 1575 he even tried to learn the art of performing *chilla-i ma'kus* (concentrating on God while suspended head down in a well for forty days and nights) from Shaikh Chaya Laddha.[27]

The influence of the pantheistic Sufic doctrine of *fana* seems to have provided an impetus to Akbar's interest in philosophy. In the company of Shaikh Mubarak, Abul Fazl, Ghazi Khan Badakhshi, Hakim Abul Fath, and other rationalist thinkers, during 1578–82, he eventually became familiar with the systematic exposition of the doctrine of *wahdat ul-wujud* by Ibn al-'Arabi in a larger philosophical perspective. As Irfan Habib points out, the pantheism of Ibn al-'Arabi, despite lacking a rational basis, was capable of becoming a strong ideological challenge to the post-Ghazali conventionalism in Islam. It was this quality of the impact of Ibn al-'Arabi's ideas on Akbar and, more importantly, on his sociopolitical perceptions during 1578–82, that is characterized by Abul Fazl as the elevation of 'intellect (*khirad*)' to a 'high pedestal' (*buland paigi*). The idea suggested by Ibn al-'Arabi that all that is not a part of divine reality is an illusion, in turn, led Akbar to the notion that all religions are either equally true or equally illusory,[28] a suggestion that was bound to be sharply denounced by all shades of orthodox opinion as a deviation from the true path. It was equally unacceptable to the Jesuit fathers then present at the court. Commenting on Akbar's assurance in 1581 to Jalala Roshani of the freedom to practise his cult, Montserrat observed: 'the King cared little that in allowing everyone to follow his religion he was in reality violating all.'[29] The emergence of this new ideological trend

[26] *Majalis*, Maktaba Ibrahimia, Haidarabad, AH 1367, p. 58.

[27] *Muntakhab ut-Tawarikh*, vol. II, p. 201; and vol. III, p. 110.

[28] Irfan Habib, 'Reason and Science in Medieval India', (cyclostyled), paper presented at the South Asian Studies Conference, Australia, 1981 (unpublished).

[29] Antonio Montserrat, *Commentary on His Journey to the Court of Akbar*, pp. 132–3.

at the court seems to have confused many of the learned regarding Akbar's worldview. 'Abdul Qadir Badauni, for instance, viewed the intellectual climate at the court around 1581 as the truimph of Shi'ism over orthodoxy.[30] This was, in any case, another decisive point of departure in Akbar's worldview, taking him much further away from the accepted Islamic beliefs and practices than was ever possible within the parameters of the pantheistic notions of Islamic mysticism.

III

The development of Akbar's worldview subsequent to his being deeply influenced by the pantheistic philosophy of Ibn al-'Arabi is identified with the concept of *sulh-i kul* (Absolute Peace). This concept was formulated by him, or for him by Abul Fazl, in such a manner that it was elevated from the status of a mystic notion alluding to the state of *fana* to that of a concept denoting a principle capable of promoting amity among divergent groups in a culturally plural situation. In a revealing restatement of Alberuni's famous passage criticizing Brahmans for their intellectual insularity, Abul Fazl tried to project the idea that social strife was caused in India primarily by the absence of the spirit of *sulh-i kul*. He goes on to suggest in the same passage that the absence of the spirit of *sulh-i kul* was in Hindustan caused mainly by the preponderance of an attitude of imitation (*taqlid*) and by the suppression of intellect and reason.[31]

After 1581, Akbar's identification with *sulh-i kul* tended to make him part company with the mainstream tendency of orthodox Islam insofar as there was no place in his vision for the prescribed prayers and the unquestioned acceptance of prophethood. It was much closer to the teachings of the contemporary *nirguna bhakti* sects which criticized both Hinduism and Islam for being formalist and divisive.

[30] *Muntakhab ut-Tawarikh*, vol. II, p. 211, where Badauni accuses Mulla Muhammad Yazdi, who had arrived from *Wilayat* (Iran) only recently, for trying to attract Akbar towards Shi'a. beliefs. In vol. III, p. 74, while commenting on Shaikh Mubarak's career, he suggests that the 'Iraqis' or Iranis (Shi'as) came to dominate Akbar's court circle at about this time.

[31] *Ain-i Akbari*, vol. III, pp. 3–4.

The conceptualization of man's relations with God articulated by Akbar in one of his less-well-known statements reveals its proximity in certain important respects to the one found in the teachings of *nirguna bhakti*. Replying to a query from Murad in 1591, Akbar tells him:

> Devotion to the Matchless one [*Bechun*] is beyond the limits of the spoken word whether in respect of form [*jism*], material attributes [*jismaniat*], letter [*harf*] or sound [*saut*]. Devotion to the Matchless one is [also] matchless. If God so wishes, [you] shall enter into the private chamber of this wonderful divine mystery. At present, the auspicious preamble [to the discourse on the subject] is this that he [*Murad*] may decorate with agreeable sincerity and praiseworthy actions the page of his disposition [*safha-i khatir*] and endeavour to gain our pleasure so that with this blessing this other fortunate house of devotion [to God] may be opened [to him].[32]

Emphasis on the absoluteness of Divine Reality and a subtle suggestion, in this passage, that one could reach it not through formal prayers but only by cultivating the self with the help of a preceptor, recall to mind the teachings of Kabir and Nanak.

It is again very much like the contemporary *bhakti* cults that in Akbar's system there was strong emphasis on the role of a preceptor. As he tells Murad, the latter may hope to have access to Divine Mystery only with the help and guidance of Akbar, who is in the position of his preceptor. The status of preceptor in Akbar's system, in turn, began to be perceived as that of the *insan-i kamil* (Perfect Man) of Islamic mysticism.

This new worldview reflected itself with its distinct tilt towards rationality as well as (with all its inconsistencies) towards the norms of moral behaviour that Akbar prescribed, not only for his personal

[32] *Akbar-nama*, MS. (possibly Abul Fazl's first draft), Br. Library, Add. 27, 247, ff. 401b–404b, carries the text of a memorandum containing Akbar's orders on queries and requests sent to him by Murad at the time of his appointment to Malwa in 1591. This memorandum is not included in the final draft. The statement of Akbar cited above can be read on f. 402a of the same MS.

devotees (*arbab-i iradat*) but also for ordinary members of the court elite. It is also revealed majestically in Abul Fazl's theoretical expositions on the concept of kingship. He defines kingship dually, as *farr-i izadi*, or Divine Light, and as originating in a social contract between society and the ruler.[33] In addition to these are Akbar's sayings,[34] and other documents reproduced by Abul Fazl, projecting a new set of cultural values rooted in rational experience but not violating the spirit of *sulh-i kul*. Some of these values appear astonishingly modern, and are imbued with compassion.

This is for example suggested by Akbar's numerous observations recorded by Abul Fazl reflecting on the duty of the ruler to work for the welfare of the common people or highlighted by statements revealing Akbar's deep respect and concern for women. His reply to Murad's request (1591) for the transfer of a *dak-chauki* man, Bahadur, to his camp, is instructive. Akbar recorded the following order: 'Bahadur's wife is not agreeable to his going [there]. If presently we [are able to] persuade her, we shall send Bahadur as well. Otherwise after a few days we shall depute him to carry a *farman* by *dak-chauki*. Then you may detain him.'[35] The regard here for Bahadur's wife's opinion, and Akbar's vague hope that he might eventually succeed in persuading her to change her mind, are revealing, especially since the person concerned is the wife of a mere *dak-chauki* messenger. Similarly, one of his sayings wherein he ridicules Hindu men for seeking salvation in the other world by inducing their wives to perish in fire, and the one in which he criticizes Muslim personal law for daughters receiving 'a smaller share in the inheritance, although it is better that the weaker should receive a large share',[36] are refreshingly original and compassionate.

[33] For Abul Fazl's expositions of these theories, see the relevant sections of *Ain-i Akbari*, particularly the section entitled *Riwa-i Rozi*.

[34] *Ain-i Akbari*, vol. III, pp. 178–91. Some of these sayings are recorded in the *Akbar-nama* as well, with reference to the actual occasions where Akbar is supposed to have uttered them.

[35] *Akbar-nama*, MS., Br. Library, Add. 27, 247, f. 403b.

[36] *Ain-i Akbari*, Lucknow, 1892, vol. III, pp. 184, 190.

Akbar's strong disapproval of meat-eating is also rooted not in his religious beliefs but basically reflects his natural compassion for living beings (*jandaran*). He shames meat-eaters for having converted 'their inner sides, where reside the mysteries of Divinity, into a burial ground of animals.' And, again: 'I wish my body made of elements (*jism-i 'unsure*) was big (*tand-o-mand*) so that these flesh-eating ignorant ones would have satisfied their hunger with my flesh, and so spared other living beings'.[37] What is important about this sentiment is that it is not sought to be supported by any religious sanction or appeal. This is one of those cultural norms recommended by Akbar that seem to carry the imprint of his very private reflections not fully assimilated into the structure of beliefs and ideas that he was trying to evolve. These were his reflections not as the *insan-i kamil* or *pir-o-murshid* of official discourse, but as a sensitive and intelligent private person who had missed a formal education.

Akbar's socio-religious outlook, based on *sulh-i kul*, developed and created an ideological space for itself, largely through a polemical dialogue with mainstream Islamic orthodoxy within the framework of comparative religion. At an ideological plane the tendency identified with *sulh-i kul* was critical of Hindu beliefs and practices as well, but this aspect remained all the time in the background, possibly because none of the Hindu sects thus criticized responded to the challenge.[38] The reaction of orthodox Muslim theologians was generally sharp. It was this continuing polemic between a large section of the orthodox theologians and the protagonists of *sulh-i kul*, which continued for

[37] Ibid., vol. III, p. 188.

[38] Akbar's rejection of the 'divine incarnation' (*hulul*) theory is reflected, as suggested by Athar Ali ('The Religious World of Jahangir', *Proceedings of the Indian History Congress*, Calcutta, 51st Session, 1990, p. 298, fn. 57), in the saying that in India no one sets a claim to prophethood because of the theory of divine incarnation. Abul Fazl's calling Todar Mal a simpleton (*sada lauh*) for his attachment to his private idols and his disapproving references to Todar Mal's bigotry (*kina tozi*) are pointers to the ideological reservations that existed between him and Todar Mal. The *Dabistan-i Mazahib* quotes a well-argued statement of Akbar criticizing Brahmans for believing in the doctrine of incarnation.

about twenty-five years (roughly the second half of Akbar's reign), that appears to have given rise to a widely held belief towards the end of Akbar's reign to the effect that he was very hostile to Islam and was trying to undermine its position within the Mughal Empire. Badauni and Shaikh Ahmad Sirhindi seem to represent the more extreme or outspoken reactions of this genre. It should, however, be kept in mind that the exaggerated reaction of Badauni and Shaikh Ahmad Sirhindi was not fully shared by many, and perhaps not by the majority of the contemporary orthodox *ulama*. A large number of such persons, noticed by Badauni himself in the third volume of *Muntakhab ut-Tawarikh* as men of great piety and learning, are also mentioned as maintaining close contacts with Akbar's court during the time when the polemics of the supporters of *sulh-i kul* against orthodox Islam were at its height. This is also suggested by some of the occasional statements of the most eminent theologians of the time, Shaikh 'Abdul Haq Muhaddis and his son Shaikh Nurul Haq. Although both were critical of some of the new ideas promoted by Akbar, they did not seemingly share the alarmist view of Akbar's policies taken by Badauni. As late as 1605 Shaikh 'Abdul Haq could find it possible to conclude his book, *Tarikh-i Haqqi*, with a prayer in which Akbar is referred to as the reigning *Padshah* who was expected to act as the defender of Islam. In the same year, Shaikh Nurul Haq went out of his way to remark that Akbar's motives in encouraging religious discussions were misunderstood by the common people.[39] These passages obviously imply an assessment of Akbar's role as king, and of his motives in starting religious discussions, as being qualitatively different from those of Badauni and Sirhindi.

IV

I should like to conclude with a few comments on the doubt raised by Athar Ali regarding Ni'amatulla's and Muhammad Sadiq's testimony corroborating Badauni's and Sirhindi's allegations that Akbar

[39] See translations of the relevant passages of *Tarikh-i Haqqi* (p. 181) and *Zubd ut-Tawarikh* (p. 191) in Elliot and Dowson, *History of India as Told by its Own Historians*, vol. VI.

had adopted a repressive attitude towards practitioners of orthodox Islam.[40]

Athar Ali doubts the veracity of these statements by pointing out that an exceptionally large mosque was built by Man Singh at Raj Mahal in 1592. Regarding this mosque he also quotes the popular tradition recorded in the Archaeological Survey's report saying the structure 'was originally intended for a temple, but was afterwards turned into the Jama Masjid for fear of the Emperor.' Athar Ali seems to argue that reports pertaining to the closing down of mosques could have been an exaggeration of difficulties caused by the reduction in 'the flow of financial patronage' to Islamic institutions. He thinks that, 'given Akbar's own religious views', 'a persecution' of the practitioners of orthodox Islam does not appear plausible.

There is, however, now available some rather more firm evidence supporting Badauni's and Sirhindi's version in its essentials, and this needs to be taken into account before one makes up one's mind on Athar Ali's view of the matter.

Before I come to an examination of this additional evidence, it may be asked why the building of a mosque by Man Singh at Raj Mahal in 1592 is relevant to the present discussion. One might suggest that the restrictive attitude with regard to Islamic practices and institutions mentioned by Badauni and Sirhindi appeared at a time later than 1592, perhaps around 1600.

There is an explicit reference to the attempt at closing down mosques and prohibiting congregational *namaz* in a '*farman*' issued by Prince Salim, during his rebellion of 1601, to local *hakims* (governors, etc.). Its text is reproduced by Rafi'uddin Ibrahim Shirazi in his *Tazkirat ul-Muluk*. As I have argued in Chapter 4 above, although Rafi'uddin (d. 1626) wrote his book at Bijapur early in the seventeenth

[40] *Tarikh-i Khan Jahani*, ed. Saiyed Muhammad Imamuddin, Dacca, Asiatic Society of Pakistan, 1962, pp. 670–1; and *Tabaqat-i Shah Jahani*, MS., Aligarh Muslim University Collection, no. 226, f. 451, cited in Athar Ali, 'Akbar and Islam', *Islamic Society and Culture,* ed. Milton Israel and N.K. Wagle, pp. 170–1.

century, he sometimes reproduces new information and documents on the history of Akbar's reign, the veracity of which cannot be reasonably doubted.[41] Salim's '*farman*' of 1601 reproduced by him seems to be one such piece:

> At the instigation of some mischievous persons, my father has abolished the arrangements for the maintenance of *khatib, mu'azzin* and *imam* in mosques and has prohibited the performance of *namaz* in congregation. He has converted many mosques into storehouses and stables. It was improper on his part to have acted in this manner. They [recipients of the '*farman*'] should resume the paying of stipends for the maintenance of the mosques, the *khatib*, the *mu'azzin* and *imam*, and should induce people to offer prayers. Anyone showing reluctance in this respect will be duly punished.[42]

This '*farman*' leaves little doubt that towards the turn of the century there was a general impression that in some mosques congregational *namaz* was prohibited by Akbar's orders. That Salim should try to win the sympathy of Muslims by playing upon this issue during his rebellion is quite understandable. It also suggests that, in Salim's perception at the time (1601), the feeling of hurt among Muslims over Akbar's attitude towards Islam was so deep and widespread that many of them could be roused to support him against his father over this issue.

A story narrated by 'Abdul Baqi Nahavandi in *Ma'asir-i Rahimi* (compiled 1614) offers corroborative evidence. He reports that, after Danyal's appointment to the newly conquered '*suba* of Deccan and Khandesh' (1601), Akbar had written to him to order him to demolish the *jama masjid* at Asirgarh 'and raise [in its place] a temple on the pattern of Hindus and [other] infidels of Hindustan.' According to this story, however, Danyal was wise enough 'not to enforce that order by ignoring it and whiling away the time' so that 'the demolition

[41] See Iqtidar Alam Khan, '*The Tazkirat u-l-Muluk* by Rafiuddin Ibrahim Shirazi as a Source on the History of Akbar's Reign', *Studies in History*, vol. II, no. 1, New Delhi, 1981, pp. 41–4 (reproduced herein as Chapter 4).

[42] *Tazkirat ul-Muluk*, MS., Br. Library, Add. 23,883, f. 224b.

of a mosque and building of a temple in its place during the time of the kings of Islam was avoided.'[43]

Regarding this story, one may note that it was recorded by 'Abdul Baqi Nahavandi in the context of his employer 'Abdur Rahim Khan-i Khanan's role in the Deccan as the *ataliq* of Danyal. There is thus an implicit suggestion in the manner this story is recorded that the credit for ignoring Akbar's extraordinary order should partly go to the Khan-i Khanan, who was then next in command to Danyal. This story is not recorded by any other known authority. Possibly 'Abdul Baqi Nahavandi's source of information for the story was 'Abdur Rahim Khan-i Khanan himself. Moreover, such a story being recorded in a text identified with 'Abdur Rahim Khan-i Khanan tends to suggest that, at the time of its writing (i.e. 1614), Akbar's restrictive measures against orthodox Islam around 1601 were such common knowledge that an allusion to them in a historical text's passing observation was not expected to be considered offensive by Jahangir as well as his courtiers.

In the memorandum already cited, containing orders recorded by Akbar on requests and queries sent by Murad from Malwa sometime in 1591, we find a query by Murad to the effect that if someone in his camp was found performing prayers 'in the manner of imitating theologians [*fuqha-i taqlid shi 'ar*]', was he to be 'forbidden' or was he to be 'left in his ways'? Akbar's response suggests that a person performing *namaz* was considered deserving 'admonition' (*nasihat*) by his superior so as to 'help' him to come to 'the path of reason' (*rah-i 'aql*]'. But Murad is also warned that such a person is not to be forced to abandon his rites of worship as this would amount to violation of *sulh-i kul.*[44] This document clearly points to two aspects of the situation: first, that some of the princes/nobles commanding armies or administering different regions were not clear in their minds, around 1591, if they should prohibit the performance of *namaz* offered by individuals serving with them; and second, that

[43] *Maasir-i Rahimi*, vol. II, ed. Hidayat Husain, Calcutta, 1925, p. 474.

[44] *Akbar-nama*, MS., Br. Library, Add. 27,247, f. 404a.

official policy at this time (1591) was for the Mughal administrators to 'admonish' but not pressurize such people to bring them 'to the path of reason'. One might suggest that this was perhaps the beginning of the drift towards a situation that, sometime prior to Salim's revolt in 1601, led to the general impression that Akbar had withdrawn all support to the maintenance of mosques, and even ordered the destruction of some.

This seems, however, to have been a brief phase. The attempt to discourage congregational *namaz* and compliance with other decrees of Islam was apparently given up by Akbar by 1601, before the *Ain-i Akbari* was completed. This is attested to by a casual statement of Abul Fazl in the *Ain-i Akbari* where he speaks of Akbar practising 'external as well as spiritual austerities in the worship [of God] which render silent the slanders [spread] by the ritualists of this age [*rasmiyan-i rozgar*].' Blochmann reads this passage as suggesting that Akbar occasionally joined 'public worship in order to hush the slandering tongues of the bigots of the present age.'[45] This rather loose rendering of the relevant line is not implausible. In the above passage the expression *riyazat-i suri* (external austerities) is perhaps an allusion to the observance of *namaz* by Akbar, which, according to Abul Fazl, silenced the 'slanderous' criticism of Akbar by *rasmiyan*, or those who considered the form or ritual of worship as of primary importance. It is a candid admission of the fact that, towards 1601, Akbar's beliefs and his attitude towards *namaz* were being widely criticized. This, perhaps, made him concerned at the reaction of common Muslims, forcing him to soften his attitude on the performance of *namaz*. One could explain the appreciative references to Akbar's role as king by Shaikh 'Abdul Haq Muhaddis and Shaikh Nurul Haq in 1605 also in the light of this possible softening in the emperor's attitude towards Islam during the last four years of his reign.

The hurt that was seemingly caused to Muslims by Akbar's hostile attitude to Islam during 1591–1601 was, apparently, healed

[45] *Ain-i Akbari*, Nawal Kishore, 1882, vol. I, p. 105. Cf. H. Blochmann, *Ain-i Akbari*, English translation, Calcutta, 1873, p. 163.

considerably in the last four years of his reign. At the time of his death, in any case, there were no signs of widespread discontent against his policies among Muslims as well as among the majority of orthodox theologians. On the other hand, at the time of Akbar's death in 1605, the impression of even a theologian like 'Abdul Haq was that, despite all his 'innovations', he remained a Muslim king.

6

The Mughal Empire and the Iranian Diaspora of the Sixteenth Century

THE EMPIRE ESTABLISHED BY the Timurid prince Zahir al-Din Babur in India (1526) was often identified by Indians of the time with the Mongols who had been invading the north-western parts of the subcontinent intermittently during the thirteenth and fourteenth centuries.[1] This identification is reflected by it being popularly designated the 'Mughal Empire' (*Saltanat-i Mughalia*).[2] In Central Asia the same empire was remembered down to the end of the seventeenth century by the familial ties of its

[1] For the earliest reference to Babur and his troops as 'Mughals' in a Persian text, see Rukn al-Din, *Lataif-i Quddusi* (completed in 1538), Delhi, 1311 H, pp. 8, 33. Compare my comment on this evidence in Iqtidar Alam Khan, 'The State in Mughal India: Re-examining the Myths of a Counter-vision', *Social Scientist,* vol. 30, nos 1–2, January–February, 2001, pp. 26–7.

[2] For example, Bernier's *Travels*, published from Paris in 1670, refers to this empire as 'the Empire of the Great Mogul (Des Etats Du Grand Mogol)'. This may indicate that it was referred to as such by the populace during the time Bernier was travelling in India. Cf. *Travels in the Mogul Empire: AD 1656–1668*, tr. Archibald Constable, second edition revised by Vincent A. Smith, London, 1916, p. xxv.

rulers with the remnants of the Chaghtai *ulus* of the Mongols then controlling parts of Xinjiang (Mughulistan). To demarcate them from Uzbek chiefs, who are also identified as descendants of Chingiz,[3] the Indian Timurids were generally referred to in Central Asian histories as Chaghtais.[4] The overall cultural profile of the Mughal Empire during its formative years was also influenced by features such as the Turko-Mongol theory of kingship, the Turani complexion of the nobility,[5] the influence of the Naqshbandi order,[6] and Eastern or Chaghtai Turkish as the lingua franca of the ruling elite[7]—all of which speak of its Central Asian ambience.

[3] The Uzbek chiefs who defeated Amir Najam at Ghajadwan (3 *Ramazan* 918H/13 November 1512) are referred to by Khwandamir *(Tarikh-i Shah Ismail Wa Tahmasp Safavi*, ed. Ali Jarrah, Tahran, 1370 Shamsi, p. 80) as *Salatin-i Chingizi.*

[4] See for example Khwaja Baha al-Din Hasan Nisari, *Muzakkar-i Ahbab* (completed in 1566), ed. S.M. Faziullah, Hyderabad, 1969, p. 93. Babur and his sons are mentioned in the category of Chaghtai rulers (*zikr-i salatin -i Chaghtai*).

[5] See R.P. Tripathi's pioneering study of the Timurid theory of kingship in his *Some Aspects of Muslim Administration,* second edition, Allahabad, 1959; and also Iqtidar Alam Khan, 'The Turko-Mongol Theory of Kingship', *Medieval India: A Miscellany,* vol. II, pp. 8–18.

[6] Cf. S.A.A. Rizvi, *Religious and Intellectual History of Muslims in Akbar's Reign,* New Delhi, 1975, p. 429. It is held that down to Akbar's time most of the Turani nobles ('Turks and Mughals') were strongly devoted to Khwaja 'Ubaidullah Ahrar's descendants. See also Baha al-Din Hasan Nisari, *Muzakkar-i Ahbab,* pp. 107–8, where Babur's second son, Mirza Kamran, is mentioned as being greatly attached to the Naqshbandi order.

[7] That Chaghtai Turkish was the spoken language at the Mughal court down to Humayun's time is borne out by many passages in the sources. From Bayazid Bayat's account (*Tazkira-i Humayun wa Akbar,* p. 101) one comes to know that at an assembly of Humayun's nobles in 1547 most of the princes repeatedly reverted to Turkish, which forced Husain Quli Sultan, an Iranian, to complain that he was not following the conversation. Recording his meeting with the Afghan chief Daulat Khan Lodi on 5 June 1525 Babur (A.S. Beveridge, *Babur-nama in English*, reprint, London, 1969, p. 459) mentions his talking to him through an interpreter. This suggests that Babur himself spoke in Turkish, which Daulat Khan found difficult to

All this should clearly set apart the nascent Mughal Empire from the Safavid Empire as it emerged under Shah Ismail (1501–24) and his successor Shah Tahmasp (1524–76) in the first half of the sixteenth century, where it was Western Turkish that was accommodated within Persian culture. The rise of the Safavids can be traced back to the Islamic revival of post-Khanid Iran, which was particularly oriented towards eradicating the remnants of Mongol paganism.[8] At the beginning of the sixteenth century this revival led to an alliance between Turkman nomads and the Iranian landed gentry (including 'clerical notables'), both of whom were bound by an allegiance to the spirit of the Safavid Sufic order. Around the same time, the Safavid order assumed a strong Shiite orientation and the Twelver Shiite doctrines came to acquire the status of a state religion; the rulers in effect claimed for themselves the role of *imams,* becoming thereby the temporal and religious heads of the Islamic community.[9] The Safavid aspiration of being acknowledged by the Timurids as their

---

follow. Muzaffar Alam ('The Pursuit of Persian: Language in Mughal Politics', *Modern Asian Studies,* vol. 32, no. 2, 1998, pp. 318–19) interprets this passage differently: He thinks Babur was speaking in Persian. It is, however, difficult to imagine that Daulat Khan would have needed an interpreter's help to understand anything spoken in Persian. Besides the fact that in its structure and vocabulary Pashto is very close to eastern Persian, one may also remember, in this regard, Muhammad Qasim Firishta's testimony (*Ta'rikh-i Firishta,*1607, vol. I, rpnt. Nawal Kishore, p. 187) that, under the Lodis, the circle of persons proficient in Persian had expanded considerably. Cf. Z. Safa in *The Cambridge History of Iran,* vol. 6, ed. Peter Jackson and Laurence Lockhart, Cambridge, 1986, pp. 913–14, for the fact that in the beginning of the sixteenth century 'the language used at the Safavid court' was Turkish, not Persian.

[8] B.S. Amoretti, 'Religion in the Timurid and Safavid Periods', *The Cambridge History of Iran,* vol. 6, ed. Peter Jackson and Laurence Lockhart, pp. 610–14, 629–34.

[9] Cf. Said Amir Arjomand, *The Shadow of God and the Hidden Imam,* Chicago, 1984, pp. 122–4; and B.S. Amoretti, op. cit., in *The Cambridge History of Iran,* vol. 6, pp. 224–40.

preceptors and spiritual guides is borne out by their offer of military assistance to Babur and Humayun in 1512 and 1545, contingent on the latter agreeing to formally enter the circle of *qizilbashes.*[10] That such an attitude on the part of the Safavids was resented by the Timurids may be gauged by the manner in which they turned their backs on their Safavid allies at Ghajdavan (13 November 1512) and Qandahar (1545).[11]

It is therefore important to discern how, with the passage of time, the Mughal Empire shed many of its Central Asian features and developed a new court culture in which the wider use of Persian, not only as the universal language of imperial administration as part of the unprecedented systematization that the Mughals attempted, but also as the main vehicle of cultural and literary discourse among the ruling elites, was an important manifestation.[12] This court culture was also infused with new artistic tastes and refinements carrying, in part, the unmistakable stamp of Persian influence.[13] Again, in this changed cultural milieu heterodox views and practices came to be tolerated to the point that a large number of Muslims, many of them Persian immigrants subscribing to *asna 'ashari* beliefs, were no longer

[10] Cf. S.A.A. Rizvi, *Religious and Intellectual History of Muslims in Akbar's Reign*, New Delhi 1975, p. 51; and Sukumar Ray, *Bairam Khan,* Karachi, 1992, p. 77. Both have noted that the donning of the Persian or Shiite cap (*taj*) by Babur and Humayun amounted to their accepting the Safavid ruler as their preceptor.

[11] See A.S. Beveridge's note in *Babur-nama in English,* p. 361; and Bayazid Bayat, *Tazkira-i Humayun wa Akbar,* p. 50. Bayazid writes that after having wrested Qandahar from Safavid officers, Humayun wrote to the Shah to lend *(batariq-i 'aryat)* him Qandahar 'for a few days'.' This was the starting point of a long Mughal –Safavid tussle over Qandahar.

[12] See Muzaffar Alam, 'The Pursuit of Persian Language in Mughal Polities', *Modern Asian Studies,* vol. 32, no. 2, 1998, pp. 325–35.

[13] Percy Brown (*Indian Architecture,* Calcutta, 1942, p. 89) emphasizes Persian cultural inspiration as an important factor shaping Mughal architecture; while, according to Milo Cleveland Beach (*Mughal and Rajput Painting, The New Cambridge History of India,* vol. I, Cambridge, 1992, pp. 31–2), Mughal court painting was dominated by the accepted artistic standards of the Iranian court.

obliged to observe subterfuges (*taqiyya*) for their rituals of piety to avoid persecution at the hands of orthodox Sunnis. So much so that we find, by the beginning of the seventeenth century, Shiites and Sunnis offering prayers in the same mosque being cited as a distinctive mark of peaceable inter-sect relations in the Mughal Empire.[14] This, in a way, was the beginning of a process of the creation of sizeable pockets of Shi'a population in many of the urban centres in North India by the latter half of the eighteenth century.[15]

Another noteworthy manifestation of this court culture was the special respect and courtesy observed by the Mughals in their relations and diplomatic exchanges with the Safavid rulers, this being in sharp contrast to the hostility and disdain generally manifested by them in their attitude towards the Shaibanids and Janids of Central Asia.[16] The element of special warmth generally discernible in Mughal–Safavid relations may also be ascribed to the close personal equations that sometimes existed between individuals belonging to the two ruling families.[17] Lastly, the inclusion of a large number of men of Iranian

[14] See Jahangir's well-known remark in *Tuzuk-i Jahangiri*, ed. Saiyid Ahmad, Ghazipur and Aligarh, 1863–4, p. 16.

[15] Cf. *Malfuzat-i Shah Abdul Aziz Dehlvi*, cited by Muhammad 'Umar, *Islam in North India: During the Eighteenth Century*, New Delhi, 1993, pp. 176–7.

[16] This is illustrated by Akbar's response to 'Abdullah Khan Uzbek's proposal in 1577 for an anti-Safavid alliance. Despite his nursing a grievance over the occupation of Qandahar by Shah Tahmasp in 1559, Akbar not only spurned the idea of a Mughal–Uzbek alliance against the Safavids, but also rebuked 'Abdullah Khan for using disrespectful language about them. Akbar knew that, following Shah Tahmasp's death (1576), the affairs of the Safavid Empire were in great confusion; yet he chose to be protective about them. This desire to appear polite survived even the outbreak of hostilities over Qandahar during 1649–53. This is borne out by letters exchanged between the two courts after Aurangzeb gained the throne in 1658. Cf. Riazul Islam, *Indo-Persian Relations*, Lahore, 1970, pp. 39–40, 52–3,102, 108–9, 113, 124–5.

[17] See for example Shah Tahmasp's letter to Akbar sent by the hand of Saiyid Beg Safavi in 1562 (Abul Fazl *Akbar-nama,* vol. II, pp. 171–2). There is a statement hinting that the Shah contemplated 'a familial connection

origin in the Mughal nobility, and the induction by marriage of women like Nur Jahan and Mumtaz Mahal from important Iranian families into the Mughal ruling family, tended to create an intellectual climate at the Mughal court where the king being a Turani was perhaps no longer of crucial significance.[18]

(*nisbat*)' with Humayun which his untimely death caused to 'remain hidden behind the veil of invisible (*dar parda-i ghaib manad*)'. This speaks of a close personal equation that appears to have developed between Tahmasp and Humayun after the latter's visit to Iran (1543–5). It was, apparently, not much affected by Humayun's going back on his promise to hand over Qandahar to the Safavid officers accompanying him in 1545. In this context, it is appropriate also to take into consideration Shah Tahmasp's supposed letter to Hamida Bano Begam, purportedly sent around the same time as the above letter. The text of this letter is included in Abul Qasim Namakin's *Munshaat-i Namakin* (MS., University Collection no. 26, f. 242 a&b); I.A. Zilli ('Early Correspondence between Shah Tahmasp and Akbar', in *Islamic Heritage in South Asian Sub-continent,* ed. Nazir Ahmad and I.H. Siddiqui, Jaipur, 2000, pp. 230–1, 232–4) treats it as a genuine letter written with the aim of inducing Hamida Bano Begam to support the restoration of friendly ties between 'the two courts'. In his view, Hamida Bano's accompanying Humayun to Iran 'presumably led the Shah to claim a special relationship with her.' But on a closer examination this letter appears to be a draft prepared by way of the literary exercise in which there is an attempt to paraphrase Shah Tahmasp's letter to Akbar. In this paraphrasing the statement: 'Regarding the late asylum of brotherhood [i.e. Humayun], we have entertained in our heart [ideas] of familial connections [*nisbat ba akhwat panah marhume nisbatha ba khatir manzur dashta*]' is changed to 'regarding that repository of Chastity [i.e. Hamida Bano Begam], we had other ideas in the dignified mind [*nisbat badan 'asmat panah digar andeshaha ba-khatiri khatir khutur dasht*].' It is, perhaps, this awkwardly worded paraphrasing that has led I.A. Zilli to imagine the Shah's claim to a 'special relationship' with Humayun's widow. I have a hunch that Riazul Islam did not include this letter in his excellent *Calendar* of documents on Indo-Persian relations because of its spuriousness. That he 'missed' this document in the *Munshaat-i Namakin,* as imagined by I.A. Zilli (fn. 1), is perhaps a hasty judgement.

[18] Cf. Athar Ali, *The Mughal Nobility under Aurangzeb,* Bombay, 1966, p. 18. Commenting on the position of Turanis at the court, Athar Ali cites an interesting anecdote recorded by M'amuri: 'An officer of Aurangzeb's court

This transformation in the Mughal court culture may be attributed to a variety of factors. Akbar's policy measures curbing the authority of orthodox *ulama* and generally encouraging the spirit of comparative religion were no doubt important in favouring this development. But the most significant circumstance contributing to this new court culture was the coming to India of a large number of Iranian immigrants in search of employment and Mughal patronage.[19] I hope here to focus on this transformation in Mughal court culture during the sixteenth century by highlighting the contributions of Iranian immigrants in various fields.

I

Both Babur and Humayun, as well as the majority of their nobles down to 1540, were more at home in Turkish than Persian. But with the possible exception of some of the chiefs who were recent immigrants from Mughulistan, and a small number of Uzbek nobles, most of them could speak Persian as well.[20] As a matter of fact, till this time, all over Central Asia, Persian was not only the language of

---

who went so far as to say in imperial presence that the word of a Turani could not be trusted, only earned a mild reproof asking him to remember that his Emperor was also a Turani.'

[19] S.A.A. Rizvi (*Religious and Intellectual History of Muslims in Akbar's Reign,* p. 262) refers to the view in *Tarikh-i Alfi* that the immigrants were attracted by the wealth of India and also by the situation in the Mughal Empire where it was possible for immigrants to rise to the status of nobles in a short time. S. Amir Arjomand (*The Shadow of God and the Hidden Imam*, Chicago, 1984, p. 198), on the other hand, attributes it to religious persecution in Iran.

[20] See fn. 7, where it is argued that Chaghtai Turkish was the spoken language at the Mughal court during the reigns of Babur and Humayun. But from a passage of Bayazid Bayat one may infer that by 1570, apart from an old Uzbek noble (Sikandar Khan), most of the persons present at a reception given by Mun'im Khan at Jaunpur were able to understand a Persian *ghazal* recited there (*Tazkira-i Humayun wa Akbar,* p. 306).

polite discourse but also the lingua franca.[21] This status of Persian in Timurid Central Asia was not disturbed by the efflorescence of Chaghtai Turkish towards the end of the fifteenth century. The foremost promoter of this literary upsurge in Eastern Turkish, Mir 'Ali Sher Navai, was also famous for starting a new trend in Persian literary writing.[22] Many of the Persian poets, scholars, and theologians present at the Mughal court during the reigns of Babur and Humayun belonged to a circle of the literati patronized in the Timurid principality of Khurasan. These literary figures included Shaikh Zain Khwafi (Babur's *sadr* and author of the *Fathnama* of the Battle of Khanua 1527);[23] Khwandamir (author of the *Habib us-Siyar* and the *Qanun-i Humayuni*);[24] and Mir Abdul Haiy (*sadr* around 1556).[25] Baha al-Din Hasan Nisari has noticed many other Persian literary men of Khurasan who eventually moved to the Mughal court in search of patronage, including the poet Qasim Kahi. Being

[21] *Babur-nama,* tr., p. 7. In Farghana the entire population of the *vilayat* of Asfara located in the hill country, sixty-five miles south-west of Marghinan, was Persian speaking.

[22] Compare Z. Safa, in the *Cambridge History of Iran,* vol. 6, p. 914.

[23] Cf. Baha al-Din Nisari, *Muzakkar-i Ahbab,* p. 245. He was a descendant of someone distantly related to the famous Sufi of fifteenth-century Khurasan, Shaikh Zain al-Din Khwafi, and is reported to have held the office of *sadr* under Babur as well as Humayun. The *Fath-nama* by him in Persian after the battle of Khanua (1527) is reproduced in the *Babur-nama.* He later expanded this document in his *Tabaqat-i Baburi,* which was also the first attempt to prepare a Persian version of Babur's memoirs.

[24] C.A. Storey, *Persian Literature: A Bio-Bibliographical Survey,* vol. I, London, 1970, pp. 101–9. Hidayat Hosain's Preface, *Qanun-i Humayuni,* Calcutta, 1940, pp. I–XXXVI. These scholarly notices of Ghiyas al-Din surnamed Khwandamir and his works are quite exhaustive. According to Babur (*Babur-nama,* tr., p. 605), finding life at Herat difficult, Khwandamir came to Hindustan in 1528 and took up service under him. His last work, *Qanun-i Humayuni,* was compiled, *c.* 1535, at Gwalior. Khwandamir died during Humayun's march to Gujarat (1535–7).

[25] Cf. Abdul Qadir Badauni, *Muntakhab ut-Tawarikh,* vol. II, p. 65; vol. III, p. 65.

a native of Kabul, to begin with he looked down upon those who were going to Hindustan in search of patronage. But eventually he came to be attached to Humayun's court at Delhi: Kahi is reported to have composed the chronogram (*Humayun az bam uftad*) which yields the year of Humayun's death. He is known to have become quite influential later, under Akbar.[26]

This early influx of Persian literary men into the Mughal court evidently began after the fall of the Timurid principality of Khurasan in 1507 and continued down to the early years of Humayun's reign. The early arrivals were those, identified with Sultan Husain Baiqara's enlightened rule, that were obliged to leave Khurasan after it was occupied by Shaibani Khan in 1507. The persecution of the Sunnis in Khurasan after its annexation by the Safavid Empire in 1510 seems to have led to the migration of many more educated Khurasanis to the Mughal court, where they were apparently employed in various capacities.[27] Several Nishapuris, Hirawis (from Herat), and Turbatis (for example, Shihabuddin Khan Nishapuri and Muzaffar Khan Turbati) were possibly Sunnis. They served under Akbar in important positions during the early part of his reign.

By the time Babur came to Hindustan, the day-to-day working of the Lodi administration was carried on in Persian. This appears to have created an ever-increasing demand for personnel with proficiency in Persian to fill minor positions in the administration. Sikandar Lodi (1491–1518) is reported to have tried to tackle this situation by promoting proficiency in Persian among non-Muslims.[28] The

[26] *Muzakkar-i Ahbab,* p. 470; also Hadi Hasan, 'Qasim Kahi (868–988 AH); His Life, Times and Work', *Islamic Culture,* Hyderabad, July 1953.

[27] Cf. Zain al-Din Wasafi, *Bada'i ul-Waqa'i Wasafi,* ed. Alexander Baldin, Moscow, 1961, pp. 2–4. There is an exaggerated notice of 'persecution' of Sunnis in Khurasan following its occupation by Shah Ismail in 1510. He cites the following couplet as a commentary on the situation: 'All the lands seized by Qizilbash, were found by the World [turned] into a garden of tulips [i.e. soaked in blood].'

[28] *Ta'rikh-i Firishta,* vol. I, p. 187 see also fn. 7.

coming of a large number of Persian literati to the Mughal Empire from Khurasan at an early stage may, therefore, be viewed as a factor enhancing the role of the Persian language in its formation. These Khurasani men of letters also appear to have brought with them novel notions of kingship and state organization. Some of these notions were sought to be adopted in the emerging Mughal polity in India, a process which, incidentally, also highlights the diminishing impact of the Mongol *tura* (customary law) on the system.[29]

One such set of notions informing the planned reorganization of administration after Humayun's accession (1530) is described by Khwandamir in his *Qanun-i Humayuni.* The central idea of this scheme was to bifurcate the administration at the plane of the central government into two compartments: (a) *sih qism*; and (b) *chahar sarkar.* The first, concerned with the management of revenue and organization of production at different levels, was entrusted to a team of professional persons not necessarily enjoying high positions in the military hierarchy; the second regulated the orderly distribution of available assets among personnel serving the state in different capacities and was looked after by high military officers. The working of these two compartments of administration was to be co-ordinated by a senior military officer (*amir*) in his capacity as the agent (*wakil*) of the king.[30] On the face of it, this arrangement appears to be an attempt to revive, in an idealized form, the bifurcation of administrative functions into civil and military compartments that sometimes obtained in the Ghaznavid Empire. There is some basis for imagining that Khwandamir himself was the prime mover of this scheme as it did not survive his death in 1534. Similarly, the idea of the 'carpet of joy' (*bisat-i nishat*) carrying a zodiacal pattern—where, in relation to high nobles and other rulers of the world, Humayun was assigned a position akin to that of the sun in the solar system,[31]

[29] Iqtidar Alam Khan, 'The State in Mughal India: Re-examining the Myths of a Counter Vision', pp. 19–20.

[30] *Qanun-i Humayuni,* pp. 34–43, 48–50.

[31] Ibid., pp. 110–12; cf. Riazul Islam, *Indo–Persian Relations,* p. 36. In a letter sent by Shah Tahmasp to Sultan Sulaiman of the Ottoman Empire

or that of 'divine-splendour (*jalwa-i quds*)' suggesting a halo of divinity round Humayun's person[32]—point to the influence of *Ishraqi* doctrines brought to the Mughal court around this time by Khurasani immigrants.[33]

II

The next large influx of Iranians of different ranks and backgrounds into Mughal service came at the time of Humayun's return to Kabul from Shah Tahmasp's court in 1545. Some of the Iranian notables who came with Humayun on this occasion already had the status of military officers under Shah Tahmasp. They were in fact deputed by the Shah to assist Humayun in his efforts to recover his lost empire. Among them one may find mention of Husain Quli Sultan (brother of Ahmad Sultan Shamlu, the governor of Sistan), Mirza Y'aqub (a maternal uncle of the prince Khuda Banda who was nominated by the Shah to act as *muhrdar* of Humayun), and Khwaja Rushdi (deputed to act as *diwan).* The Shah also permitted the Uzbek chief Haidar Sultan Shaibani, and his sons 'Ali Quli and Bahadur—known for their bravery and distinguished ancestry—to accompany Humayun to Kabul.[34] Along with these notables, there had followed Humayun, at this time, many other men of lower rank, such as Bayazid Bayat himself, in the hope of finding employment as functionaries in one

---

sometime before 1543, he complains that the rulers of Iran, Turkey, and Central Asia were assigned places in this arrangement in a manner suggesting they were Humayun's subordinates.

[32] Rafi' al-Din Ibrahim Shirazi, *Tazkirat ul-Muluk*, MS., Br. Library, Add. 23,883, f.158a & b; also see Shah Tahmasp's letter to the Ottoman Sultan cited above in fn. 31, where this practice is denounced as amounting to claiming divine powers.

[33] See Irfan Habib, 'A Political Theory for the Mughal Empire—A Study of the Ideas of Abu'l Fazl', *Proceedings of the Indian History Congress,* 59th (Patiala) Session (1998), pp. 332–4, where the influcncc of the *ishraqi* theory on Abul Fazl's doctrine of *farr-i izidi* is discussed.

[34] Bayazid Bayat, *Tazkira-i Humayun wa Akbar*, pp. 35–6.

of the royal establishments or in the *sarkars* of high nobles. Names of some of these men are incidentally recorded by Bayazid in three separate lists of persons who came to India in 1555 in the retinues of Humayun, Akbar, and Bairam Khan.[35] In these lists one comes across the names of several persons who rose to the rank of nobles during the early years of Akbar's reign. The influx of Iranians to the Mughal court in search of patronage and employment continued throughout the period of Humayun's later stay at Kabul (1545–55) and in the period of Bairam Khan's regency (1556–60) in India. It was during this time that Mir 'Abdul Latif Qazvini and his relations, as well as the well-known painters Khwaja 'Abd al-Samad, Maulana Dost, and Maulana Saiyid 'Ali, came to the Mughal court.

The arrival of these men, some of whom had already earned distinction in their special fields, appears to have given the initial push to the intellectual and artistic trends that matured in the latter part of Akbar's reign. For example, from Abul Fazl's much-quoted passage noticing 'Abdul Latif Qazvini's arrival in 1556, one may infer that he had by then already earned for himself a reputation of being above sectarian differences. Abul Fazl also hints that he was in the process of arriving at a worldview imbued with the spirit of 'universal reconciliation (*sulh-i kul*)'.[36] Similarly, the painters Mir Saiyid 'Ali, 'Abd al-Samad, Dost Muhammad, and Mir Musavvir, as well as Sayyid Muhammad Mirak (the Khurasanian architect), may be credited for laying the foundation of subsequent achievements in the fields of painting and architecture.

The early illustrations prepared by 'Abd al-Samad and other Iranian painters at Humayun's court, preserved in the Fitzwilliam Album, Cambridge, indicate the attempt to introduce 'a fully imperial Persian style into the Mughal atelier.' In the early illustrations of Akbar's reign, namely those of *Tuti-nama, Hamza-nama* (1570), and *Anwar-i Suhaili*, a synthesis of the Persian style brought in by immigrants with

[35] Ibid., pp. 176–87.

[36] *Akbar-nama,* vol. II, p. 18.

that of local artists with whom they collaborated can be seen to be in gestation.[37] In this new style the quality of decorative perfection in Persian painting was sought to be combined with art traditions of local origin.[38] The synthesis of these two styles in Mughal painting, according to Beach, 'is among the most fascinating episodes of Indian or Islamic art.'[39] The inclination to erect buildings resembling those of Timurid Khurasan was quite manifest among the Indian Mughals from the very beginning. The *Chahar bagh-i padshahi* of Babur at Agra, according to Ebba Koch, was the first attempt at introducing the Khurasani scheme of a walled garden in India. *Sabz-burj* raised at Delhi in the early part of Humayun's reign (1530–40) carries features like the portico (*peshtaq*), modelled after post-Timurid forms; it is present in the shrine of Momo Sharifan at Ghazni *(c.* 1500) with its octangular complex of chambers (*hasht-bahisht*). Combined with its 'Mughalized elevation', *Sabz-burj* served as a standard model for small mausoleums and garden pavilions of Mughal India during the sixteenth century.[40] Humayun's tomb, designed by Saiyid Muhammad Mirak, with its 'high dome, great arched alcove that gives character to its facade' and 'complex of rooms and corridors forming the interior arrangements characterizes it', according to Percy Brown, 'as an example of synthesis of two traditions of building art: the Persian and the Indian': an 'Indian interpretation' of 'Persian conception'. Such a synthesis in its varying manifestations remained a distinctive feature of Mughal architecture as it flowered under Akbar and his successors.[41]

[37] Beach, 'Mughal and Rajput Painting', in *The New Cambridge History of India*, Cambridge, 1992, pp. 16, 20–1, 25, 28–9.

[38] S.P. Verma, 'Akbar's School of Painting', in Iqtidar Alam Khan, ed., *Akbar and His Age*, New Delhi, 1999, pp. 273–4.

[39] Beach, 'Mughal and Rajput Painting', p. 31.

[40] Ebba Koch, *Mughal Architecture: An Outline of Its History and Development,* Munich, 1991, pp. 33–4, 37.

[41] Percy Brown, *Indian Architecture,* pp. 89–90. For a notice of Saiyid Muhamad Mirak, under whose supervision Humayun's tomb was built on the model of Nawsherwan's burial place, see *Muzakkar-i Ahbab,* p. 103.

The most significant impact of the Iranian influx, however, was a perceptible change in the composition of the Mughal nobility which surfaced dramatically in the first twenty years of Akbar's reign. Among fifty-one nobles who came with Humayun to India in 1555, sixteen (31.37 per cent) were Iranis or Khurasanis, while the number of Turani nobles was twenty-seven (52.9 per cent). During the first twenty years of Akbar's reign, i.e. 1556–75, among the high nobles enjoying *mansabs* of 500 and above the Iranis and Khurasanis, many of whom were known Shiites or Tafzilis, represented 38.58 per cent of the total strength. This placed them almost at par with the Turanis, representing 39.58 per cent of the total in the same set of ranks.[42]

The Iranis seem to have improved their positions in the nobility during 1562–7 mainly by earning promotions in the course of military operations against rebellious Turani nobles. Many of the Turanis on Akbar's side were rather lukewarm, while the Iranis were usually steadfast and unsparing in their support of the royal cause.[43] This should partly also explain why some tension developed between the two groups during 1564–7 and why many of the Turanis came to distrust their Irani colleagues.[44]

The contrary pulls of this situation within the nobility combined with the orthodox intolerance of *Sadr-us-Sadur.* Shaikh 'Abd al-Nabi seems to have goaded Akbar into adopting a paradoxical policy with regard to Shiites down to 1575. On the one hand he is reported to have extended patronage and favours to many Irani nobles as well as theologians known for their Shiite leanings. On the other there are on record two instances of his inflicting in the early 1570s capital

[42] Cf. Iqtidar Alam Khan, 'The Nobility under Akbar and the Development of his Religious Policy, 1560–80', *Journal of the Royal Asiatic Society.* London, nos. 1 and 2, 1968, pp. 30, 35, Appendix I (reproduced herein as Chapter 3).

[43] Ibid., pp. 30–1.

[44] *Akbar-nama,* vol. III, pp. 162, 178. The Turanis were unhappy over Khan-i Jahan's appointment in 1576 as commander of the Mughal army in Bangal. They did not cooperate with him because he was perceived as an Irani and Shiite.

punishments on highly placed persons charged with Shiite 'heresy'.[45] The exhumation of the body of the universally respected Shiite divine Murtaza Sharifi Shirazi from the proximity of Amir Khusrau's tomb in 1566 was, perhaps, the most blatant of Akbar's actions of this nature.[46]

This paradox became still more manifest in Akbar's attempt to win recognition, through the famous *mahzar* of 1579, as *Sultan-i Islam* with the authority to arbitrate between different schools of Sunni jurisprudence. It virtually amounted to the theologians assigning to him headship of Sunni Muslims in India at a time when the nobility created by him was already a group in which Iranis (many of them Shiites) and Rajputs and other Hindus put together represented 33.1 per cent (Iranis, 17.27 per cent and Rajputs plus other Hindus, 15.83 per cent) of the total strength.[47] In the immediate context, the *mahzar* was possibly aimed at mobilizing support for Akbar among the ruling elite in order to overcome the rising discontent among the nobles over the introduction of branding regulations. This regulation was sought to be enforced rigorously by Akbar from 1574 with the help of a team of able and energetic officers, amongst whom men of Khurasani and Irani origin (for example, Muzaffar Khan Turbati, Khwaja Shah Mansur Shirazi) were conspicuous for their zeal.[48] The branding regulation, which adversely affected the autonomy

[45] The examples of theologians with Shiite leanings patronized by Akbar during this early period are those of Mir 'Ala al-Din Lari and Mir Murtaza Sharifi Shirazi. See 'Abdul Qadir Badauni, *Muntakhab-ut tawarikh* vol. II, pp. 55, 84, 198, and255; vol. III, pp. 67, 84. See also Rafi'uddin Shirazi, *Tazkirat ul-Muluk*, British Library Add. 23,883, MS., f. 177b.

[46] Abdul Qadir Badauni, *Muntakhab-ut tawarikh,* vol. II, p. 99; vol. III, p. 442.

[47] Iqtidar Alam Khan, 'The Nobility under Akbar', pp. 34–5.

[48] Both were Iranis who met violent deaths in 1580. Muzaffar Khan died fighting the rebels in Bengal and Shah Mansur was executed by Akbar on the charge of conspiring with Mirza Hakim. This charge was based on a forged letter planted by Shah Mansur's enemies at the court. See *Akbar-nama*, vol. III, pp. 116–18, 227, 290–4, 304, 501.

and benefits of the nobles, particularly alienated a large number of Turanis who till this time represented the largest racial grouping in the nobility. Many of the Iranis, whose strength in the higher ranks of the nobility had become sizeable by 1575, were possibly also alarmed by the measure.

Both these powerful groups appear to have reacted adversely to the *mahzar*. The Sunnis as well as the Shiites would have been put off by the suggestion of assigning the role of supreme arbiter in the interpretation of sources of Islamic law (*ijtihad*) to Akbar, for this smacked of an attempt to attribute to him the status of a true guide (*Mahdi*). Insofar as the *mahzar* implicitly restricted the scope of study and interpretation of the Islamic law (*ijtihad*) to orthodox schools, the *'asharis* were bound to perceive it as a move towards further restricting space for the practise of their faith in the Mughal Empire. It is significant that, subsequent to the *mahzar,* a *fatwa* of *kufr* against Akbar was issued by a Shiite divine, Mulla Muhammad Yazdi, who, according to Badauni, was earlier allowed by Akbar to make statements in his presence that were hurtful to Sunnis.[49] The text of Yazdi's *fatwa* is nowhere reproduced. But the circumstances suggest that its main point of reference was the *mahzar* signed exclusively by six leading Sunni divines of the realm, though five of them did so reluctantly.[50] One cannot but connect Mulla Muhammad Yazdi's response to the *mahzar* with the fact that in the rebellion of nobles during 1580–1, unlike the revolts of 1564–7, an appreciable number of Iranis were involved.[51] In short, the *mahzar* not only failed to

[49] Ibid., p. 309; *Muntakhab-ut Tawarikh,* vol. II, pp. 211, 276. Cf. S.A.A. Rizvi, *Religious and Intellectual History of Muslims in Akbar's Reign,* pp. 158, 161, 211.

[50] Cf. *Muntakhab-ut tawarikh,* vol. II, p. 270. The signatories were (1) Abdullah Sultanpuri (*Makhdum ul-Mulk*); (2) Shaikh 'Abdul Nabi; (3) Qazi Jalal al-Din of Multan; (4) Sadr-i Jahan, the *Mufti*; (5) Shaikh Mubarak; (6) Ghazi Khan Badakhshi.

[51] For the racial break-up of the total number of nobles participating in the revolt of 1580–1, see *Journal of the Royal Asiatic Society* (London), 1968, nos1 & 2, p. 36 (Appendix 4).

strengthen Akbar's hands but also tended to open up the sensitive issue of *ijtihad* that had the potential of alienating a very large section of Irani nobles as well.[52]

It is therefore understandable that soon after it was issued the *mahzar* was consigned to cold storage—to the extent that in 1594 Abul Fazl found it embarrassing to reproduce the text of this document as drafted by his own father, Shaikh Mubarak.

III

Akbar's turning away from the *mahzar* of 1579, and his recourse to a policy of total tolerance under the principle of *sulh-i kul* (Absolute Peace), appears to have paved the way for a fresh influx of Irani notables into the Mughal Empire. Shah 'Abbas I's harsh treatment of some of the local dignitaries and members of heterodox sects appears to have contributed significantly to this influx. As Arjomand puts it, 'many Nuqtawis, including a truly impressive number of poets, fled to India, Emperor Akbar's land of religious freedom.'[53] A letter written by Abul Fazl on Akbar's behalf to Mir Saiyed Ahmad Kashi, a Nuqtawi leader of Iran, as well as a revealing passage about him in *'Alam Ara-i 'Abbasi*, indicate that Akbar kept himself informed about the Nuqtawis and was also eager to win them over to his doctrine of *sulh-i kul.*[54]

Within this background, Akbar's advice to Shah Abbas in 1594 to follow his own example of making no distinction among his subjects on the basis of 'cult or creed' assumes special significance.[55] Shah 'Abbas, obviously, was not amused by this preaching of *sulh-i kul* by Akbar, not only because it militated against the *asna-i 'ashari* doctrines, but also because it amounted to interfering in the affairs of his empire.

[52] For a contrary argument, see S.A.A. Rizvi, *Religious and Intellectual History of Muslims* in *Akbar's Reign*, p. 158.

[53] Arjomand, *The Shadow of God and the Hidden Imam*, p. 198.

[54] Cf. Riazul Islam, *The Calendar of Documents on Indo-Persian Relations, 1500–1750,* vol. I, pp. 101-4.

[55] See ibid., vol. I, pp. 123–4 [Calendar no. A36].

This is reflected in one of Shah 'Abbas' letters to Akbar sent in 1599. While being respectful to the extent of comparing their mutual relations with those between a father and son, Shah 'Abbas expresses his disagreement with Akbar's doctrine of *sulh-i kul* and points out that all prophets have condemned lawless people (*ashqiya*).[56]

The Irani notables who came to the Mughal court during this time included distinguished men of letters like Nurullah Shustri, Shah Fath ul-lah Shirazi, Hakim Lutf ul-lah, Mulla Huzuni, Mulla Mirza, Jan Muzaffar Husain Sabzwari, and Jamal al-Din Anju. Some others who had arrived in India before 1580 but became famous at Akbar's court now included Hakim Abul Fath, his brothers Hakim Hammam and Hakim Nur al-Din, and also Saiyid Muhammad Jamal al-Din 'Urfi Shirazi and Sharif Amuli. Among them, perhaps the most distinguished was 'Urfi who, during his short stay at the court, earned enduring literary fame.[57] This accretion in the strength of the Iranis occupying high positions in the nobility, and Akbar's close personal association with many of them,[58] appear to have created the general impression that they were gaining an upper hand in the administration after sidelining the Turani and Rajput nobles.[59] It was perhaps this situation that was characterized by Badauni as the time when Iraqis (i.e. Shiite Iranis) were in great favour. At another place in the same context he speaks of Shiites having become predominant (*ghalib*) and Sunnis the conquered people (*maghlub*).[60]

[56] Ibid., vol. I, pp. 128–9 [Calendar no. A39].

[57] Cf. *Ruqa'at-i Hakim Abul Fath*, pp. 5, 19–20, 33; Badauni, *Muntakhab-ut Tawarikh*, vol. II, pp. 246–8, 315–16; vol. III, 137–8, 167–8, 285. See also S.A.A. Rizvi, *Religious and Intellectual History of Muslims in Akbar's Reign*, pp. 123–4, 191.

[58] Akbar's personal proximity to Shah Fath Ullah Shirazi is borne out by the following couplet composed by Faizi on his death. 'The Emperor of the world had his eyes full of tears at his death, Alexander wept tears of regret because Plato left the World.'

[59] See Aziz Koka's letter to Jahangir in an untitled collection of documents in Br. Library, MS., Add. 16, 859.

[60] Abu'l Fazl (*Akbar-nama*, vol. III, p. 273) admits that some 'wicked people had come to allege around this time that Akbar had become a Shiite.

IV

The increasing impact of Akbar's worldview, informed by his commitment to *sulh-i kul,* freed him entirely by the early 1580s from the constraints of orthodoxy.[61] In this new situation the Shiites among the Iranian nobles and state officials came for the first time to enjoy the freedom to openly practice their religious rites. According to Badauni, Shah Fath ul-lah Shirazi performed with great composure his Shiite prayers (*namaz*) inside the state hall (*diwan-khana-i khas*),[62] notwithstanding Akbar's disapproval of *namaz* of any kind.[63] It was from the early 1580s that Akbar began giving ecclesiastical Islamic offices of *qazis* and *sadrs* of *subas* as well as of the central government to known Shiites. Important appointments were those of Shah Fath Ullah Shirazi as *sadr us Sudur,*[64] of Nur ul-lah Shustari (known for his strong views on the question of *imamat* and commitment to *fiqh-i*

According to him, this misunderstanding was created by Akbar's policy of allowing the Shiites to present their point of view frankly in the discussions of the *Ibadatkhana.* For Badauni's comment on this situation, see *Muntakhab-ut tawarikh,* vol. II, p. 308. My attention to this evidence was directed by its citation in Nawab Muhammad Abbas Talib Safavi's scholarly Urdu work *Din-i Ilahi ke anasir-i arb'a,* Lucknow, 1556, p. 83.

[61] See my paper in the *Journal of the Royal Asiatic Society,* London, nos. 1&2, 1968, where I have studied the development of Akbar's religious policy of the earlier phase ending in the 'debacle' of the *mahzar* (1579). It is suggested that, subsequent to 1580–1, Akbar's enlightened religious policy based on his philosophy of *sulh-i kul* unfolded more or less smoothly.

[62] Badauni, *Muntakhab-ut Tawarikh,* vol. II, p. 316.

[63] See *Akbar-nama,* MS. Br. Library, Add. 27, 247, f.404a, for a memorandum recorded by Akbar on requests and queries by his son Murad, then deputed to govern Malwa, sometime in 1591. To a query on whether performing *namaz* inside the army was to be 'forbidden', Akbar replied that a person performing *namaz* deserved 'admonition [*nasihat*]' so as to help him see 'the path of reason [*rah-i 'aql*].' But if he persisted in his ways, such a person was not to be forced to abandon his rites of worship as that would amount to a violation of *sulh-i kul.* See also Iqtidar Alam Khan, 'Akbar's Personality Traits and World Outlook—A Critical Reappraisal', in *Akbar and His India,* ed. Irfan Habib, Delhi, 1997, p. 95.

[64] Badauni, *Muntakhab-ut Tawarikh,* vol. II, p. 343.

Ja'fria) as the *qazi* of Lahore,[65] and of Hakim Hammam as *sadr* of the region 'to the east of Ganges'. [66]

This was obviously a new situation, where even ordinary persons subscribing to *asna-i 'ashari* doctrines would no longer be obliged to resort to subterfuges (*taqiyya*) for the practice of their piety. The example of some of the nobles and highly placed officials of Iranian origin observing *asna-i 'ashari* rites publicly and with great ceremony could also draw to them many Indian Muslims with a *tafzili* bent of mind. The *tafzili* trend was strong among Indian Muslims from quite an early date. It was, for example, inherent in the teaching and rites of the Chishti *sufis,* the most influencial mystic order in India.[67] Several other popular cults centring round semi-mythical figures of *darweshes* and *qalandars* in different parts of the subcontinent also popularized the idea of 'Ali being the first (*'Ali ka pahla number* in a modern popular formula) after the Prophet in the Islamic spiritual hierarchy.[68] A near-*tafzili* attitude rooted in Islamic mysticism is also discernible in the beliefs of some of the Turani nobles influenced by the confluence of orthodox and *imamia* doctrines in Timurid Khurasan under Sultan Husain Baiqara.[69] The surviving relatives of Babur's nobles, like Muhammad Qasim Khan Shaibani and others who had been with Sultan Husain Baiqara before joining Babur in 1506, as well as the grandchildren of Sultan Husain Baiqara—some of whom were still with Akbar in the 1580s—may be counted in

[65] Ibid., vol. III, p. 138.

[66] Ibid., vol. II, p. 296.

[67] For Shaikh Nizam al-Din's sayings emphasizing the *Fazilat* of 'Ali, see *Fawaid ul Fawad,* rpnt with Urdu translation by Hasan Sani Nizami, New Delhi, 1999, pp. 329–30, 422–3.

[68] For example the cult of Shahbaz Qalandar in Sind. The Urdu line (*Ali ka pahla number*) is from a devotional song of the cult. Cf. *Dabistan-i Mazahib,* Lucknow, Nawal Kishore, 1904, pp. 215–16, for the notice on the cult of Saiyid Jalal Bukhari: the practitioners justified their practices with reference to Safavid customs.

[69] On the trend towards Shiism in Khurasan under Sultan Husain Baiqara, see S.A.A. Rizvi, *Religious and Intellectual History of Muslims in Akbar's Reign,* p. 48; B.S. Amoretti in *Cambridge History of Iran,* vol. 6, p. 612.

this category of Turanis. The Mughal ruling family was also not immune to the attraction of *tafzili* ideas. Among Babur's sons, for example, Mirza Kamran was a staunch Sunni. Such an assertion cannot, however, be made with any measure of certainty about Humayun, 'Askari, and Hindal. Humayun's commitment to Sunnism was tempered by his scholarly inquiries into its precepts as well as by his interest in Greek philosophy and *Ishraqi* doctrines, to the point of his sometimes claiming *tafzili* beliefs and outlook. Kamran's own brother 'Askari also had a mystic bent of mind; for him 'the source of inspiration [*mushrab*]' was more important than 'the religious order [*mazhab*]'.[70] Another close relation of the ruling family, Mirza Sulaiman of Badakhshan is known to have been greatly devoted to the Shaikhs of the Chishti order.[71]

In short, the wide prevalence of *tafzili* sentiment combined with the presence of a large number of Shiite Iranis—who had the freedom to observe their rites openly in the latter half of Akbar's reign—appears to have favoured the emergence of a community of Shiite Muslims in Mughal India in the sixteenth century. That already by the early 1580s urban pockets of Shiite Muslim population existed in the Mughal Empire is borne out by Montserrat's description of the 'Musalmans' observing Muharram with 'lamentation and tears' and by walking over fire, all the time shrieking "Asson Hossen" [Hasan-Husain].' This description conforms to the mourning over the martyrdom of Imam Husain as practised by Shiites. But it also, very significantly, indicates that all the Muslims of a town participated in the gathering of the tenth day of Muharram, and no one there objected to the Shiite form of mourning.[72] Ordinary Muslims apparently accepted a coexistence which theologians found unacceptable.

[70] *Muzakkar-i Ahbab,* pp. 107–?7, 216; Muhammad Qasim Firishta (*Tarikh-i Firishta,* vol. I, p. 237) quotes Humayun as saying to Shah Tahmasp that, unlike his brother Mirza Kamran, he always had 'love for the family of the Prophet [*muhabbat-i khandan-i risalat*]'.

[71] Ibid., p. 124.

[72] Montserrat, *The Commentary of Father Montserrat,* tr. J.S. Hoyland and S.N. Banerji, Oxford, 1922, pp. 21–2. I owe this reference to Dr S. Ali Nadeem Rezavi.

Bibliography

For the reader's convenience, pre-modern sources appear below first in a chronological order, then in alphabetical order

Pre-modern Sources (in Chronological Order)

'Ali ibn Hamid Kufi, *Chach-namah* (1216–17), ed. Umar ibn Daudpota, Haiderābad, 1939.

Juvaini, *Tarikh-i Jahankushai* (1260), ed. Mirza Muhammad Qazvini, vol. II, London, 1912.

Fawaid ul- fawad (1309), compiled by Amir Hasan Sanjari, Urdu translation by Hasan Sani Nizami, New Delhi, 1999.

Ibn-i Khaldun, *The Muqaddimah* (1379), tr. F.R. Rosenthal, vol. I, London, 1958.

Babur's Order, text published in *The Oriental College Magazine*, May 1933.

Tuzuk-i Baburi, MS., Br. Library Or. 3714.

Babur-nama, tr. A.S. Beveridge, London, 1912; rpnt, 1969.

Zain al-Din Khwafi (d. 1533–4), *Fath-nama* describing the battle of Khanua, reproduced by Babur; see A.S. Beveridge, *The Babur-nama in English*, London, 1912.

Zain-al Din Wasafi (d. 1539), *Badai 'ul- Waqa'i Wasafi*, ed. Alexander Baldin, Moscow, 1961.

Ruknuddin, *Lataif-i Quddusi* (1538), Delhi, 1311 AH/AD 1894.

Maktubat-i Quddusiya (collection of Shaikh 'Abdul Quddus' letters), Matb'-i Ahmadi, Delhi (no date).

Khwandamir, *Tarikh-i Shah Ismail wa Tahmasp Safavi,* ed. Ali Jarrah, Tahran, 1370 Shamsi.

Khwandamir, *Qanun-i Humayuni* (1533–4), ed. Hidayat Husain, Calcutta, 1940.

Mirza Haidar Doghlat, *Tarikh-i Rashidi* (*circa* 1546), tr. Denison Ross, London, 1895–8, and also Aligarh MS. University Collection, no. 34.

Sidi Ali Reis, *Travels and Adventures of a Turkish. Admiral (1553–56)*, tr. A. Vamberey, London, 1899.

Khwarshah b. Qubad-al Husaini, *Tarikh-i Ilchi-i Nizam Shah* (1562–3), MS., British Library (Rieu, I, 107a, Suppt 32).

'Alaud Daula Qazwini, *Nafais ul-Maasir* (1565–6), MS., British Library, Add 22,831 (Rieu i, 404).

Khwaja Baha al-Din Hasan Nisari, *Muzakkar-i Ahbab* (1566), ed. S.M. Faziullah, Hyderabad, 1969.

Amir Mahmud b. Khwand-Amir, *Tarikh-i Shah Ismail wa Tahmasp Safavi* (1576), ed. Ali Jarrah, Tahran, 1370 Shamsi.

Miyan Mustafa Bandagi, *Majalis*, Mataba Ibrahimia, Haiderabad, AH 1367.

Gulbadan Begum, *Humayun-nama* (1578), ed. A.S. Beveridge, London, 1902.

'Abbas Khan, *Tarikh-i Sher Shahi* (1579), MS., India Office, Ethe, 219.

Monserrat, Antonio, *Commentary on his Journey to the Court of Akbar* (1580–3), tr. J.S. Hoyland, annotated by S.N. Banerjee, Calcutta, 1922.

Bayazid Bayat, *Tazkira-i Humayun wa Akbar* (1585), ed. Hidayat Husain, Calcutta, 1941.

Rizqullah Mushtaqi (d. 1581), *Waqiat-i Mushtaqi*, MS., British Library, Or. 1929.

'Arif Qandahari, *Tarikh-i Akbari* (1584), Aligarh transcript of Rampur MS., ed. Imtiyaz 'Ali 'Arish, Rampur, 1962.

Jauhar Aftabchi, *Tazkirat ul- Waqi'at* (1586–7), MS., British Library, Add, 16.711.

Ruqq'at-i Hakim Abu'l Fath Gilalni (1588–9), ed. Muhammad Bashir Husain, Lahore, 1968.

'Abdul Haq Muhaddis, *Akhbar ul- Akhyar* (1588), Delhi (1322 AH).

Tarikh-i Alfi, (1588–9), MS. India Office, Ethe 12.

John Leyden and William Erskine, *Memoirs of Zehir-ed-Din Muhammad Babar (mainly from Persian Version prepared by 'Abdul Rahim Khan-i Khanan in 1589–90)*, London, 1826.

Faizi Sirhindi (d. 1592–3), *Akbar-nama*, MS., Br. Library, Or. 169.

Nizam al-Din Ahmad, *Tabaqat-i Akbari* (1593–4), Lucknow, Nawal Kishore, 1875.

Nizam al-Din Ahmad, *Tabaqat-i Akbari* (1593–4), ed. B. De, Calcutta, 1913.

Abul Fazl, *Akbar-nama* (1594) first draft, MS. Br. Library Ad. 27247.

Abul Fazal, *Akbar-nama* (1594), ed. Agha Ahmad Ali, *et al.*, Calcutta, 1827.

Abul Fazal, *Ain-i Akbari* (1598–9), ed. H. Blochmann, Calcutta, 1868.

Abul Fazal, *Ain-i Akbari* (1598–9), Lucknow, Nawal Kishore, 1892.

'Abdul Qadir Badauni (d. 1595–6 or 1597–8), *Muntakhab-ut-Tawarikh*, vol. I, Calcutta, 1864–9; vol. II, Calcutta, 1877 or 1895–9; vol. III, Calcutta, 1864–9.

'Abdul Haq Muhaddis, *Tarikh-i Haqqi*, (1596–7), tr. Henry Eliot, *History of India*, vol. VI, reprint, Allahabad, 1964.

'Abul Qasim Namakin, *Munshiat-i Namakin* (1605–9), MS., University Collection, no. 26, Maulana Azad Library, AMU, Aligarh.

'Aziz Koka's Letter to Jahangir, Br. Library MS., Add. 16, 859.

Nur al- Din Khaqani, *Akhlaq-i Jahangiri*, MS., Subhanullah (AMU, Aligarh), MS. 891.0026.

Muhammad Qasim Hindu Shah, *Tarikh-i Firishta* (1606–7), Lucknow, Nawal Kishore, 1884.

Rafi'uddin Ibrahim Shirazi, *Tazkirat ul-Mulk* (1609), MS., British Library, Add. 23,883.

Ni'amat-ul-lah, *Tarikh-i Khan Jahani* (1613), ed. Imad-ud Din, Dacca, 1960.

Gausi Shattari, *Gulzar-i Abrar* (1613), MS. John Rylands Library.

Ahmad Yadgar, *Tarikh-i Shahi* (1614), ed. Hidayat Husain, Bib. Ind. Series.

Sikandar b. Manjhu, *Mirat-i Sikandari* (1615), tr. F.L. Faridi, Bombay, 1899.

'Abdul Baqi Nahawandi, *Maasir-i Rahimi* (1616), ed. Hidayat Husain, Calcutta, 1910–31.

Mirza Kamran, *Mirza-nama* (1618–19), text and English translation published by Hidayat Husain, *Journal of the Asiatic Society of Bengal*, 1913.

Mutamad Khan, *Iqbalnama-i Jahagiri* (1620), Lucknow, Nawal Kishore, 1870.

Jahangir (d. 1627), *Tuzuk-i Jahangiri*, ed. Saiyid Ahmad, Ghazipur and Aligarh, 1863–4.

F.S. Manrique, *Travels 1629–43*, tr. C.E. Luard and H. Hoston, London, 1927.

Yusuf Mirak, *Mazhar-i Shahjahani* (1634), ed. Pir Hasamuddin Rashidi, Part 2, Karachi, 1961.

Shaikh Nurul Haq (d. 1662), *Zubdat-ut Tawarikh*, tr. H.M. Elliot and John Dowson, *History of India as told by its own Historians*, vol. VI, London, 1964.

Bernier François, *Travels in the Mughal Empire, A.D. 1668*, tr. Archibald Constable, second revised edn, ed. Vincent A. Smith, London, 1916.

Niccolao Manucci, *Storia do Mogor, 1656–1712*, tr. William Irvine, vol. I (London, 1907–8), reprint, Calcutta, 1965.

'Abdullah, *Tarikh-i Daudi* (1669), ed. Shaikh 'Abdul Rashid, Aligarh, 1969.

'Mobid', Dabistan-i Mazahib, ed. Nazar Ashraf, Calcutta, 1809, reprint, Lucknow, Nawal Kishore, 1904.

Sheikh Farid Bhakkari, *Zakhiratul Khwanin* (mid seventeenth century), ed. Moinul Haq, Karachi, 1961.

'Inayat-ul-lah Kanboh (d. 1674–5), *Tarikh-i Dilkusha*, MS., Cambridge, King's, 71.

Waqa'i Sarkar Ajmer wa Ranthambhor (1678–80), MS., Asafia Library, Hyderabad, *Fan-i Tarikh*, Aligarh transcription.

Bhimsen, *Nuskha-i Dilkusha* (1708–9), Br. Library, Or. 23.

Mahmud Shivani, *Faiz Aam* (a summary of mathnavi written in AH 1141/AD 1728–9.

Khafi Khan, *Muntakhab al-Lubab* (1731), ed. Maulana Kabir al-Din Ahmad, 2 pts, Calcutta, 1860–70.

Iqbal-nama (anonymous author eyewitness down to 1734), Rampur MS.

Tek Chand Bahar, *Bahar-i 'Ajam* 1739–40), Lucknow, Nawal Kishore, 1336/1916.

Shah Nawaz Khan, *Ma'asir-ul Umara* (1742–7), ed. Ashraf Ali, Calcutta, 1888–91.

'Ali Ahmad Khan, *Mirat-i Ahmadi* (1761), ed. Nawab 'Ali, vol. I, Baroda, 1928.

Muhammad Baksh Ashob, *Tarikh-i Shahdat-i Farrukh-siyar w julus-i Muhammad Shah* (1782), Br. Library MS., Rieu, III, 944–5.

Ghulam Husian, *Riaz us-Salatin: A History of Bangal* (1787–8), tr. Abdus Salam, rpnt, Delhi, 1975.

Nand Ram Khayasth, *Siyaq-nama*, Lucknow, 1879.

Haft Risala-i Taqwim al-Buldan (18th century?), MS., 45, Buhar Collection, National Library, Calcutta.

Sharaif-i 'Usmani (a local history of Bilgram compiled in the eighteenth century carrying texts of a large number of documents), MS., Department of History, AMU, Aligarh.

Shyamaldas, *Vir Vinod* (nineteenth-century Rajasthani text), vol. 4, Udaipur (year of publication not indicate).

Muhammad Ghiyasuddin, *Ghiyas ul-Lughat* (1825–6), Kanpur, Nawal Kishore, 1878.

Pre-modern Sources (in Alphabetical Order)

Abul Fath Gilani, *Ruqq'at-i Hakim Abul Fath Gilani* (1988–9), ed. Muhammad Bashir Husain, Lahore, 1968.

'Abbas Khan, *Tarikh-i Sher Shahi* (1579), MS., India Office, Ethe, 219.

Abul Fazl, *Ain-i Akbari*, ed. H. Blochmann, Calcutta, 1868.

———, *Ain-i Akbari*, Lucknow, Nawal Kishore, 1892.

———, *Akbar-nama* (1594), ed. Agha Ahmad Ali, *et al.*, Calcutta, 1827.

———, *Akbar-nama* (first draft) MS, Br. Library, Ad. 27247.

'Abdul Baqi Nahawandi, *Maasir-i Rahimi* (1616), ed. Hidayat Husain, Calcutta, 1910–31.

'Abdul Haq Muhaddis, *Tarikh-i Haqqi* (1596–7), tr. H.M. Eliot, *History of India*, vol. VI, reprint, Allahabad, 1964.

'Abdul Haq Muhaddis, *Akhbar ul-Akhyar* (1590), Delhi (1322 AH).

Abdullah, *Tarikh-i Dandi* (1669), ed. Shaikh 'Abdul Rashid, Aligarh, 1969.

'Abdul Qadir Badauni (d. 1595–6 or 1597–8), *Muntakhab-ut-Tawarikh*, vol. I, Calcutta, 1864–9; vol. II, Calcutta, 1877 or 1895–9; vol. III, Calcutta, 1864–9.

'Abul Qasim Namakin, *Munshiat-i Namakin* (1605–9), MS., University Collection, no. 26, Maulana Azad Library, AMU, Aligarh.

Alaud Daula Qazwini, *Nafais ul-Maasir* (1565–6), 1574–5, MS., British Library. Add 22,831 (Rieu i, 404).

'Ali Ahmad Khan, *Mirat-i Ahmadi* (1761), ed. Nawab 'Ali, vol. I, Baroda, 1928.

'Ali ibn Hamid Kufi, *Chach-namah* (1216-17), ed. Umar ibn Daudpota, Haiderābad, 1939.

Amir Hasan Sanjari, *Fawaid ul- fawad* (1309), Urdu translation by Hasan Nizami, New Delhi, 1999.

'Arif Qandahari, *Tarikh-i Akbari* (1584), Aligarh transcript of Rampur MS., ed. Imtiyaz 'Ali 'Arish, Rampur, 1962.

Ahmad Yadgar, *Tarikh-i Shahi* (1614), ed. Hidayat Husain, Bib. Ind. Series.

Amir Mahmud b. Khwand-Amir, *Tarikh-i Shah Ismail wa Tahmasp Safavi* (1576), ed. Ali Jarrah, Tahran, 1370 Shamsi.

'Aziz Koka's Letter to Jahangir, Br. Library MS., Add. 16, 859.

Babur-nama, tr. by A.S. Beveridge, London, 1912; rpnt, 1969.

Babur, *Tuzuk-i Baburi*, MS., Br. Library Or. 3714.

Babur's order, text published in *The Oriental College Magazine*, May 1933.

Baha al-Din Hasan Nisari, Khwaja, *Muzakkar-i Ahbab* (1566), ed. S.M. Faziullah, Hyderabad, 1969.

Bayazid Bayat, *Tazkira-i Humayun wa Akbar* (1585), ed. Hidayat Husain, Calcutta, 1941.

Bernier, François, *Travels in the Mughal Empire, A.D. 1668*, tr. Archibald Constable, second edition, revised by Vincent A. Smith, London, 1916.

Bhimsen, *Nuskha-i Dilkusha* (1708–9), Br. Library, Or. 23.

Dabistan-i Mazahib, ed. Nazar Ashraf, Lucknow, Nawal Kishore, 1904, rpnt Calcutta, 1809.

Faizi Sirhindi (d. 1592–3), *Akbar-nama*, MS., Br. Library, Or. 169.

Farid Bukhari, Sheikh, *Zakhiratul khwanin* (mid seventeenth century), ed. Moinul Haq, Karachi, 1961.

Gausi Shattari, *Gulzar-i Abrar* (1613), MS. John Rylands Library.

Ghulam Husain, *Riaz us-Salatin: A History of Bangal* (1787–8), tr. Abdus Salam, rpnt, Delhi, 1975.

Gulbadan Begum, *Humayun-nama* (1578), ed. A.S. Beveridge, London, 1902.

Haft Risala-i Taqwim al-Buldan, MS., 45, Buhar Collection, National Library, Calcutta.

Ibn-i Khaldun, *The Muqaddimah* (1379), tr. F.R. Rosenthal, vol. I, London, 1958.

'Inayat-ul-lah Kanboh (d. 1674–5), *Tarikh-i Dilkusha*, MS., Cambridge, King's, 71.

Iqbal-nama (anonymous author, eyewitness down to 1734), Rampur MS.

Jahangir (d. 1627), *Tuzuk-i Jahangiri*, ed. Saiyid Ahmad, Ghazipur and Aligarh, 1863–4.

Jauhar Aftabchi, *Tazkirat ul-Waqi'at* (1586–7), MS., British Library, Add. 16.711.

Juvaini, *Tarikh-i Jahankushai* (1260), ed. Mirza Muhammad Qazvini, vol. II, London, 1912.

Khafi Khan, *Muntakhab al-Lubab* (1731), ed. Maulana Kabir al-Din Ahmad, 2 pts, Calcutta, 1860–70.

Khwandamir, *Qanun-i Humayuni* (1533–4), ed. Hidayat Husain, Calcutta, 1940.

———, *Tarikh-i Shah Ismail wa Tahmasp Safavi,* ed. Ali Jarrah, Tahran, 1370 Shamsi.

Khwarshah b. Qubad-al Husaini, *Tarikh-i Ilchi-i Nizam Shah* (1562–3), MS., British Library (Rieu, I, 107 a, Suppt 32).

Leyden, John and William Erskine, *Memoirs of Zehir-ed-Din Muhammad Babar (Mainly from the Persian version),* London, 1826.

Mahmud Shirani, *Faiz-i 'Aam* (a summary of a *mathnavi* written in AH 1141/AD 1728–9), *Oriental College Magazine*, 1940.

Maktubat-i Quddusiya (collection of Shaikh Abdul Quddus' letters), Matb'a-i Ahmadi, Delhi (no date).

Manrique, F.S., *Travels 1629–43*, tr. C.E. Luard and H.Hoston, London, 1927.

Manucci, Niccolao, *Storia do Mogor, 1656–1712*, tr. William Irvine, vol. I (London, 1907–8), reprint, Calcutta, 1965.

Mirza Haidar Doghlat, *Tarikh-i Rashidi* (*circa* 1545), Aligarh MS. University Collection, no. 34; and translation by Denison Ross, London, 1895–8.

Mirza Kamran, *Mirza-nama* (1618–19), text and English translation published by Hidayat Husain, *Journal of the Asiatic Society of Bengal*, 1913.

Miyan Mustafa Bandagi, *Majalis*, Mataba Ibrahimia, Haiderabad, AH 1367.

'Mobid', *Dabistan-i Mazahib*, ed. Nazar Ashraf, Calcutta, 1809, reprint, Lucknow, Nawal Kishore, 1904.

Monserrat, Antonio, *Commentary on His Journey to the Court of Akbar*, tr. J.S. Hoyland and annotated by S.N. Banerjee, Calcutta, 1922.

Muhammad Baksh Ashob, *Tarikh-i Shahdat-i Farrukh-siyar w julus-i Muhammad Shah* (1782), Br. Library MS., Rieu, III, 944–5.

Muhammad Ghiyasuddin, *Ghiyas ul-Lughat* (1825–6), Kanpur, Nawal Kishore, 1878.

Muhammad Qasim Hindu Shah, *Tarikh-i Firishta* (1606–7), Lucknow, Nawal Kishore, 1884.

Mutamad Khan, *Iqbalnama-i Jahangiri* (1620), Lucknow, Nawal Kishore, 1870.

Nand Ram Khayasth, *Siyaq-nama*, Lucknow, 1879.

Ni'amat-ul-lah, *Tarikh-i Khan Jahani* (1613), ed. Imad-ud Din, Dacca, 1960.

Nizam al-Din Ahmad, *Tabaqat-i Akbari* (1593–4), ed. B. De, Calcutta, 1913.

Nizam al-Din Ahmad, *Tabaqat-i Akbari* (1593–4), Lucknow, Nawal Kishore, 1875.

Nur al-Din Khaqani, *Akhlaq-i Jahangiri*, MS., Subhanullah (AMU, Aligarh), MS. 891.0026.

Rafi'uddin Ibrahim Shirazi, *Tazkirat ul-Muluk* (1609), MS., British Library, Add. 23,883.

Rizqullah Mushtaqi (d. 1581), *Waqiat-i Mushtaqi*, MS., British Library, Or. 1929.

Ruknuddin, *Lataif-i Quddusi* (1538), Delhi, AH 1311/AD 1894.

Shah Nawaz Khan, *Ma'asir-ul Umara* (1742–7), ed. Ashraf Ali, Calcutta, 1888–91.

Shaikh Nurul Haq (d. 1662), *Zubdat-ut Tawarikh*, tr. H.M. Elliot and John Dowson, *History of India as Told by its Own Historians*, vol. VI, London, 1964.

Sharaif-i 'Usmani (a local history of Bilgram compiled in the eighteenth century carrying texts of a large number of documents), MS., Department of History, AMU, Aligarh.

Sheikh Farid Bhakkari, *Zakhiratul Khwanin* (mid seventeenth century), ed. Moinul Haq, Karachi, 1961.

Shyamaldas, *Vir Vinod* (nineteenth-century Rajasthani text), vol. 4, Udaipur, year of publication not indicated.

Sidi 'Ali Reis, *Travels and Adventures of a Turkish Admiral (1553-56)*, tr. A. Vamberey, London, 1899.

Sikandar b. Manjhu, *Mirat-i Sikandari* (1615), tr. F.L. Faridi, Bombay, 1899.

Tarikh-i Alfi (1588–9), MS. India Office, Ethe 12.

Tek Chand Bahar, *Bahar-i 'Ajam*, (1739–40), Lucknow, Nawal Kishore, 1336/1916.

Waqa'i Sarkar Ajmer wa Ranthambhor (1678–80), MS., Asafia Library, Hyderabad, *Fan-i Tarikh*, Aligarh transcription.

Yusuf Mirak, *Mazhar-i Shahhjahani* (1634), ed. Pir Hasamuddin Rashidi, Part 2, Karachi, 1961.

Zain al-Din Khwafi (d. 1533–4), *Fath-nama* describing the battle of Khanua, reproduced by Babur; see A.S.Beveridge, *The Babur-nama in English*.

Zain-al Din Wasafi (d. 1539), *Bada'i ul-Waqa'i Wasafi*, ed. Alexander Baldin, Moscow, 1961.

Modern Works

Afzal Husain, 'Growth of Irani Elements in Akbar's Nobility' *Proceedings of the History Congress*, 36th Session 1975.

Alam, Muzaffar, *The Languages of Political Islam in India, c. 1200–1800*, New Delhi, 2004.

——— and Sanjay Subrahmanyam (ed.), *The Mughal State, 1626–1750*, Delhi, 1998.

Amorett, B.S., 'Religion in the Timurid and Safavid Period', in *The Cambridge History of Iran*, vol. 6, ed. Peter Jackson and Laurence Lockhart, Cambridge, 1986.

Asher, Catherine B. and Cynthia Tablot, in *India before Europe*, New Delhi, 2005.

Arjomand, S.A., *The Shadow of God and the Hidden Imam*, Chicago, 1984.

Athar Ali, *The Mughal Nobility under Aurangzeb*, Bombay, 1966.

———, 'Mughal Empire in History', Presidential Address, Section II (Medieval India), *Indian History Congress*, 33rd Session, Muzaffarpur, 1972.

———, 'Towards an Interpretation of the Mughal Empire', *Journal of the Royal Asiatic Society*, London, no. 1, 1978.

———, 'Akbar and Islam', in *Islamic Society and Culture: Essays in Honour of Professor Aziz Ahmad*, ed. Milton Israel and N.K. Wagle, New Delhi, 1983.

———, 'The Religious World of Jahangir', *Proceedings of the Indian History Congress*, 51st Session, Calcutta, 1990.

———, *Mughal India: Studies in Polity, Ideas, Society and Culture*, New Delhi, 2006.

Ayalon, David, *Gunpowder and Firearms in the Mamluk Kingdom*, London, 1962.

Bausani, A. in *Cambridge History of Iran*, vol. 4, ed. J.A. Boyle, 1968.

Beach, Milo Cleveland, 'Mughal Rajput Painting', in *The New Cambridge History of India*, vol. I, Cambridge, 1992.

Brown, Percy, *Indian Architecture*, Calcutta, 1942.

Chandra, Satish, *Parties and Politics at the Mughal Court*, Bombay, 1979.

Digby, Simon, 'Shaikh 'Abdul Quddus Gangohi (AD 1456–1537): The Personality and Attitude of a Medieval Indian Sufi', *Medieval India: A Miscellany*, vol. III, Aligarh, 1975.

Fuhrer, A., *The Monumental Antiquities and Inscriptions in Western Provinces and Oudh*, Allahabad, 1891.

Gommans, Jos, *Mughal Warfare*, London, 2002.

Grewal, J.S., ed., *The State and Society in Medieval India*, New Delhi, 2005.

Habib, Irfan, 'The Political Role of Shaikh Ahmad Sirhind and Shah Waliullah', *Proceedings of the Indian History Congress*, Aligarh, 23rd Session, 1960.

———, *Agrarian System of Mughal India*, Bombay, 1963.

———, 'Aspects of Agrarian Relations and Economics in a Region of Uttar Pradesh during the Sixteenth Century, *The Indian Economic and Social History Review*, vol. IV, no. 3, September 1967.

———, 'Reason and Science in Medieval India' cyclostyled paper presented at the South Asian Studies Conference, Australia, 1981 (unpublished).

———, *An Atlas of the Mughal Empire*, Delhi, 1982.

———, 'A Political Theory for the Mughal Empire—A Study of the Ideas of Abu'l Fazl', *Proceedings of the Indian History Congress*, 59th Session, Patiala, 1998.

———, ed., *Religion in Indian History*, New Delhi, 2007.

Hadi Hasan, 'Qasim Kahi (AH 868–988), His Life, Times and Work', *Islamic Culture*, Hyderabad, July 1953.

Haider, Najaf, 'Coins and Silver Crises', in *Economic History of Medieval India, 1200–1500*, ed. Irfan Habib, New Delhi, 2011.

Hasan, Nurul, 'The *Mahzar*' of Akbar's Reign', *Journal of U.P. History Society*, vol. XVI, pt I, 1943.

Hodiwala, S.H., *Historical Studies in Mughal Numismatics*, Calcutta, 1923.

———, *Studies in Indo-Muslim History*, Bombay, 1957.

Ibn Hasan, *Central Structure of the Mughal Empire*, London, 1936.

Khan, A.R., 'Babur's Settlement of His Conquests in Hindustan', *Proceedings of the Indian History Congress*, Patiala, 1967 (Patna, 1968).

———, 'Gradation of Nobility under Babur', *Islamic Culture*, vol. IX, no. 1, Hyderabad, January 1986.

Khan, Iqtidar Alam, 'The Nobility under Akbar and the Development of his Religious Policy, 1560–80', *Journal of Royal Asiatic Society*, London, nos 1 and 2, 1968.

———, 'Mughal Court Politics during Bairam Khan's Regency', *Medieval India—A Miscellany*, I, Aligarh/Bombay, 1969.

———, 'The Turko-Mongol Theory of Kingship', *Medieval India: A Miscellany*, vol. II, 1972.

———, *The Political Biography of a Mughal Noble: Mun'im Khan Khan-i Khanan, 1497–1575*, New Delhi, 1973.

———, 'The Kawansarays of Mughal India, A Study of Surviving Structures', *Indian Historical Review*, vol. XIV, nos 1-2, July 1987 and January 1988.

———, 'The Mughal Assignment System during Akbar's Early Years, 1556–1575', *Medieval India—1: Researches in the History of India*, ed. Irfan Habib, Delhi, 1992.

———, 'Nature of Gunpowder Artillery in India during the Sixteenth century: A Reappraisal of the Impact of European Gunnery', *Journal of the Royal Asiatic Society*, London, third series, vol. 9, pt I, April 1999.

———, 'State in Mughal India: Re-examining the Myths of a Counter Vision', *Social Scientist*, vol. 30, nos 1-2, January–February, 2001.

———, *Gunpowder and Firearms: Warfare in Medieval India*, New Delhi, 2004.

———, 'Hindu Chiefs in Sultanate Polity (13th and 14th Centuries)', *Studies in Peoples' History*, vol. I, issue I, June 2014.

———, 'Wizarat under Humayun (1545–1555)', *Medieval India Quarterly*, vol. V, no.1.

———, ed., *Akbar and His Age*, Indian Council of Historical Research, New Delhi, 1999.

Koch, Ebba, *Mughal Architecture: An Outline of its History and Development*, Munich, 1991.

Kolff, D.H., *Naukar, Rajput and Sepoy: The Ethnohistory of the Military Labour Market of Hindustan, 1450–1850*, Cambridge, 1991.

Kondo, Osama, *The Early Modern Monarchies in Mughal India*, Kyoto, 2012.

Laski, Harold, 'Social Contract', in *Encyclopaedia of Social Science*, vols. XIII and XIV, 1932.

McAuliffe, M.A., *The Sikh Religion: Sacred Writings and Authors*, vol. I, Oxford, 1909, rpnt, 1963.

Mehdi Hasan, *Tughlaq Dynasty: The Study of a Civilization*, New Delhi, 2007.

Moosvi, Shireen, 'Formulation Land Revenue Rates under Akbar until 1596–7', *Journal of the Royal Asiatic Society*, London, no. 2, 1980.

———, 'The Evolution of the *Mansabdari* System under Akbar until 1596–7', *Journal of the Royal Asiatic Society*, London, no. 1, 1981.

Moreland, W.H., *The Agrarian System of Mughal India*, rpnt, Delhi, 1968.

———, *The Agrarian System of Muslim India, 1600–1800*, Cambridge, 1929, rpnt, Allahabad.

Muhammad Abbas Talib Safavi, *Din-i Ilahi ke anasir-i arb'a*, Lucknow, 1956.

Mukherjee, Taropad and Irfan Habib, 'Akbar and the Temples of Mathura and Its Environs', *Proceedings of the Indian History Congress*, 1987.

Nizami, K.A., *Tarikh-i Mashaikh-i Chisht*, Delhi, 1957.

———, *Salatin-i Delhi ke Mazhabi Rujhanat*, Delhi, 1958.

Prasad, Ishwari, *The Mughal Empire*, Allahabad, 1976.

Platts, John T. *A Dictionary of Urdu, Classical Hindi and English*, London, rpnt, New Delhi, 1977.

Qanungo, K.R., in *History of Bengal*, ed. J.N. Sarkar, Dacca, 1948.

Qureshi, I.H., *The Administration of the Mughal Empire*, Karachi, 1966.

Qazi Mukhtar Ahmad, 'Was Bairam Khan a Rebel?', *Islamic Culture*, 1947.

Ray, S.K., *Bairam Khan*, Karachi, 1992.

——, 'The Execution of Tardi Beg Khan', *Indian Historical Quarterly*, June 1952.

Riazul Islam, *Indo–Persian Relations*, Lahore, 1970.

——, *The Calendar of Documents on Indo–Persian Relations, 1500–1750*, vol. I.

Richard, J.F., *The New Cambridge History of India: The Mughal Empire*, Cambridge, 1993.

Rieu, Charles, *Catalogue of Persian Manuscripts in the British Museum*, London, 1895.

Rizvi, S.A.A., *Muslim Revivalist Movements in Northern India in the Sixteenth and Seventeenth Centuries*, Agra, 1964.

——, *Religious and Intellectual Histrory of Muslims in Akbar's Reign with Reference to Abul Fazl*, New Delhi, 1975.

Rushbrook Williams, *An Empire Builder of the Sixteenth Century*, Delhi, S. Chand & Co., rpnt (no date line), New Delhi.

Safa, Z., 'Persian Literature in the Safavid Period', in *The Cambridge History of Iran*, vol. 6, ed. Peter Jackson and Laurence Lockhart, Cambridge, 1986.

———, *Mughal Administration*, Calcutta, 1921, fourth edition.

Sarkar, J.N., *History of Bangal*, Patna, 1973.

Sharma, S.R., *The Religious Policy of the Mughal Emperors*, Bombay, 1962.

Siddiqui, I.H., *Some Aspects of Afghan Despotism in India*, Aligarh, 1969.

Smith, V., *Akbar the Great Mughal*, Delhi, 1962.

Srivastava, A.L. *Akbar the Great*, vol. 2, Agra, 1967.

Steingass, F., *Persian–English Dictionary*, Indian edition, 1973.

Stewart, Charles, *History of Bengal*, Calcutta, 1910.

Storey, C.A., *Persian Literature: A Bio-Bibliographical Survey*, 2 vols, London, 1970.

Streusand, Douglas E., *The Formation of the Mughal Empire*, Delhi, 1989.

Studies in Indian Textile Industry, Calico Museum of Textiles, Ahmedabad, 1966.

Tripathi, R.P., 'Akbar and Maham Anaga', *Journal of Indian History*, vol. I, 1922.

———, *Rise and Fall of the Mughal Empire*, Allahabad, 1956.

———, *Some Aspects of Muslim Administration*, Allahabad, 1959.

Umar, Muhammad, *Islam in North India: During the Eighteenth Century*, New Delhi, 1993.

Verma, S.P., 'Akbar's School of Paintings', in *Akbar and His India*, ed. Iqtidar Alam Khan, New Delhi, 1999.

Wilson, H.H., *A Glossary of the Judicial and Revenue Terms*, Delhi, 1968.

Zilli, I.A. 'Early Correspondence between Shah Tahmasp and Akbar', in *Islamic Heritage in South Asian Sub-continent*, ed. Nazir Ahmad and I.H. Siddiqui, Jaipur, 2000.

Index

Names and terms in the tables of Appendixes 1, 2, and 3 of chapter 1 (pp. 41–92) are not included